PACKMEN, CA
& PACKHORSE

TRADE AND COMMUNICATIONS IN NORTH DERBYSHIRE AND SOUTH YORKSHIRE

David Hey

'Along the ridge ran a faint foot-track,
which the lady followed. Those who knew it well called
it a path, and, while a mere visitor would have passed it unnoticed even by day,
the regular haunters of the heath were at no loss for it at midnight. The whole
secret of following these incipient paths, when there was not light enough in
the atmosphere to show a turnpike-road, lay in the development of the sense
of touch in the feet, which comes with years of night-rambling in little-trodden
spots. To a walker practised in such places a difference between impact on
maiden herbage, and on the crippled stalks of a slight footway,
is perceptible through the thickest boot or shoe'.

Thomas Hardy, *The Return of the Native* (1878)

'He came to a place, where by keeping the extremest track
to the right, it was just barely possible for a human creature to miss his way.
This track, however, he did keep, as indeed he had a wonderful capacity
at these kinds of bare possibilities'.

Henry Fielding, *Joseph Andrews* (1742)

PACKMEN, CARRIERS & PACKHORSE ROADS

TRADE AND COMMUNICATIONS IN NORTH DERBYSHIRE AND SOUTH YORKSHIRE

David Hey

Published by
Landmark Publishing Ltd,
Ashbourne Hall, Cokayne Ave, Ashbourne, Derbyshire DE6 1EJ England
Tel: (01335) 347349 Fax: (01335) 347303
e-mail: landmark@clara.net
web site: www.landmarkpublishing.co.uk

ISBN 1 84306 132 5

Landmark 2nd Edition 2004

British Library Cataloguing in Publication Data: a catalogue
record for this book is available from the British Library.

Print: Cambrian Printers, Aberystwyth
Design: Mark Titterton
Cover by James Allsopp

Front cover: Ancient causeway, near Whitby, from S. Smiles, *Lives of the Engineers.*

Back cover: Bakewell Bridge. *C.L.M. Porter.*

Page One: "Watering Place by the Roadside near Grindleford Bridge" by Sir Francis Chantrey, from Rhodes' *Peak Scenery.*

Page Three: Causeway descending Stanage Edge. *C.L.M. Porter.*

Contents

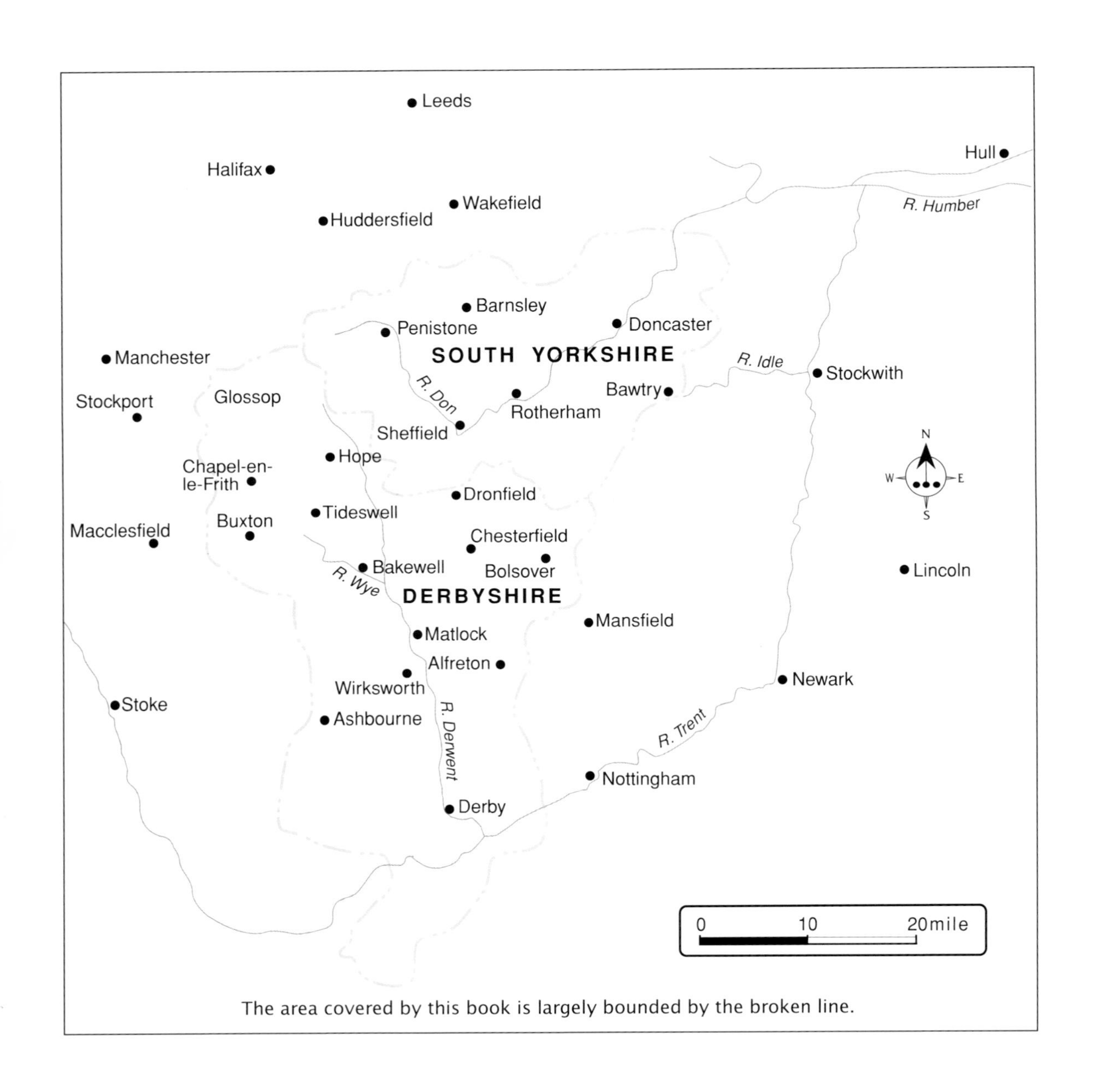

The area covered by this book is largely bounded by the broken line.

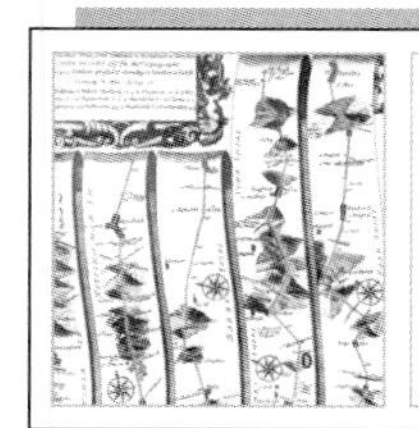

PREFACE

The first edition of this book was published in 1980 by Leicester University Press and quickly went out of print. When I was asked by Landmark to bring the book up to date in a new edition I leaped at the chance, for amongst the books that I have written this has always been a firm favourite of mine. I have made some minor alterations and have added new information that has come to light in the last twenty years, but the structure and spirit of the old book are preserved. At the time that it was first written academic interest in inland trade was stirring after years of neglect, but researchers rarely combined the documentary approach of the social-and-economic historian with that of the field archaeologist who searched for evidence on the ground. The Peak District and adjacent parts provided the ideal opportunity to look for abandoned tracks, holloways, causeys, bridges and guide stoops inscribed with the names of market towns in order to reconstruct the ancient pattern of highways and byways. This was a most enjoyable subject to research.

My enthusiasm was shared by a lively and knowledgeable group who met as an extramural class under my supervision at the University of Sheffield. I owe much to their reports and our discussions. The class members were Mary Bramhill, Roy Bullen, Alex Chatwin, John Civico, Jesse Clarke, Robert Clinging, Valerie Clinging, Evelyn Evison, George Fowler, Vincent Hopkinson, Bill Owen, Stephen Penny, Michael Price, Ted Spencer, Jon Whiting and Philip Young. Since then, I have lectured to audiences far and wide on 'Packhorse routes of the Peak District' and have learned a lot from comments and discussions. The subject has a strong appeal to all those who love to walk in the local countryside, for there is much to catch the eye of the observant rambler.

I am particularly grateful to Stephen Penny and Howard Smith for sharing their knowledge of local roads with me. I also give warm thanks to Dr Sheila Edwards and Brian Edwards for their excellent photographs and drawings, also B. Haines, P. Deakin, C.L.M. Porter and H. Smith for their photographs.

David Hey
Dronfield Woodhouse
2001

1 INTRODUCTION

1 'A waste and houling wilderness'

Above: Winnats Pass, from Rhodes' *Peak Scenery*, drawn by Sir F. L. Chantrey.

Seventeenth- and eighteenth-century travellers were agreed that the Peak District contained some of the wildest, most difficult terrain in the whole of England. When Daniel Defoe paused at the top of the cliff above Chatsworth in the early eighteenth century, he viewed with apprehension the 'vast extended moor or waste, which, for fifteen or sixteen miles together due north, presents you with neither hedge, house or tree, but a waste and houling wilderness, over which when strangers travel, they are obliged to take guides, or it would be next to impossible not to lose their way'.[1] Other famous travellers had used this fearsome moorland route before him and were equally impressed by the dangers that faced them. In 1698 Celia Fiennes remarked on 'the steepness and hazard of the Wayes — if you take a wrong Way there is no passing — you are forced to have Guides as in all parts of Darbyshire', [2] and when Edward and Thomas, the young sons of Sir Thomas Browne, made the same journey on a stormy day in September 1662, they were thankful to have Bakewell men to guide them over 'this strange mountainous, misty, moorish, rocky, wild country'. They marvelled at 'the great quantity of rain that fell [which] came down in floods from the tops of the hills, washing downe mud and so making a bog in every valley, the craggy ascents, the rocky unevenness of the roade, the high peaks and the almost perpendicular descents, that we were to ride down'. [3]

Dangers and Difficulties

As late as 1809, a decade or so before the Snake Pass was opened, William Hutchinson could describe his journey up Lady Clough, in another part of the Peak District, in these terms:

> *The road is extremely dangerous, on the side of a steep hill, where there is not above a foot and a half left for a horse to travel, and in some parts the wall, raised as a kind of battlement, has fallen down, so that it is scarcely passable. One false step would bring destruction to the rider and his horse. After a tedious passage through the dreary Lady Clough, we attained the summit of the moor ... The descent was down a dreadful steep pass, nearly two hundred feet perpendicular. The traveller should be extremely careful, and if his horse gets forward at one mile an hour this is good work.* [4]

Outsiders were not the only ones to fear the moors. The Nonconformist parson and apothecary, Revd James Clegg of Chapel en le Frith, set out for Crich on 5 February 1735, dined at Baslow, and wrote later that 'a kind providence directed me safely over the East more and I got in in good time'. His diary records several accidents on late journeys, as for instance on 10 March 1730 when he narrowly escaped a dangerous fall when his mare jumped into a stone pit in the dark, and on his return from a visit to his parents in Rochdale on 30 January 1723, when he found that the snow was thawing quickly and the waters were rising so fast that

he and his mare were swept downstream in the ford below Bugsworth Hall. 'Thro' the mercy of God', he wrote, 'I continued to sit her and with much struggling got her through the river.' [5] Adam Eyre, the parliamentary captain of Hazlehead Hall, had similar distressing experiences and reacted in the same way. On 22 October 1647 he wrote, 'This night, as I came home, the Lord delivered me from hurt of a very dangerous fall from my horse, on the Bents beyond Bullhouse, praysed and ever glorifyed be His name therfore', and on Christmas Eve that year he heard 'Ralph Wordsworth, my soldier, say that Captain Rich was in danger to have beene

Above: Curbar gap. The gritstone edge high above the River Derwent formed a barrier to traffic heading from the White Peak to the river ports and market towns further east. This natural gap in the escarpment acted as a funnel for many routes that struck out across the Big Moor. *Sheila Edwards.*

Right: Guide Stoop on Big Moor on the path to Baslow. *C.L.M. Porter.*

Below: Stanedge Pole. boundary and way marker. *B. Haines.*

drowned in coming from Peniston yesternight; and thereupon I resolved never hereafter to stay out in the night again'. [6]

Even local people sometimes found it necessary to hire a guide. On 9 January 1647 Adam Eyre gave twopence 'to a guide as wee came homewards, when wee had lost our way in the night beyond Honley', even though he was less than ten miles away from home. [7] Strangers had no alternative. On 5 September 1639 John Taylor, the water poet, found a guide to take him from Wortley to Halifax and found that 'the ways were so rocky, stony, boggy and mountainous, that it was a day's journey to ride so short a way'. [8] The mortal dangers that threatened those who travelled without guides are evident from entries in the Penistone burial register: '10 March 1755. Wm. Wordsworth Starv'd to Death on the Moors', '15 February 1763. Jos. Charlesworth from Burton lost in Snow', and '6 March 1764. James Marsh starv'd in the Snow', or in the Bradfield burial register for 25 August 1718: 'Memorandum - a coffin put in the earth with Bones of a Person found upon the high Moors, thought to be Richard Steade'. The *Journal of Mr. John Hobson*, of Dodworth Green, notes that on 31 December 1725 Mr Baines, the parson of Barlow and schoolmaster of Dronfield, met his death in a great snowfall on Froggatt Moss while on his way to Grindleford Bridge. Next winter Hobson wrote that Tuesday, 13 December 1726, 'was such an ill day for frost, snow and wind, that severall people had like to have perished in comming over the moors from Woodhead, and some lost their lives in going from Sheffield to Heithersedge'. [9]

Nevertheless, despite these dangers and difficulties, diaries such as those of Clegg, Eyre and Hobson record a great deal of movement within a ten- or twenty-mile radius, as people visited friends and relations, took up work in neighbouring parishes, or sold their produce and made purchases in the market towns. Occasionally, they undertook much longer journeys, say to York or the capital. The poor condition of the highways caused many a grumble, but the sensational accounts of travellers should not lead us to suppose that the routes along which they journeyed were hardly used. Some of the wildest, least hospitable moors were in fact criss-crossed with numerous tracks worn hollow by traffic taking industrial goods to the market towns and inland ports and returning with corn and malt. Though strangers were filled with awe at the prospect of an uncomfortable journey across desolate tracts of land, the like of which they had never seen before, the jaggers, salters, badgers and carriers did not feel the same terror, for they were familiar with the moors in all their changing moods and appearances.

The effect of Physical Geography

The complex local pattern of highways and byways was determined by the physical geography of the region, by the needs of the local population, and by external demand for its produce. The basic geological structure, formed during the Carboniferous period, has been the constant factor through the ages: human needs have changed from time to time, but the restrictions imposed by the landscape have remained unaltered. Travellers in the White Peak could usually find a firm footing on the thin soils that overlie the limestone, though the going was rough over the uncultivated commons and across the deep valleys, and wind and rain frequently hindered progress. The greatest difficulties were encountered further east in the Dark Peak where the shales and sandstones have been overlain with peat. Men and horses were soon fatigued by the spongy surface and the need to make detours around the fens and mosses and they naturally sought the shortest and most direct routes wherever possible. The local distribution and depth of peat must have been an important factor in fixing the best ways across the moors. The thickness of the peat on the Big Moor is usually nine or ten inches, with local variations from six to twelve inches, which is much less than deposits ranging from two feet to twenty feet in depth on the moors further north and nearby in Leash Fen. Large areas of saturated moorland dominated by cotton grass were avoided by travellers who went for drier parts marked by heather, bilberry or grass. Where a bog had to be crossed, the route invariably took the narrowest practical crossing even if this meant a detour in the approach. [10] Still further to the east, the Coal Measures sandstones offered easier access, but even there the steep hills and well-wooded valleys often provided formidable obstacles.

Wherever possible, travellers sought ridgeways that avoided the woods and swamps and provided a clear, unrestricted view of their destination. The pattern of through routes was moulded by the landscape, for moorland spurs controlled the flow of traffic, channelling it along the line of the deep river valleys, but high above the tree-line and the flood-plain. Even where the valleys have been cleared in modern times, their former impenetrable nature is sometimes revealed by place-names such as Deepcar, the 'deep marsh' or 'deep, well-wooded valley' dominated by alders. The ancient highways which crossed the Pennines from Cheshire and Lancashire avoided this difficult area on their way to Rotherham and Sheffield and sought instead the ridges at Hunshelf Bank and Bolsterstone; no one travelled along the valley bottom through Deepcar until the Wadsley and Langsett turnpike road was opened in 1805. Local lanes, however, followed much more varied lines, for human needs were a more important factor than physical restrictions in creating a network that linked isolated farms and hamlets with each other and with the parochial and manorial centres.

On long journeys major river crossings were unavoidable and routes were funnelled towards a few key fording or bridging points. A series of roads heading south from Yorkshire converged on the medieval bridges over the Don at Doncaster, Rotherham and Sheffield, and though travellers who were passing south through Derbyshire could generally avoid the Derwent, some had to cross the Wye at Ashford or Bakewell or the Lathkill at Alport. Sometimes there was no alternative but to go across the grain of the land, up and down steep valley sides. Thus, the route across the Strines from Bamford to Penistone crosses five major river valleys within thirteen miles. Yet the continued importance of this ancient track is evident from the decision

The track from left side to mid bottom of the photograph climbs up Stanage. The Roman road must have passed nearby, but this later track was probably used for moving millstones. *C.L.M. Porter.*

in 1771 to make it a turnpike road. Even the most difficult terrain could be overcome if necessary. Thankfully, the dreary summits of Bleaklow and Kinderscout could be avoided, though even here packhorse tracks traversed the edges. Perhaps the most difficult journeys of all involved the carriage of millstones and lead from the western parts of Derbyshire across the deep valleys or the wide and frequently turbulent Derwent, up one of the steep cliffs such as Curbar Edge, then over the bleak moors in the direction of Bawtry; yet such journeys were made regularly with heavy and bulky goods. The difficulties were not insuperable.

Three Shires Head. Packhorse bridge over the River Dane at Panniers Pool, near Flash where Derbyshire meets Cheshire and Staffordshire. The bridge has been widened upstream. Four packhorse routes converged on this bridge.

2 Streets, ways and gates

Fieldwork and aerial archaeology over the past few decades have shown that large parts of south Yorkshire and north Derbyshire were settled before the arrival of the Romans in the first century A.D. Given that the choice of routes was severely limited by the nature of the

The Port Way, near Winster. The names attached to country lanes often provide a clue to their former significance. The track branching left leads into the fields, but the one on the right is part of an old route from Wirksworth to Bakewell, still known in the eighteenth century as the Portway, i.e. the market road. *Sheila Edwards.*

Left: The valley to the right (above the bridge) marks the start of the Cut Gate path from Slippery Stones to Langsett and Penistone. *C.L.M. Porter.*

Below: The descent into Bonsall's village centre was know as the Clatterway. *C.L.M. Porter.*

landscape, it is likely that the major highways of the Middle Ages followed tracks that had been used by early settlers. These routes were unplanned but became accepted by trial and error as the most convenient ways across the country. This theme will not be explored in detail here, but two examples will suffice. In the first place, the road via Chapel en le Frith and Castleton is no doubt an early route across the Pennines, for the way down the Winnats Pass has been guarded by a succession of important forts. Impressive earthworks going back to the Bronze and Iron Ages embrace Mam Tor; three miles down the valley the Roman fort of Anavio can still be traced in outline at Brough; and between them Peveril Castle dominates the small Norman borough of Castleton. Each fort is very close to the highway. Another ancient moorland track is that which climbs up Longdendale via Woodhead and Saltersbrook and then follows the summit of the great ridge that separates Penistone from Stocksbridge. Turnpiked in 1732-41, it has always been a major highway across south Yorkshire. So important was this route in early times that when county boundaries were fixed in the tenth or eleventh century Cheshire assumed a most peculiar shape with a long, narrow extension guarding the Longdendale valley. This was the way that Cheshire salters came towards the West Riding market towns.

Ancient Highways

The Romans used existing tracks and added the first artificial or planned roads; in fact the only roads that were planned before the turnpike trustees and enclosure commissioners set to work in the eighteenth century. The Anglo-Saxons referred to Roman roads as *straets* and often used them as parish and estate boundaries, so even where the course of such roads is not known by fieldwork or excavation, map and place-name evidence can sometimes indicate a general line. For example, several street names have been located along a forgotten highway that ran along the crest of the Magnesian Limestone in a north-south direction through the centre of south Yorkshire. It crossed the rivers Don and Dearne at Mexborough and Conisbrough at Strafford Sands, the 'street-ford' which later became the meeting place for the wapentake of Strafforth. Its former course can be traced approximately along the boundaries of several medieval parishes and in part along country lanes, notably Packman Lane in the south and Street Lane, which still serves as the boundary between Brodsworth and Hooton Pagnell.

The lost place-name Ricknieldthorpe, near Kiveton Park railway station, shows that this route was once the great Ricknield Street that headed for York, and a number of prehistoric sites alongside suggest that it was an even older ridgeway which the Romans adapted for their own purposes. [11] In the eastern lowlands of south Yorkshire the road that later formed the basis of the Great North Road was Roman in origin, connecting forts at Bawtry, Rossington Bridge and Robin Hood's Well. It served as a boundary for several medieval parishes and it can still be followed for 3½ miles along a rough track between the Sun Inn and Red House to the west of Adwick le Street. Similarly, the Roman road from Derby along the watershed between the Dove and the Wye to Buxton and Manchester was prominent enough in later times to be used by several parishes as a boundary and it was still a great highway when John Ogilby produced his volume of road maps in the late seventeenth century.

In other cases it is not yet known whether the medieval highway stuck closely to the Roman road or whether a new line was preferred. The road which connected the Roman forts of Danum and Templeborough, for instance, may well underlie parts of the present road from Doncaster to Rotherham. Undoubtedly, some Roman roads fell into disuse, but on the other hand many seem to have survived in part, with later diversions to take account of new economic realities. The general line of a Roman road which presumably came from Bawtry follows the Cricket Inn Road and goes through the centre of Sheffield out towards Anavio (Brough) along Lydgate Lane and Sandygate Road, but the medieval track now known as the Long Causeway departs from the Roman road to pass Stanedge Pole; the Roman road descended Stanage Edge at a point that has not been discovered with certainty. Beyond Brough, the road to the Roman baths at Buxton was still evident in the Elizabethan period and was described in 1572 as 'an high way forced over the moors, all paved, of such antiquity as none can expresse, called Bathgate'. [12] More generally known as Batham Gate, and referred to as such in 1400, it can still be followed for much of the way along lanes that were improved by the enclosure commissioners, and the post-Roman Grey Ditch that barred this route is still visible at Bradwell. The footpath known as Doctor's Gate, or 'Docto Talbotes Gate' as it was called in 1627 is no longer considered to be Roman in origin. [13]

No Anglo-Saxon charters survive for this region, so it is not possible to establish the antiquity of local roads by documentary evidence. Local charters and deeds survive only from the middle of the twelfth century. Such a record is the agreement made in 1161 between Richard de Louvetot, lord of Hallamshire, and the Benedictine monks of the abbey of St Wandrille in Normandy, the owners of an estate associated with Ecclesfield priory. By this agreement Richard kept the land on the left side of the way (now the A6135) from Sheffield to Ecclesfield and the monks had the clearings on the other side. Moreover, the road that linked the church at Ecclesfield with its chapel-of-ease at Bradfield divided the clearings that lay further west; the charter specifically mentions the Birley Stone which is still a landmark at the top of Jaw Bone Hill, where the road starts to descend from Grenoside to Oughtibridge. Many local highways and byways are named as boundaries in medieval charters, but the region does not have earlier records going back well before the Norman Conquest such as have been used profitably in other parts of the country. For the earliest periods we have to rely just on the evidence of place-names and topography.

Differing Nomenclature

The Anglo-Saxons did not use the word *road* but spoke instead of *ways*. It thus became natural to speak of highways and byways, wayfarers, the wayside and highwaymen, to assert one's right of way along an immemorial route, and to ask the way when lost. Occasionally, small settlements took their names from the ancient thoroughfares on which they were sited. Bradway was on the broad way across the hills to the south of Sheffield towards Bakewell, Ridgeway developed alongside a ridge-road, Troway was unusual in that its name is derived from a road that linked the farms in the bottom of a valley, and a sunken track in central Derbyshire was already so worn by the first decade of the thirteenth century that the hamlet alongside it had taken the name of Holloway. [14] Routes that led to market towns were called portways and elsewhere a few distinctive tracks acquired special names of their own. The clatter of loose stones as horses descended the hill into Bonsall caused the locals to name the track Clatterway. More mysteriously, in 1356 a plot of ground in Staveley was said to 'lie upon Tychwaye'. [15]

Before the seventeenth century highways were rarely described as roads. Shakespeare used 'road' in only one of his plays and the word is found only once in the King James Bible. [16] Celia Fiennes was familiar with the word at the end of the seventeenth century but normally stuck to the older usage. Early local records, in the form of charters, deeds, manorial accounts and wills, nearly always use the Latin *via* or speak of ways, highways or common ways. However, as early as 1617 the route from Rotherham to Whiston was described as 'the Auncient Rode way or London way for carryers' and in 1644 the justices of the peace for the West Riding mused over the poor state of 'the public road from Bakewell to Wakefield'. [17] W. B. Crump suggested that the new word became popular after John Ogilby's 'Book of the Road' was published as *Britannia Depicta* in 1675. [18] Certainly the Derbyshire guide stoops, which were erected in 1709, used 'road' much more frequently than 'way' in their inscriptions. Not long afterwards the major highways were made into turnpike roads and, although the old usage has never been forgotten, people gradually came to describe their thoroughfares in the new manner, and 'anyroad' has replaced 'anyway' as a local expression.

The Scandinavian settlers of northern and eastern England used *gate* in much the same sense as the Saxons used *way* to mean anything from a 'road' to 'small track'. The street-names of our local towns and many other places in the old Danelaw, notably York, retain this usage. In south Yorkshire Darfield and Rotherham each have a Doncaster Gate and Sheffield, Wath and Wombwell have roads with the descriptive name of Sandy Gate. Many upland villages have their Towngates, and the route from Langsett over the moors to the Upper Derwent valley goes via Cut Gate, which has dug deep into the peat. In 1703 two of the minor routes of the Derbyshire village of Brampton were known as Church Gate and Sungate and in the Cordwell valley byways to local farms known as Fanshaw Gate, Horsleygate and Johnnygate take their names not from supposed entrances to Holmesfield park but from the Scandinavian *gata*, meaning way; thus in 1496 the Holmesfield manor court rolls refer to 'the way called Horsleygate'. [19] The Scandinavian form was used naturally and freely as an alternative to the Anglo-Saxon word. Hollowgate has the same meaning as Holloway and whereas the ancient route by which salt was brought from Cheshire across the Pennines to Wakefield market was called Salterway in a medieval bounder of the Graveship of Holme, it was described as Saltergate in the 1828 enclosure award for the township of Thurlstone. [20]

On her visit to Yorkshire in the 1690s Celia Fiennes was puzzled by the two words which are now spelt 'gate'; the Scandinavian *gata*, meaning way, and the Old English *geat*, meaning a bar or barrier that could be opened, in the sense of the four medieval bars at York, the West Bar at Sheffield and the bars to Chesterfield market. In common speech *geat* became yate and several Lidyates or Lidgetts survive where a swing-gate once opened the way to the commons. The Scandinavian sense is preserved in the word gait, which the *Oxford English Dictionary* defines as 'manner of walking, bearing or carriage as one walks'. On her way from York to Aberford Celia Fiennes observed that:

> *the ordinary people ... tell you its very good gate, instead of saying it is good way, and they call their gates yates, and do not esteem it uphill unless so steep as a house or precipice; they say it is good levell gate all along, when it may be there are severall great hills to pass, but this account did encrease on us the nearer we came to Derbyshire.* [21]

Another old name that is still in common use is lane. In town and countryside alike it retains its original meaning of a minor way or gate, though just occasionally it was used more loosely and applied to a more important route like Derbyshire Lane, the ancient southern exit from Sheffield. The usual sense is of a track enclosed by fields or woods rather than of a route across open moors. Modern roads are rarely, if ever, named in this way, so the word usually denotes a byway of some antiquity. It was in local use by the thirteenth century when Bent Lane acted as a property boundary in Loxley, and no doubt was a familiar word long before such records were kept. [22] Lanes are most commonly named after the village, hamlet or farmstead towards which they are heading, such as 'the lane or hye way called Wombwell, or Ardsley lane', which in 1611 was said to be badly in need of repair. [23] Beyond the settlement the lane would assume another name.

Celia Fiennes used this road between Chatsworth and Bakewell in her trip through Derbyshire.
C.L.M. Porter.

Some lanes, however, were named after the salters, badgers, packmen and other traders who used them and these are amongst the most interesting to follow on the map or the ground. Others acquired descriptive names like Long Lane or Back Lane, or nicknames like Blind Lane for a cul-de-sac or Dog Leg Lane for a road with a sharp bend in it. The narrowness of many of these lanes is brought to light by their descriptions in documents of the Tudor and Stuart period, such as 'a certain narrow lane called Ellet Lane' near Ecclesfield, 'a narrow lane which led towards Shiregreen' from Wincobank, and 'a common lane, or narrow way' at Neepsend. [24] Some lanes were so narrow that they were little more than bridleways; indeed in 1718 a track was described as the 'Strait Lane or Bridlesty leading towards Owlerton Hall'. [25] Sty was derived from Old English and Scandinavian words meaning a path and often appears in local records. For example, 'a bridle stye' at Ecclesall was referred to in 1573 and 'a Bridlesty way' at Midhope was mentioned in a document of 1704, while in 1772 the low inquest at Eckington gave permission to John Rodgers to 'hang a gate in the Bridle Stie at Howbrooke Lane, as formerly'. [26]

Simple footpaths can be equally as old. A perambulation of the boundaries of the Peak Forest in 1285 followed the Longdendale valley up to Woodhead and proceeded by 'an ancient footpath' (*veterem semitam*) to the head of the River Derwent; in other words, the path was already considered old by the thirteenth century. [27] Of course, many people could not afford to keep a horse and often had to travel great distances on foot. James Clegg noted in his diary on 10 March 1736 that a man who had come to ask his medical advice had walked all the way from Southwell to Chapel en le Frith, a journey of about forty-five miles over difficult country. Paths were also known by the dialect word *rack*. Rakes Close, a Mexborough field name, was known as 'The Rackes' in 1633, Wreakes Lane in Dronfield was Rakes Lane in 1623 and Oxton Rakes near Barlow was referred to in 1330 as the 'Oxrakes de Barley', meaning 'ox or oxen paths' to the commons. [28] The lane from Stannington to Walkley known as the Racker Way may also be derived in this manner, rather than from the 'racking gait of horses', which was T. W. Hall's suggestion. [29] Another interesting dialect word is *bar*, which was formerly used in Derbyshire to describe a horseway up a steep hill. The eighteenth-century antiquary, Samuel Pegge, wrote, 'In the Peak of Derbyshire all those steep and precipitous roads which run down from the cliffs to the valleys, where the villages are generally plac'd, they call Bars, whence Bakewell Bar, Beeley Bar, Baslow Bar, Rowsley Bar, etc.' [30] Some later bar names, however, are derived from the position of a toll bar across a turnpike road.

Churchways

In the large parishes that straddled the Pennines and the western parts of the Coal Measures, hamlets and isolated farmsteads sometimes lay several miles away from the parish church and so special paths were needed to connect them. These distinctive tracks were known as churchways or kirkgates. In 1262 the way from Midhope to the church at Bradfield formed the boundary of land known as Ekilrode and the way to Bradfield church from Oughtibridge acted as the boundary to another piece of property in 1370. [31] The special nature of such gates was recognised by the jurors of Bradfield manor court in 1657 when they ordered that the occupiers of Walker House and their neighbours in Low Bradfield 'should not hereafter lead any carts or carriages down the causeway to the Hoyles being the church way'. [32] In the neighbouring parish of Penistone the kirkgate from Carlecotes was referred to in an arbitration award of the 1570s, and in 1602 disputed common land at Snowden Hill was said to be bounden by the Church Way. [33] Such routes acquired an aura of their own as hallowed ways for burial parties. Revd J. C. Atkinson's memorable account of Danby on the North York Moors in *Forty Years in a Moorland Parish* records the fears of burial parties that a dead person would 'come again' to haunt them if the traditional route was not used, for the deceased would not 'rest easy in his grave'. A funeral party which refused to take a short cut from the hallowed way arrived two hours late after a difficult journey of nearly twelve miles. [34]

Perhaps such beliefs did not survive quite so long in the West Riding, but they seem to have been important in earlier times. On 11 April 1640 the jurors for the township of Ossett within the large manor of Wakefield ordered that, 'Thomas Akeroyde Thomas Hemingway and Roberte Whitakers doe make the lane sufficient betwixt pilldars lane and Chickingley which is our Churchway for carieyinge our corpes'. [35] When the inhabitants of Holmfirth petitioned the Commonwealth leaders to elevate their chapel-of-ease to parochial status, they claimed that in times of heavy snows burial parties sometimes took two days to get to the parish church at Kirkburton. Their kirkgate is still known by name and is marked by flagstones beyond the river crossing north of New Mill; it approaches the church not by the present detour through the hamlet of Riley but along the unmetalled track that led directly to the churchyard, This track is marked on a map of 1753 as 'Corpse Way". [36] Further south, Joseph Kenworthy noted that a causeway at the side of the Canyards leading towards Hanson Cross was known to old people in the early twentieth century as the church-walk, along which burial parties traditionally made their way to Bradfield. [37] In north Derbyshire Hollins cross was a traditional stop and place for prayer, for burial parties crossing the ridge from Edale to Castleton. Additionally a track that descends from Highlow and crosses the Derwent towards Hathersage was known in 1720 as the 'corps way to church'. [38]

3 Responsibility

The Statute of Winchester (1285) placed responsibility for the maintenance of highways upon the landowners in each manor and ordered that if a track became impassable another should be made alongside it. Manorial courts spent a great deal of time dealing with this responsibility. In 1440-42, for example, the Sheffield manor court noted that common ways had been obstructed at Cowley, Dawfield Head and Fox Lane, that a common way at Brightside was full of mud because a water course had not been scoured, and that Ralph of Leghe ought to repair part of a public highway in Ecclesall. [39] In return, manorial lords claimed the right to levy tolls on strangers who carried goods through their lands. In 1441-42 the lord of Sheffield received the sum of 10s.8d. from 'divers persons crossing through the lord's lordship to the fairs of Chesterfield and Ripon'. [40] Even as late as the seventeenth century some lords still levied such tolls. Amongst the manorial perquisites of the honour of Tickhill in 1649 were 'The tolls of waggons, cartes and all other carriages and drifts passing in or through the way or streete called Sunderland' and in the following year parliamentary surveyors noted the claim of the lord of the manor of High Peak to 'the passage and through Toll paide for Packs and Carryages passing att Hayfield and Walley Bridge'. [41] Furthermore, in 1617 the feoffees of Rotherham (a charitable body whose duties included the repair of local highways) were said to have regularly made a special payment to the lord of Whiston in lieu of tolls 'for passing directly from the Mile Okes in Whiston feilde to the topp of Rotheram more'. [42]

Overseers and Statute Labour

The inability of manorial courts to cope with the increasing amount of traffic led Tudor governments to establish a new system. Henceforth, the inhabitants of the ancient ecclesiastical parishes were responsible to the justices of the peace at the county quarter sessions for the upkeep of the highways and byways within their boundaries. Where parishes were large, responsibility was delegated to various divisions, such as a township or hamlet; for example, the huge parish of Ecclesfield had sixteen divisions until highway boards were set up in 1861.

Stone breakers on the road. This illustration from George Walker, *The Costume of Yorkshire* (1814) shows how highways were repaired under the statutory labour system.

Under the terms of an act of 1555 unpaid overseers of the highways had to be elected annually by each parish vestry and every householder was ordered to work on the roads for four days a year under the supervision of the overseer, or else he had to pay someone to do the work for him. In 1563 this liability was increased to six days. Undoubtedly, as William Harrison, an Essex parson, observed in his *Description of England* (1577), this obligation was 'much evaded'; nevertheless, the system worked in a rough and ready way for the next three centuries, supplemented by the moneys received from numerous bequests in local wills towards the repair of highways and bridges. [43] A glimpse of the local organisation at work is provided by Adam Eyre, who noted in his diary on 30 May 1647, 'This morne I went to Peniston, to church, on foote, and writ a note for Fr. Haigh, to be read in church, for mending the way to Denby bridge', and on 22 October that same year, 'This day Edw. Mitchell's servants broke an ox neck, in coming from the common day works, vzt from leading stone to Denby bridge, as they were bringing goods home in the wayne'. [44]

The eighteenth-century bridge over the Barlow Brook by the site of the old smelting mill displays rare evidence of the responsibility of local officers. It is inscribed underneath: 'John Ingham the mason & Hugh Rippon the thirdbaro'; the thirdborough was an alternative term for a constable. Justices of the Peace regularly ordered parish overseers to repair their highways and bridges if they were not up to standard and they supported any overseer who encountered local difficulties. In 1715, for instance, Richard Cope of Buxton was indicted at the Derby quarter sessions 'for not sending his cart to the mending of the highways according to notice given in church', and among the routine orders of the West Riding J.P.s is one referring to the bizarre case of Joseph Nightingale of Rotherham, who in 1737 had erected 'a boghouse and a swine coat in or near a certain place called the Market Place' and had deposited there 'twenty cartloads of dung by means whereof not only the air there is rendered offensive and unwholesome, but also the road is obstructed by this evil example'. [45]

Manorial courts were also prepared to lend their support, for the old system continued to operate alongside the new. In 1609 the great court leet of the manor of Sheffield resolved that, 'The overseers of the high wayes shall not discharge any man of his six dayes labour for the common dayes worke under 6d. a man, or else to have a lawfull labourer except such as have draughts and those to worke according to the statut', and four years later the Stainborough manor court ordered that, 'all inhabitants and residents within the manor should provide yearly and send sufficient and able workmen and their carts, with sufficient instruments and tools to provide for the repair of the highways, at such times as by the overseers of other roads might be fixed; they should be under pain for every offence' ten shillings. [46] Further north, the court of the great manor of Wakefield, meeting on 15 October 1639, ordered every householder within the Graveship of Holme to 'come or send a sufficient labourer to the mending of the high wayes and turfe gates', and on 11 April 1640 the constable and sworn men of Ardsley West presented the owners and occupiers of William Lindley's land 'for not doinge five Common day workes with a draught this yeare last past'. [47]

The influence of the local J.P.

By the middle of the seventeenth century the common days work system was already deemed unsatisfactory in some places. Although no statutory authority existed, Derbyshire J.P.s acted upon local petitions and levied a highway rate at Newbold and Dunston in 1649 and at Calow in 1650. J.P.s were given formal power to order a parish assessment during the Commonwealth period by an Act of 1654, but this Act was repealed at the Restoration. A generation later, they again acquired such power by an Act of 1691 and special levies soon became normal practice. In April 1692, for example, the Derbyshire J.P.s granted a petition for an assessment at Brampton as the highways 'are very Large and at this time in great decay'. [48]

The J.P.s also acted as arbiters in disputes over responsibility. For instance, in 1752 the inhabitants of Chapeltown, one of the sixteen divisions of Ecclesfield parish, were indicted for not repairing Nether Lane. They claimed that forty or fifty years previously Nether Lane had indeed been the public highway from Sheffield to Chapeltown but that as it had been replaced as such by Coit Lane they now rarely used it and its bad state was the result of heavy carriages going to and from the pits at Hesley. The rest of the parish blamed Housley Freeman of Housley Hall, 'who unfortunately for his neighbours had such an Education in Law as to make him very troublesome [and] has taken it into his head that Nether Lane ought to be taken off [Chapeltown] Division and repaired by the Parishioners in general'. As for the claim that the turnpiking of the Saltersbrook-Rotherham road had been costly to the inhabitants of Chapeltown, 'The Truth is they did very little at their Highways before the Turnpike was made, and would do no more now if they could help it'. Unfortunately, we do not have the J.P.s' verdict, just the weary comment that 'the Highways in Every Division have at one time or other been indicted at the Quarter Sessions'. [49]

Early accounts of the parochial surveyors of the highways do not survive locally. The earliest date from the 1770s and though they are not particularly informative they do demonstrate the primitive ways in which the roads were maintained. We read that 1s.6d. was spent at Dore in 1770 'for mending Ouday Lane in winter' and that the Totley overseer spent 15s.1d. in 1779 on 'stone getting and breaking and a bridge making'; in 1800 '3 Days leveling and forming Ground for Causway' at Worsbrough cost 7s.6d., and the payments made by the overseer of Ecclesfield Lower Division in 1812-13 included threepence to Ben Turner for spreading a load of cinders and 1s.4d. 'At Street Muck Selling'. The tools belonging to that division consisted simply of a shovel, a rake, a mattock and a few hammers. [50] When Horace Walpole visited Wentworth Castle in 1756, he wrote, 'During my residence here I have made two little excursions, and I assure you it requires resolution. The roads are insufferable; they mend them — I should call it spoil them — with large pieces of stone'. [51] But then, the 1769-72 accounts of Saintforth Wroe, the surveyor of the Sheffield-Wakefield turnpike road, do not seem very different from those of the parish overseers when they record 'Leading Cinders from Chapeltown furnace with 2 Carts' and 'ditching both sides of the Road, cleaning the Dirt of the whole breadth of the Road, and filling up Ruts'. [52] Real improvements in the techniques of road maintenance still lay a long way ahead.

Above: Chapel Gate packhorse way on Rushup Edge. *C.L.M. Porter.*

Right: The cross base of Knowsley cross near Stanton, west of Ashbourne. The packhorse way east from here has a short length of cut stone blocks suggesting a long forgotten causeway. *C.L.M. Porter.*

Below: Okeover Mill on the River Dove. First mentioned in the Domesday Book, it has been the focus of roadways for nearly a millennia. Many other water-powered mills in the Peak became the focus of roads which still survive long after the mill has stopped work or even disappeared. *C.L.M. Porter.*

2 FINDING THE WAY

1 Waymarkers

Before the eighteenth century travellers received very little guidance on how to cross the difficult terrain of the Peak district. 'All Derbyshire is full of steep hills' wrote Celia Fiennes in 1697, 'and nothing but the peakes of hills as thick one by another is seen in most of the County which are very steepe which makes travelling tedious, and the miles long, you see neither hedge nor tree but only low drye stone walls round some ground, else its only hills and dales as thick as you can imagine'. On her way from Haddon Hall to Buxton she observed, 'Its very difficult to find the wayes here for you see only tops of hills and so many roads by reason of the best wayes up and down that its impossible for Coach or Waggon to pass some of them, and you scarce see a tree and no hedge all over the Country, only dry stone walls that incloses ground no other fence'. [1]

The going could be just as difficult for the locals. When Leonard Wheatcroft lost his way on the moors between Ashover and Chatsworth on 25 September 1670 he was so relieved to recognise a landmark that he composed a few lines of doggerel and inscribed them upon it:

Great Monement for my content
I'le rest me heare a while;
Had'st thou not beene, for me to've seene
I'de wandred many a mile.

Ten days later he and his son 'erected by the way 4 heapes of stones betwixt Matlock and Ashover which we judged would stand to many generations', a tradition of cairn-building that ramblers have continued to this day. Wheatcroft's experience obviously made a deep impression on him, for a decade later, on 20 July 1680, he 'set up 3 heapes of stones for hey-way marks betwixt Matlock and Ashover'. [2] No doubt many others did the same elsewhere. John Wilson, the Broomhead Hall antiquary, noted in 1777 that Abraham Ibbotson, aged sixty-six, of Tinker Brook:

> *says he has heard that Rowland Thompson's sons of Brightholmlee and Edward Waterhouse sons of Swinnock Hall, who he can remember, tho' grown up, when he was a lad, set up the following stones or crosses at every half mile. One cross at Brightholmlee facing Thomas Burdekin's barn, half a mile to Swinnock Hall nook. The Second upon the green at Tinker Brook. The Third Short cross at Benthill against Thomas Greaves of the Coit below the road to Sheffield; set up since he was born. He has heard old John Swinden of Spouthouse say so.* [3]

Above: Squeezers to the rocks, Curbar. This kind of narrow stile is distinctive to the Derbyshire part of the Peak District.

Slab bridge and waymarker, the Big Moor. The single slab that bridges this moorland stream is marked by an upright post of unknown date, so that travellers could readily find the crossing on their way from the Hope Valley to Sheffield. *Sheila Edwards.*

A similar set of stone stoops still mark the Stannington to Derwent bridleway near Moscar and other moorland routes.

Natural landmarks and specially-erected stones often served a dual purpose as waymarkers and boundary points. It is difficult to decide whether roads subsequently headed for these marks or whether a road was an ancient landscape feature that could serve as a convenient boundary and therefore had a stone erected alongside it. Several shallow holloways go past the Lady Cross on Big Moor, which acted as a boundary mark for an estate that had been granted to Beauchief Abbey by 1263, and another Lady Cross near Saltersbrook not only marked the limit of lands within the manor of Glossop, which were granted to the Cistercian abbey of Basingwerk in the thirteenth century, but acted as a welcome indication that the steep climb up the ancient track through Longdendale was over. In both these cases it seems likely that boundary stones were erected alongside existing highways. [4] Similarly, a 1784 survey shows that Ones Moor Cross and Rotherham Cross both stood along the line of the road from Bradfield to Worrall, [5] and the wooden poles that mark the county boundary at Stanage and an old parish and manorial boundary to the west of Totley Moss are successors of ancient ones whose other function was to guide the traveller over the craggy edges that pierced the skyline east of the River Derwent.

Finding the way was a curiously primitive task even for the mightiest subjects in the land. During the 1720s Joseph Ludlam was employed by Thomas Watson-Wentworth (later the first Marquis of Rockingham) to survey the roads from Wentworth Woodhouse to various places of importance. His description of the way to Blyth and so on to the Great North Road is quoted here to illustrate the simple manner in which the passing miles were recorded:

Wentworth House

The first Close on the other side Swallow wood gate a Oak Tree marked 1, Stubin Lane a Large Stone Right Hand marked 2, Burkwood a Cross on the Right Hand on the Farr Side Some Trees 1, Swinton Common a Cross on the other Side the Road betwixt Swinton and Rothem. 1, Kilnhurst Lane a Cross on the Swarf on the other Side the Cutt Bridge 1, Hooton Common a Cross on the Swarf meeting Rotherham Road 1, Conisbrough Lane to a great Stone mark'd 8 on the Right Hand 1, On the other Sid Conisbrough going up the Hill a Large Stone marke 9 on the Right Hand 1, Mr Woodyears an Oake Tree just in the turn mark'd with an X 1, Entering upon Cockhill a Cross on the Swarf 1, This end of a Moor on the other Side Cockhill Swarf mark'd XII 1, Wilsick a Loop hole in Wm. Gills Barn end 1, Wilsick Lane a Maple Tree marked XIII a Little Behind Some Ouller Roots Left hand 1, Wilsick Lane mark'd in the Swarf 11 near a Hay Stack Left Hand 1, Tickhill paper Miln the Corner of the Miln 1, Harworth Field an Ash Tree 1 Chain above measure Standing near a Corner on the Right Hand Marked X 1, Harworth Field on the Other Side the Town an Oak tree mark'd with a Cross X at the Further of a Clump 1, Harworth Field a Cross in the Swarf and a Stake driven down opposite to an Elder 1, Blyth opposite to the Sign of the wool pack 1, To the Angel gates 0.2.4.0. = 20.2.4.0. Blth Lane a Large ash Tree Mark'd with a Cross is 50 Links beyond the mile 1, Torworth Field a Cross in the Swarf on the Right Hand 1, Forrest 2 Chains behind Bilbie gate a Cross in Swarf 1, Bilbie Forrest a Cross on the Swarf on the Right Hand 4 chains on this side a Thorne Tree 1, To the meeting of London Road at a guide Stoop 0.5.7 = 4.5.7. Wentworth House to London by the Way of Blyth is 159 Miles.

The Marquis of Rockingham was later to write, 'In the year 1750 I made severall Copper plates and Maps drawing and graving of which came to more than £500. A great deal was done in repairing the neighbouring Roads [and] setting up mile stones'. [6]

2 Guide stoops

In 1697 Parliament responded to the difficulties of the rising number of travellers who were trying to follow the correct lines of the lonely highways and byways by authorising Justices of the Peace to order the erection of guide posts or stoops where crossroads were remote from towns and villages. The Lancashire J.P.s reacted immediately, and the following year, after completing her journey from Garstang to Lancaster, Celia Fiennes noted, 'They have one good thing in most parts of this principality ... that at all cross wayes there are Posts with Hands pointing to each road with the names of the great town or market towns that it leads to, which does make up for the length of the miles that strangers may not loose their road and have it to goe back againe'. [7] The West Riding J.P.s waited until 1700 before they ordered 'Stoops to be sett up in Crosse highways; inscribed with 'the name of the next Market Town to which each of the joining highways leede', and even then they do not appear to have enforced their order. [8] None of the surviving south Yorkshire stoops seems to be earlier than those erected under a new order of 1733.

In Derbyshire, a stoop opposite Sycamore Farm, Hopton, is inscribed 1705 on all four sides and marks the roads to Ashbourne, Bakewell, Derby and Wirksworth. Perhaps it was erected on the order of Philip Gell of Hopton Hall, who was an M.P. at the time, for it is four years earlier than the county's other stoops. When the Derbyshire J.P.s used their powers in 1709 they acted firmly to ensure that their order was obeyed. We have the record of their decision in the quarter sessions order book and also the instruction to the overseers of the highways within the hundred of Scarsdale that 'For the better convenience of Travelling, where two or

Above left and right: stoop on Beeley Moor. Two sides of a Derbyshire guide stoop of 1709, directing the traveller to Chesterfield and to 'Offerton' (Alfreton). The stoop has four sides and block capitals in the usual Derbyshire manner.

Left: Longshaw Park stoop. Dated 1709, this is typical of Derbyshire stoops except for its unusually long inscription, pointing the way to Hathersage and Chapel en le Frith.

All Photogrpahs: *Sheila Edwards.*

more cross Highways meet in your said Liberty you are required forthwith ... to erect or fix ... in the most convenient place, where such ways join, a Stone or Post with an inscription theron in large Letters, containing the Name of the next Market Town to which each of the said joyning Highways leads'. [9] A further order was made at the July 1712 meeting of the quarter sessions warning those who had failed to obey the original instruction.

The characteristic Derbyshire and West Riding stoops are rectangular blocks of Millstone Grit, standing from three to well over five feet high and resembling farm gateposts in size and shape. No other part of the country can match this invaluable visual record of the network of highways and byways in use during the two or three generations that preceded the turnpike era. This is largely due to the durable nature of such large blocks of stone and to the need for routes on the Pennines to be signposted. In counties like Leicestershire or Nottinghamshire, where villages were close together, stoops were not needed as the traveller could always ask the way. In other counties stoops may have been erected but may not have survived because, in the absence of local stone, they were made of wood. Nevertheless, the Derbyshire and Yorkshire stoops also bear witness to the regular use of a large number of routes across difficult terrain. The trouble and expense of erecting stoops could not have been justified unless a considerable number of traders were to benefit from them.

A few stoops are embellished with pointing fingers but usually the traveller had to work on the tacit assumption that he should turn right from the face that marked the required destination. Nowhere is this rule stated, but it can be proved from an examination of surviving stoops, unless they have fallen or have been removed to serve as gateposts. Normally, the Derbyshire stoops are inscribed on all four sides, even if some of the market towns that are named could not be reached easily and directly. However, local circumstances sometimes led to different methods. A lonely marker by a moorland track from Curbar Gap to Owler Bar is inscribed with pointing fingers and the words 'BAKEWEL WAY' and 'SHEFIELD WAY' on two of its sides, but as it does not stand at a junction the other sides are blank. Similarly, a stoop at Pudding Pie Farm, which marks the road from Chesterfield to Bakewell, has two sides which are blank. More unusually, a stoop on the southern edge of Big Moor is marked 'CHESTERFEILD ROADE' on one side but is unmarked on all three others, for its sole function was to point the way across the Bar Brook. Finally, a stoop at Ball Cross on the route that Celia Fiennes and Daniel Defoe took through Chatsworth and Edensor on their way to Bakewell and another stoop alongside Fox Lane have only three sides marked because they stand at junctions where only three inscriptions were necessary. [10]

Many of the Derbyshire stoops have the date 1709 cut into them, but unlike some of the stoops in the heart of the West Riding, they do not normally display the name of the local surveyor or constable. [11] One that does is the stoop at Curbar Gap which heralds the end of the steep climb from the crossing of the Derwent and the beginning of a new hazard, the Big Moor. In favourable conditions it is still just possible to read the faint directions to Sheffield, Dronfield, Chesterfield and Tideswell, with the name of 'HUMPHERY GREGORY SUPERVISOR' and the date 1709. A mile-and-a-half further north on the moor, a stoop on White Edge is remarkable for the clarity of its inscriptions and is designed in the typical Derbyshire manner. It reads:

BAKE	DRON	SHEF	TIDS
WELL	FEILD	EILD	WALL
ROAD	ROAD	ROAD	ROAD
			1709

Above left: Dyson Cote stoop. The only six-sided stoop in the region, dated 1734. The traveller followed the usual principle of turning right from the face of the stoop marking his destination. *Sheila Edwards.*

Above right: Hartcliff stoop. Several stoops have been moved from their original positions. This one now serves as a farm gatepost and is partly defaced. It was erected in accordance with an order of the West Riding J.P.s of 1738. *Sheila Edwards.*

Left: The buried stoop on Beeley Moor (see p.29). *D. Hey.*

Some stoops were erected a little later than this; that at Alport by Wirksworth is marked 1710, one on Longstone Edge above Rowland is dated 1717, and seven stoops that are inscribed 1737 suggest that the J.P.s made a fresh order in that year, though no record of this has been found. At Bleak House a stoop that directs the traveller to Bakewell, Stoney Middleton, Dronfield and Chesterfield was put up as late as 1743. Otherwise, even where the date of erection is not stated, the style of the Derbyshire stoops suggests that they can usually be assigned to the year 1709. [12]

The stoop at Ball Cross, which marks the ways to Bakewell, Sheffield and Chesterfield with pointing hands, and a similar stoop on Fox Lane, which shows the ways to Bakewell, Dronfield and Chesterfield, are unusual among Derbyshire stoops in using lower case, not capital letters. Unlike the West Riding stoops, the Derbyshire ones are normally carved in large, block capitals. Derbyshire practice also differs from Yorkshire in never recording distances and rarely naming any settlement smaller than a market town. A stoop on Beeley Moor directs the traveller to Chatsworth, another in Longshaw Park marks the way to Hathersage, [13] and the stoop at Bleak House is inscribed on one side with the name of (Stoney) Middleton, none of which places held the right to hold a market or fair, but generally speaking the men who erected the stoops stuck strictly to the terms of the 1709 order. It may be objected that the same stoop on Beeley Moor also has the inscription 'OFFERTON ROADE' and that this must refer to Offerton Hall on the edge of Offerton Moor, ten difficult miles away, but the answer to this is that Offerton is merely a phonetic spelling of the market town of Alfreton, which lies in a completely different direction, but which satisfies the usual principle that one should turn to the right from the face of the stoop. The use of phonetic spellings adds greatly to the antiquarian interest of these stones. Many ramblers find pleasure in reading them for their own sake without trying to fit them into an overall pattern of routes, and none is more amusing than the stoop in Longshaw Park which is inscribed, 'TO HA-THAR-SICH-AND-So-TO CH-APIL I-N Lee-FRITH / TO-SHAFILD-1709 / TO-TIDSWeL / T0-CHAS-TER-FILD'. Though many packmen probably could not read very well, no doubt they could distinguish a few key words which could be recognised as pictures, sufficient to direct them on their way. [14]

In recent years Howard Smith has made a thorough investigation of the seventy or so surviving stoops of Derbyshire and south-west Yorkshire and has re-discovered many that were lost, while Jim McAllister and other members of the Holymoorside and District History Society have been active in re-erecting stoops in their original positions. Some of these had been moved by farmers or gamekeepers, others had been buried by the Home Guard during the Second World War. In 1995 the first stoop to be unearthed and re-erected was that on Beeley Moor, which had been buried in 1940. A photograph taken in 1914, the first edition of the six-inch Ordnance Survey map, surveying techniques and prodding with a steel rod led to the discovery of the stoop six to nine inches below the surface. It had been made in 1709 to mark the ways to 'Backwell, Worksworth, Shefeld and Chestterfeld'. [15]

Stoops were unnecessary in the eastern parts of the region where the traveller had ample opportunity to ask the way if in doubt. The real difficulties were encountered on the wild moorlands that overlie the grits and shales of the Pennines and the western edges of the exposed coalfield. At the quarter sessions held at Pontefract on 3 April 1733 the West Riding J.P.s decided that:

for the better Convenience of Travellers ... all and every the Surveyors of the highways of any parish or place within the said Riding on Notice hereof to them respectively given Do forthwith Erect or Cause to be Erected or fixed in the most Convenient place where two or more Cross highways within their said Respective precincts Do meet or Joyn, a Stone or post with an Inscription theron in Large Letters Containing the name of the next Markett Town to which Each of the said Joyning Highways Leads.

Above left and right: Guide stoop, near Gladwin's Mark (SK 316667), points the way to Bakewell, Chesterfield, and (on another side) to Winster. It was re-erected in 1997 by the Holymoorside and District History Society. *D. Hey and H. Smith.*

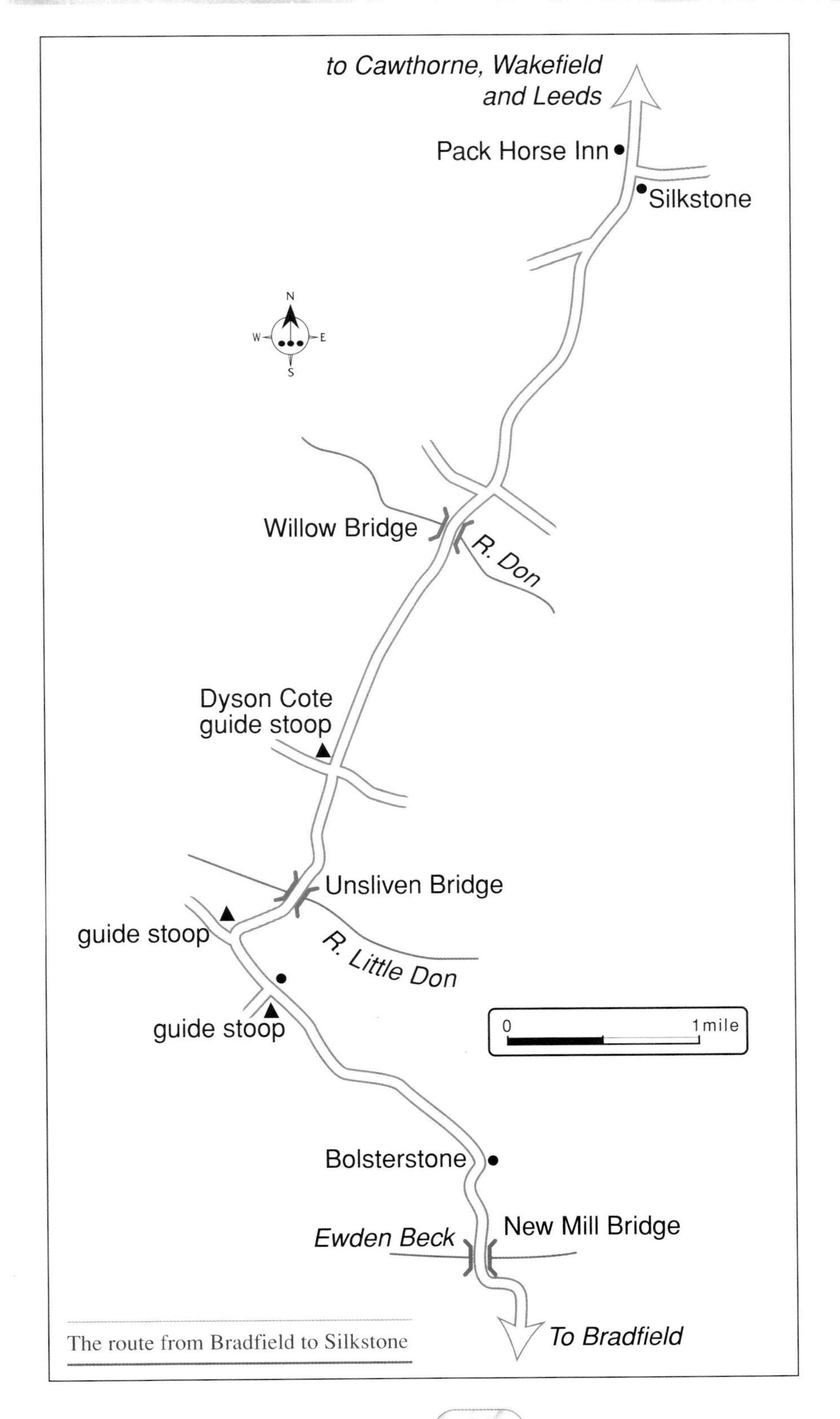

The route from Bradfield to Silkstone

The instructions to the parish surveyors recognised that 'upon large Moors and Commons where intelligence is difficult to be had' it was not much use simply to inscribe the names of distant market towns. [16] Stoops erected under the terms of this order therefore commonly point the way to villages and hamlets and, in at least one case, to an isolated farm which stood a few hundred yards up the lane at the next junction.

West Riding stoops are similar in appearance to Derbyshire ones but the inscriptions are in lower case letters and it is usual for only three sides of the stone to be used. At the various meetings of the quarter sessions in 1738, such as the one held at Sheffield on 11 October, the J.P.s issued fresh orders, insisting that the number of miles should also be recorded. [17] These orders are a great help in dating some existing stoops, for any stone that displays the name of a settlement smaller than that of a market town but does not indicate the mileage can be placed between 1733 and 1738. Two such stoops can be found on the hills west of Stocksbridge on a forgotten route from Bradfield and Bolsterstone to Silkstone and Cawthorne and so on to Wakefield and Leeds. At Green Farm a crudely hewn block of Millstone Grit standing sixty-six inches high is engraved on three of its sides 'Uden / Peniston / Bolster-stone'. The Penistone sign indicates the way down the lane to the next junction, where another huge stone, fashioned in a similar manner, is marked 'Un-sliven-bridge / Middop / Green'. [18] It seems that the various local authorities made a deliberate attempt to improve this highway in the years immediately preceding the turnpike era, for the former New Mill bridge over the Ewden Beck (now re-erected in Glen Howe park) can be dated by documentary evidence to 1734 and Unsliven bridge and Willow bridge on the same route were probably rebuilt about the same time.

The destination of this particular highway is revealed by another guide stoop, which stands at Dyson Cote on the great ridge between the Don and the Little Don. [19] It confirms what has been said above by having the date 1734 carved on one of its sides. Though the inscriptions are of the normal style of the years 1733-38, the stoop is unusual in having six sides; nevertheless, the traveller still followed the method of turning right from the face marking his destination. The route down to Unsliven bridge is marked 'Underbank [and] Bradfield' and the continuation of this neglected highway via Willow bridge, Silkstone and Cawthorne is indicated as leading eventually to 'Wakefield & Leeds'. Cutting across this highway is the older and more important ridgeway coming from 'Woodhead [and] Mottram' and leading to 'Sheffield & Rotterham', the east-west route used by the Cheshire salters and turnpiked in 1741 as the Hartcliff-Rotherham branch of the Saltersbrook-Doncaster road. North of the stoop, the lines of the old tracks across the common were altered considerably by the early nineteenth-century enclosure commissioners, but a short holloway indicates the turning to 'Penistone, Huthersfield & Hallifax' and the other side of the stoop, which is marked 'Barnsley & Pontefract. 1734. Doncaster', pointed the way down to Oxspring bridge, thence up Bower Hill to Coates farm and along past Eastfield, Stainborough and Keresforth.

Once they had outlived their purpose and were no longer used by travellers, several stoops were moved and now it is often difficult to determine their original sites. One of the gateposts leading into the field containing Hartcliff tower, west of Penistone, is a guide stoop which has been moved, but the enclosure of the common on which it once stood has made its precise former location uncertain. Pointing hands mark the way on two sides and it is still possible to read 'Penistone 2 Miles / Rotharam [1]2 Miles / Bar[ns]ley 8 M[ile]s'. Now at first sight this mileage is rather puzzling, for 400 yards away a small turnpike milestone indicates that Rotherham is fifteen miles distant. [20] The explanation is that the turnpike surveyors used the statutory mile of 1,760 yards, whereas guide stoops were erected by parish officers who used the old customary mile, which varied in different parts of the country but in Yorkshire and Derbyshire was reckoned to be about 2,200 yards, or a mile-and-a-quarter in modern reckoning. [21] When the Earl of Oxford's party made a circuitous journey from Barnsley to Sheffield via Rotherham in 1725 they were surprised to learn that they had covered no more

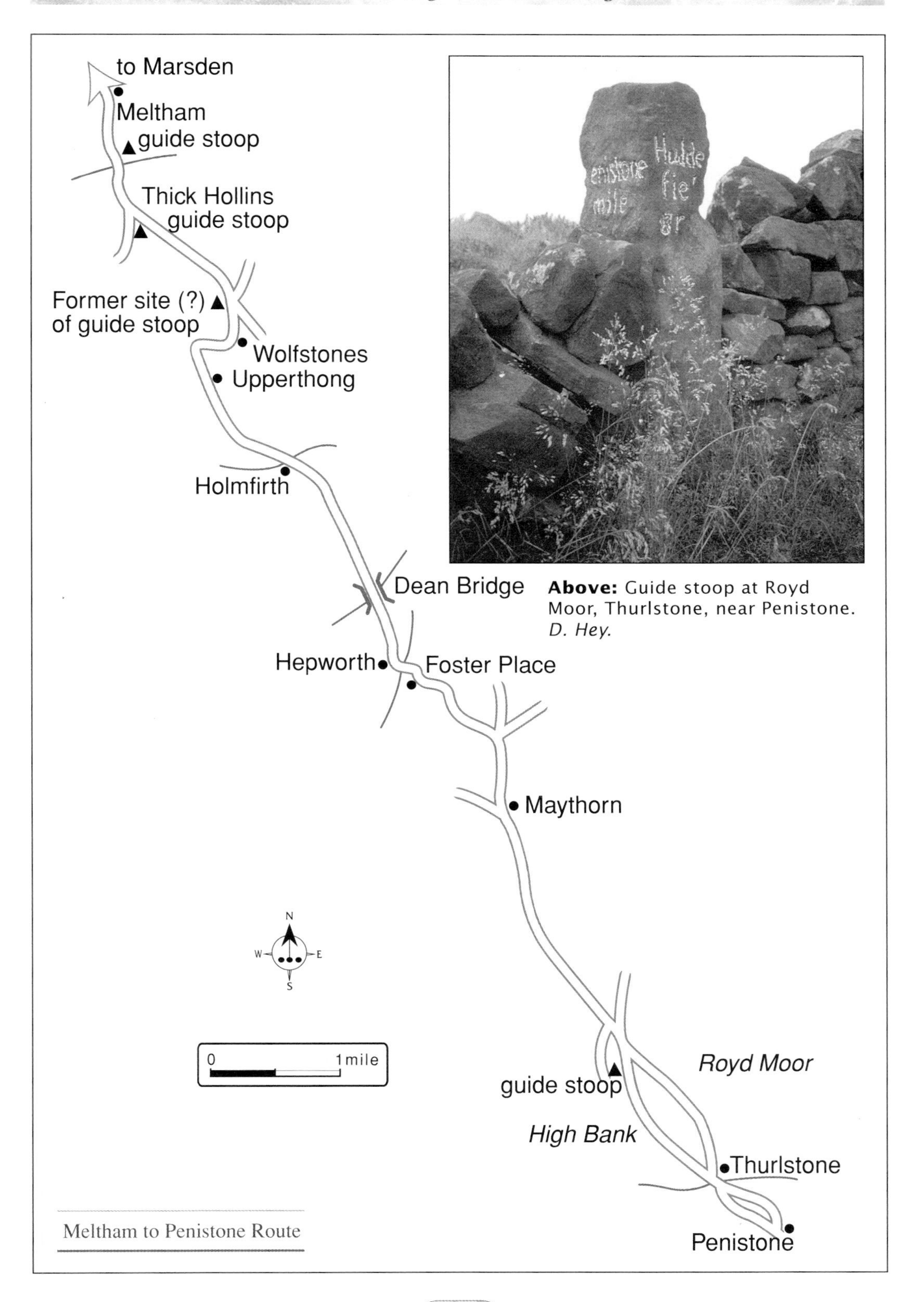

Above: Guide stoop at Royd Moor, Thurlstone, near Penistone. *D. Hey.*

Meltham to Penistone Route

than fourteen miles, 'according to the generous way of computation we met with in this country'. [22]

Stoops were erected at irregular intervals in lonely parts of the West Riding long after 1738. A stone known as Hanson Cross, which guided travellers to Penistone and Bradfield or along a track to Sheffield was erected in 1753. One old customary mile further along this highway to Penistone, just past the Bar Dyke at the junction with the route over the Strines, is a small stoop, which was placed there in 1740 to mark the routes to Bradfield (2 miles), Hope (9), Penistone (5) and Sheffield (9). [23] A stoop in Tolson museum, Huddersfield, that once stood at Shelley Bank Bottom, indicating the ways to Huddersfield, Penistone, Sheffield and Wakefield, was erected as late as 1758, according to its inscription. Several late stoops in the Oughtibridge-Brightholmlee-Bradfield area were not constructed until 1860. [24] Their inscriptions were chipped away during the Second World War so that enemy parachutists would be unable to find their way on the local hills and moors. New directions have since been painted on these stoops, but they are not necessarily the same as the old ones.

Detective work using Stoops

Despite these difficulties it is still possible to identify some old packhorse routes by the guide stoops alongside them. An old hill route that has been driven into oblivion by newer routes along the valley bottoms connects Marsden and Meltham, two typical West Riding textile settlements, with the former cloth market at Penistone. Like so many ancient routes, it is surprisingly direct on the map. [25] Entering Meltham along the present road from Marsden, it drops down the hill and crosses a stream on the way to Thick Hollins. Just by the bridge is a well-worn stoop on which can just be read, 'Honley 2½ Miles / Penistone 11 Miles / Marsden [?] Miles' on three of its sides. Following the Penistone sign we come to another stoop at the junction of the Netherthong and Ford Inn roads, which reads, 'Marsden 4 miles / Penis[tone] 11 mil[es] / Holmfirth 2 miles. 1761'. The Penistone side now points in the wrong direction, so the stoop must have been moved. Further on, a stoop that was probably erected at the Wilshaw-Netherthong and Honley-Ford Inn crossroads was later used as a gate post, then as a top-stone for a field wall in Netherthong and has now disappeared. It was carved 'Marsden 5 Miles / Penyston 8 Miles / Huddersfield 5 Miles'.

For the next few miles the route is not signposted, but it probably went via Wolfstones and Upperthong into Holmfirth, then up the steep South Lane to Cinderhills and along to Hepworth via Sandy Gate and Dean bridge. It then zig-zagged across a steep valley and climbed past Foster Place to Maythorn, an ancient boundary marker between the Graveship of Holme and Thurlstone township. In sharp contrast, the 1821 turnpike road extension from the Flouch Inn to New Mill follows the line of the river; the older route deliberately sought the hills. Having reached the summit, the old road followed the ridge towards Thurlstone and Penistone. Thomas Jeffreys' map of 1767-72 shows that the line was identical with the present lane, which was straightened and set out at a standard width of thirty feet by the Thurlstone enclosure commissioners in 1812-16. One more stoop remains to mark the way. It now forms part of the wall on the right-hand side of the unmetalled lane that forks right at the top of Royd Moor and descends High Bank into Thurlstone, but no doubt it once stood at the crossroads. This battered guide stoop preserves a tenuous link with the past and confirms that this hill-route was indeed an old pack-way, for it reads, 'Holmfirth 4 mile[s] / Hudde[rs]fie[d] 8 M[iles] / [P]enistone [?] mile[s]'.

So four stoops still stand alongside this forgotten Pennine highway. Both in Yorkshire and Derbyshire stoops survive in the western hills and on the moors where they were most needed. None has been found east of a line between Chesterfield, Sheffield and Barnsley, where it was easier to find or ask the way. Yet perhaps a few stoops were erected in the more lonely spots in the east, even if none survives, for how else can we explain the field-name 'Guide Stoop Close', which was marked by the crossroads on Ravenfield common in a sketch in a surveyor's notebook in 1766? [26]

A large number of guide stoops can be found further north in the textile district of the West Riding and a few more can be seen on the North York Moors, but the ones that Celia Fiennes saw in Lancashire have gone and no other part of England has such a rich heritage of waymarkers before the era of turnpike roads. They are invaluable evidence of the network of routes that were in use in the first half of the eighteenth century.

3 Maps

According to W. B. Crump, [27] the pioneer historian of old packhorse roads, the earliest reference in English literature to a traveller consulting a map to find his way appears near the end of the second part of *Pilgrim's Progress*, when Greatheart was guiding Christiana and her family through the Enchanted Ground:

> *I saw then in my dream that they went on ... till they came to a place at which a man is apt to lose his way. Now, though when it was light their guide could well enough tell how to miss those ways that led wrong, yet in the dark he was put to a stand. But he had in his pocket a map of all ways leading to or from the Celestial City; where-fore he struck a light (for he never goes without his tinder box) and takes a view of his book or map, which bids him to be careful in that place to turn to the right hand ...*
>
> *Then thought I with myself, who that goeth on pilgrimage but would have one of these maps about him, that he may look when he is at a stand which is the way he must take?*

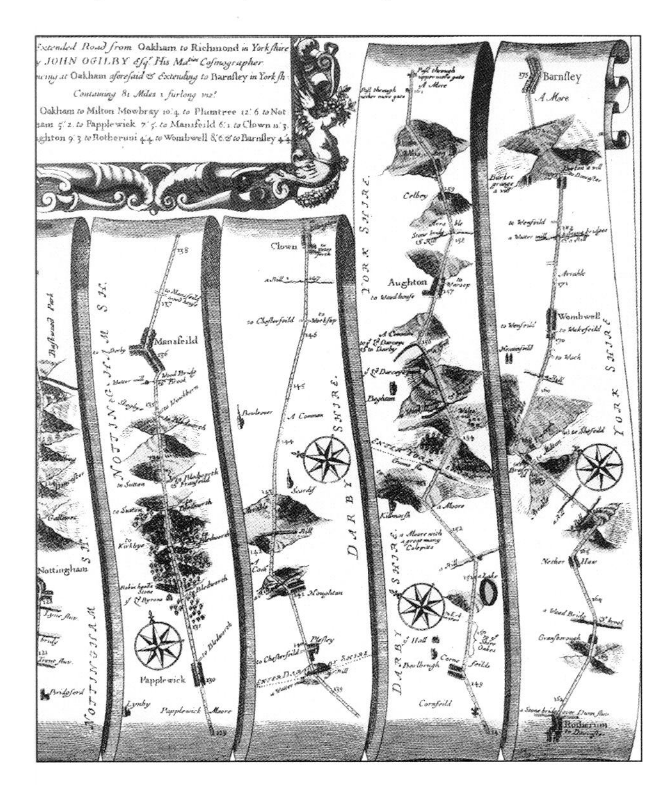

Left: Part of John Ogilby's map of the London-Richmond road.

Bunyan's tale was published in 1685, only ten years after John Ogilby's *Britannia Depicta*, the country's first collection of road maps. Ogilby's maps were clearly the model that Bunyan had in mind.

The general lines of some of the great medieval highways, including one from Lichfield and Derby to Chesterfield and so on to Doncaster, had been marked on Gough's national map of about 1360, but the scale was far too small to be of any use to the traveller. The first county maps did not appear until Christopher Saxton began to publish his work in 1574. Saxton was authorised by the queen's council to travel the country and take innumerable compass bearings from church towers and other view points and to collect information from knowledgeable local inhabitants. The maps of Derbyshire and his native Yorkshire were published in 1577 and they formed the basis of many maps that were redrawn and re-published under different names for well over a century. [28] These maps were attractively produced and were no doubt a pleasure for gentlemen to peruse in the library or study, but it is doubtful whether they offered much practical assistance to the traveller. They were normally issued in atlases and were too big to be carried on a journey: moreover, although they placed settlements in their correct geographical relationship and marked the major bridges, they did not indicate the roads. A map of England and Wales by Wencelaus Holler in 1644 showed a few roads, but their courses were marked only roughly. Otherwise, highways were not included until Ogilby's roads were grafted on to a Saxton or Speed base map.

Elizabethan and Stuart travellers had to rely instead upon the experience of local guides and on printed chronicles, starting with Grafton's *Abridgement of the Chronicles of England* (1572), which contained lists or tables of highways with the distances from town to town. No doubt it was also regular practice for travellers to make notes based on their own experiences or on the advice of friends. An example of such a collection of notes, which has been preserved amongst the records of the Wortley family, contains jottings on routes and distances from Wharncliffe lodge during the period, 1731-56. [29] One page reads, 'From the lodge to Eckington 12 Miles thus: To Jessops [Broom Hall] 6 Miles, from Mr. Jessops to little Sheffield 1, Hely 1, Gladely 1, Marsburgh 2, Eckington 1', with an alternative route via Rotherham, proceeding 'to Whiston 1, Aughton 2, Bayton 1, Eckington 2'. A journey from Middleham in the North Riding down the Great North Road, which was made in a chaise on 16 August 1744, was recorded for future reference as 'To Borough bridge, Wetherby, Aberforth, Castleforth Bridge', then via 'Sr. R. Wins [Nostell Priory], Stairfoot by Roiston, Pilley, Lodge'. Three days later, after ruefully reflecting on the arduous nature of a journey which had lasted from 4.20 a.m. until 9.15 p.m., with two hours thirty-five minutes allowed for 'baiting', the writer jotted down the observations of Mr Spencer of Cannon Hall, in the following manner:

> *From Barnsley to Chevet 4, To Castleford bridge 7 / 11 miles, From Barnesly to Heath 6, To Castleford Bridge 6 / 12 miles. The first of these two he says is the best for a Chais and better than to go by Pontefract, the roads to which are better. He agrees the Road from Barnsley to Pontefract is 9, From Pontefract to Castleford bridge 3 / 12. NB Mr Walker is Confident that for a Chais or Coach the Road by Pontefract is best being made Level when the roads are dry, less deep when they are not — better than the road by Heath.*

Such discussion must have preceded and followed many a journey both before and after the publication of adequate maps; even today the choice of the quickest and least troublesome route is an endless topic of conversation amongst motorists.

The traditions of the early mapmakers and the chroniclers were brought together in a successful and enduring manner in 1675 with the publication of John Ogilby's *Britannia Depicta*. Ogilby was approaching the end of a remarkably varied career when he obtained the patronage of Charles II for his project. His volume depicted the seventy-five principal highways of the kingdom in a series of 100 double folio copper plates and each road was followed by means of a strip map, a device still used in the publications of motoring organisations at the present time. The illustrations which embellish some of the plates show Ogilby's surveyors at work. One portrait shows a man pushing a simple wheel, which is geared to a comptometer that measures distances on a dial. The unit of measurement was the statutory mile of 1,760 yards rather than the various customary miles that were still commonly used. Another drawing shows a man on horseback, carrying an azimuth compass to record major changes of direction. Every highway was measured accurately by the surveyor and every detail about crossroads, junctions, bends, bridges, names of towns and villages, the destinations of

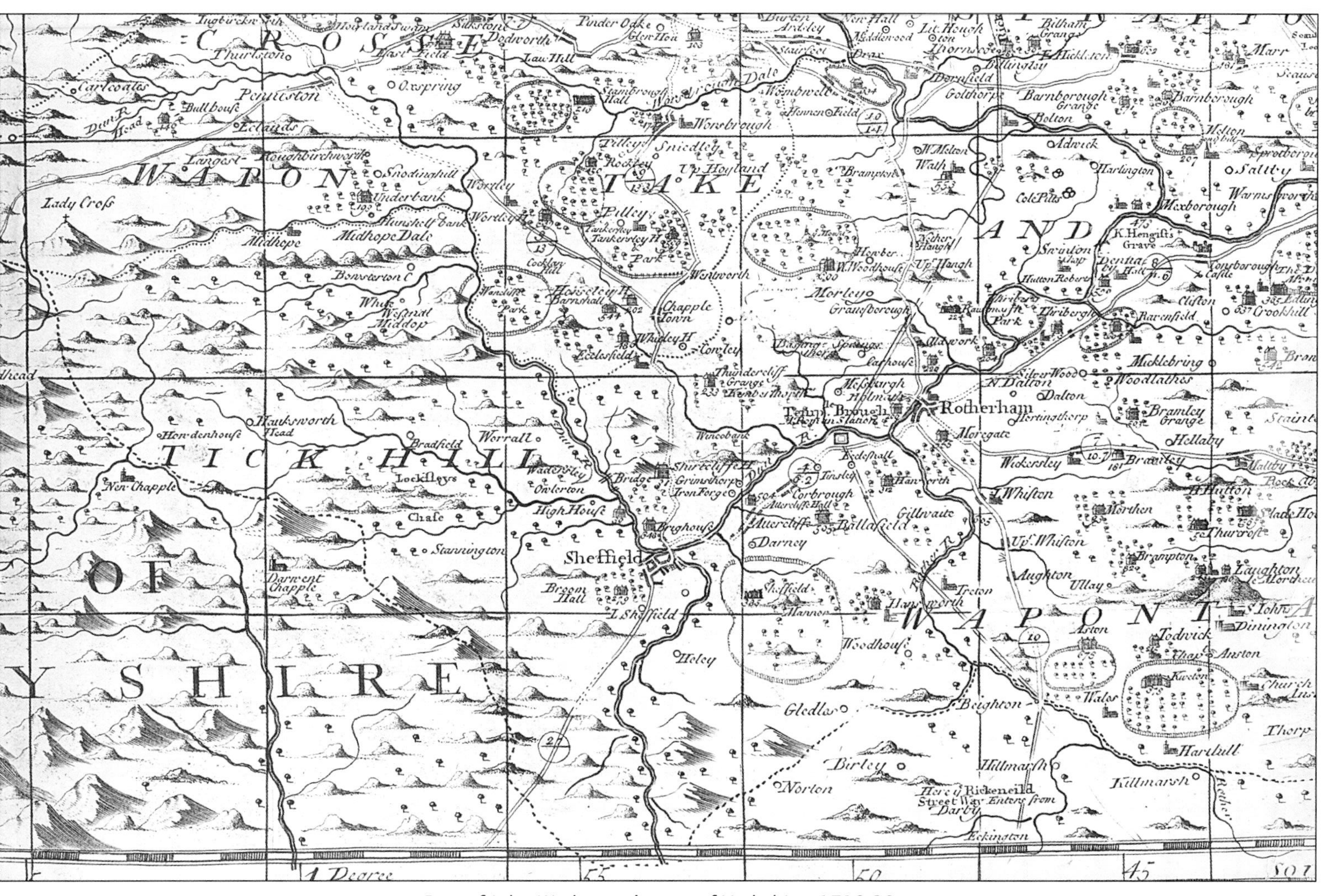

Part of John Warburton's map of Yorkshire. 1718-20

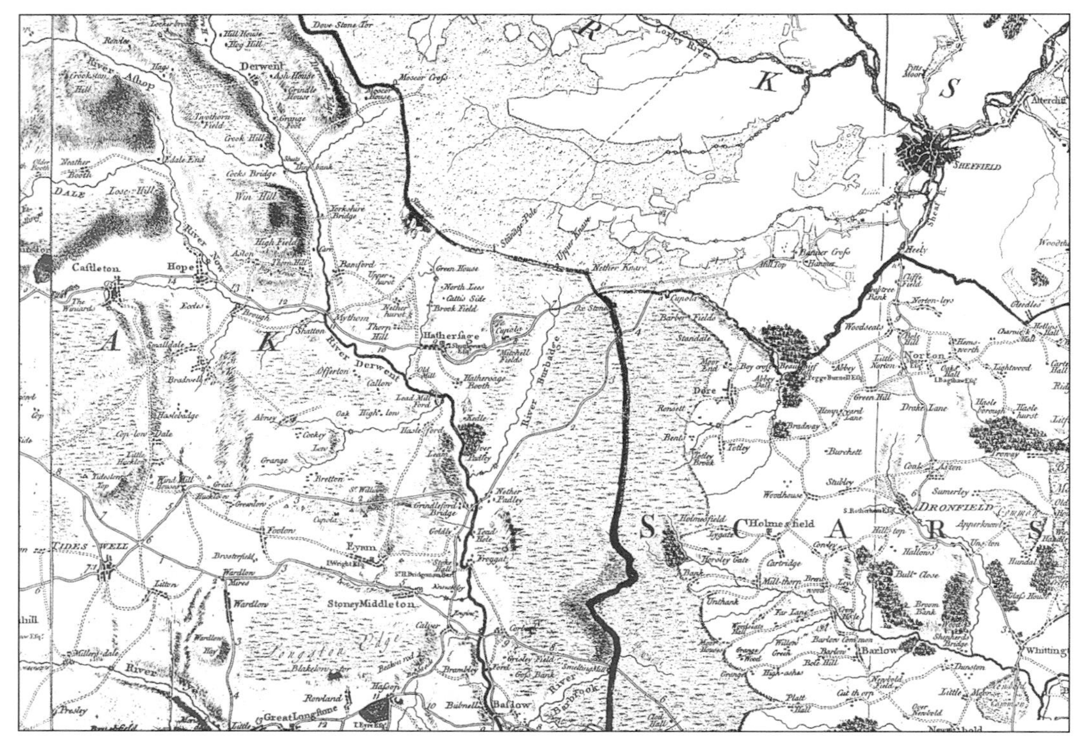

Part of P. P. Burdett's map of Derbyshire, 1763-67.

side roads and much miscellaneous information was based upon personal observation. Ogilby's volume was a major advance in mapping and though it was too large for the traveller to carry, relevant sections could be copied or noted quite easily.

Nevertheless, each volume could deal with relatively few of the numerous highways then in use; only three of Ogilby's roads passed through our region. The principal historical interest of his maps is that they show what were thought to be the major routes of his day. It is no surprise to find that he marks the Great North Road, entering south Yorkshire at Bawtry and proceeding via Rossington Bridge and Doncaster to Wentbridge, but the other two roads are unexpected; one is an old Roman road which had not yet been by-passed by the roads of the turnpike trustees and enclosure commissioners, the other is an ancient hill route which in its northern stretch is now completely forgotten. The old Roman road connected Derby and Manchester along the watershed between the Dove and the Wye, via Kedleston, Hognaston and Brassington. The exact line of the Roman road was not observed in the southern stretch but it was picked up on the approach to Chelmorton and was followed into Buxton.

From there, the highway stuck to the present route via Whaley Bridge, Disley and Stockport to Manchester. Ogilby's other road through the region was the London-Oakham-Rotherham-Halifax-Richmond route, which declined in status during the eighteenth century after the improving of the Aire and Calder navigation and the turnpiking of the Halifax-Doncaster highway offered a good connection with the capital. The old route deliberately sought the hills and though its course now seems strange to us it followed the shortest line that the local topography allowed. Letters and diaries from the first half of the eighteenth century show that the Spencers of Cannon Hall, the south Yorkshire ironmasters, invariably rode along this route to Nottingham (where they hired a coach to the capital) and that London merchants sometimes came this way in the opposite direction. This was the route along which Charles I was brought as a prisoner when the Scots army delivered him up to Parliament, as local witnesses were to remember for the rest of their lives. [30]

At the end of the seventeenth century James Paterson brought out a revised version of Ogilby that was to prove very popular. By 1826 Paterson's *Roads*, as it was known, was in its eighteenth edition, though considerably amended and enlarged. Its original title set forth its aims:

> *The Traveller's Guide: a most exact Description of the Roads of England. Being Mr Ogilby's Actual Survey and Mensuration by the Wheel of the Great Roads to all the Considerable Cities and Towns in England and Wales, together with the Cross Roads from one City or Eminent Town to another ... Wherein is Shown the Distance from Place to Place and plain Directions given to find the way, by setting down every Town, Village, River, Brook, Bridge, Common, Forest, Wood, Copse, Heath, Moor, etc., that occur in passing the Roads. And for the better Illustration thereof there are added Tables wherin the Names of the Places with their Distances, are set down in Column, in so plain a manner that a meer Stranger may Travel all over England without any other Guide.* [31]

In most parts of the country no further advance in mapping roads was made until almost a century after Ogilby, but Yorkshire is fortunate in having John Warburton's survey of 1718-20, which marks all the highways between the various market towns. When he began his survey, Warburton was an excise officer in Bedale, but he was soon to be elected F.R.S. and F.S.A. and to be appointed Somerset Herald. He travelled the county in a gig, soliciting subscriptions from gentry families while his assistants measured the roads with a wheel and took compass bearings from church towers and other high points. Only subscribers received

Part of Thomas Jeffreys's map of Yorkshire, 1767-72.

maps and copies are now rare, but Warburton's detailed notebooks are preserved in the Lansdowne collection in the British Library. [32] The notebooks show that he questioned local people as he went along and recorded names as he heard them pronounced: Stainber for Stainborough, Worspordale for Worsbrough Dale, Huiston for Whiston, Stenton for Stainton, and so on. Crossroads and streams, or 'rills', were always noted and other landmarks and points of interest jotted down. On the road between Penistone and Barnsley, for instance, he wrote:

Enter Silkstone town end the town strikkes Southwards, on the Rt The Church Tower Steeple 6 Bells. Mr Clarkson Parson. Cross A Rill at the Bottom. The Glass house on the Rt. Ascend A hill thro' A spring of wood.

Approaching Barnsley, he took three compass bearings and noted,

NE 490 Old Barnsley B[earing] NE 190 Descend A hill Leasurely two Coalpits on the Lt. Old Barnsley T[own]. B[earing] NE 40 at the Bottom A Rill which Crosses the way & runs along on my Rt ... Ascent into the Town ... Market day on Wednesday. 2 fairs only a Constable Barnsley is Remarkable for Coalls & Wires.

Distances between market towns were given on the map in both customary ('computed') and statutory miles; thus from Penistone to Sheffield the mileage was given as nine or thirteen and that from Barnsley to Rotherham as ten or fourteen. Churches, great houses and parks were marked, but hills and woods were indicated only in the rough manner of Saxon and in the western parts the details were poor and sometimes wrong. [33] Even so, Warburton's map as a considerable advance on previous publications and it is of great historical interest in outlining the major highways of his day. Above all, the map shows that the turnpike roads two or three generations later simply followed ancient routes that were well-established by 1720 and probably well before.

New maps of a far better calibre than anything produced previously were published during the third quarter of the eighteenth century. In 1762 the Royal Society of Arts, then known as the Society for the Encouragement of Arts, Manufactures, and Commerce, offered prizes of £100 for new county maps on the scale of one inch to one mile. Peter Perez Burdett, who started work on Derbyshire in 1763, had his map published in 1767 and Thomas Jefferys, who began his survey of Yorkshire in 1767, produced his map in sections in 1771-72. Both maps soon ran to further editions, They are invaluable to historians for marking the extent of commons and wastes on the eve of enclosure, the area devoted to parks and woodland, the sites of coal pits, lead mines, smelting cupolas, windmills, water-powered corn mills, textile mills, forges and cutlers' grinding wheels, and not only the major highways but many of the lanes as well. The early turnpike roads are accurately delineated and milestones recorded along them. They depict the pattern of highways and byways on the eve of the changes associated with parliamentary enclosure and the creation of new routes by some of the turnpike authorities. [34]

Most of the lanes and highways that are shown on Burdett's and Jefferys's maps are still in use today. Those marked by Burdett in the old parish of Dronfield are still recognisable as Stubley Lane, Mickley Lane, Cowley Lane, and so on, but the present route from Sheffield to Chesterfield, via Meadowhead, was not created until 1795. Burdett shows the line of the ancient highway, which was made into a turnpike road in 1756. It left Yorkshire by Heeley Bridge and followed Derbyshire Lane through Norton Park, where it continued as Dyche Lane (or Drake Lane as Burdett mistakenly labels it) to Coal Aston and so down Green Lane to Dronfield. On reaching Unstone it climbed up what is now a narrow lane to Old Whittington instead of taking its present course through Whittington Common. Its original purpose had been not to take the quickest route between the two market towns but to connect all the villages on the way.

3 The Evidence on the Ground

1 Holloways

Many of our present-day roads and lanes are ancient routes which have been levelled and provided with a firm surface. Even now the traveller is sometimes aware that he is well below the level of the surrounding fields or woods, that what he is following is a former holloway which has been improved for the benefit of modern traffic. Elsewhere, in many parts of the countryside, particularly on the slopes of hills, abandoned and overgrown tracks retain their sunken appearance. Often they survive only in short stretches, but some, like that which connects Milnthorpe with Johnnygate in the Cordwell Valley, can still be followed for hundreds of yards. They are instantly recognisable as an ancient feature of the landscape, immediately redolent of a previous era of transport.

Holloways are an ancient feature of the landscape, for some can be dated to prehistoric times. Place-names recorded in local medieval deeds and charters show that the constant wear of traffic had produced sunken tracks by the time of our earliest documents. The hamlet of Holloway, three miles south of Matlock, had acquired its name by the first decade of the

Holloways converging on Bar Brook; their origins are unknown, but they may have been turf-gates. *H. Smith.*

thirteenth century and may have stood at the junction of two or more sunken tracks, for the persistence of the plural form of the name is noteworthy. A field near Baslow was known as Holweyrode in 1356 and the present Holloway Lane at Youlgreave is probably the 'Holeweye' of 1314. Nor were holloways merely a rural phenomenon, for in 1532 John Holland of Sheffield left two shillings in his will 'to the mending of Howlow Layne' and Rotherham has its Hollow Gate along which travellers once left the town on their way to London. Wath upon Dearne, Mosborough and Charlton Brook, near Chapeltown, each have a Hollowgate, though modern surfaces disguise their ancient character. Dark Lane at Alport and Dyche Lane at Coal Aston (or Dikes Lane as it was called in 1592) were holloways under other names and some of the numerous tracks that have been nicknamed Mucky Lane were routes that were so churned up by horses and carts that they became unpleasant to use. [1]

The old ridgeways rarely degenerated into holloways, except when they crossed the peat moors, for they could normally rely upon a firm surface, but when tracks left the summits to descend the steep hills they often cut deep into the sub-soil. Soon they formed gullies for heavy rains and served as natural drains for the land alongside. Samuel Smiles aptly described them as horse tracks in summer and rivulets in winter. The rain washed away the loose soil and when horses and wheeled vehicles churned up the wet surface, the ways got deeper and deeper. In time they became unusable in bad weather and if land was available another track was formed alongside and eventually abandoned in turn.

In 1788 Gilbert White wrote that among the singularities of his beloved Hampshire village of Selborne were two rocky lanes, which

> *by the traffic of ages, and the fretting of water, [were] worn down through the first stratum of our freestone, and partly through the second; so that they look more like water-courses than roads; and are bedded with naked rag for furlongs together. In many places they are reduced sixteen or eighteen feet beneath the level of the fields; and after floods, and in frost, exhibit very grotesque and wild appearances, from the tangled roots that are twisted among the strata, and from the torrents rushing down their broken sides; and especially when those cascades are frozen into icicles, hanging in all the fanciful shapes of frost-work. These rugged, gloomy scenes affright the ladies when they peep down into them from the paths above, and make timid horsemen shudder while they ride along them; but delight the naturalist with their various botany, and particularly with their curious filices with which they abound.*

On the moors, where choice of route was unrestricted, the holloways are sometimes little more than a series of shallow tracks that fan out over a wide area. Often they are concealed by heather and can be seen to advantage only after a moorland fire. But even on the moors holloways are sometimes several feet deep as they descend the steeper hills. Jeffrey Radley identified over sixty moorland packways and branch tracks heading from west to east from Beeley Moor in the south to Stanedge Pole in the north and over forty packways aligned north-west to south or south-east between Stanage and Kinderscout. Big Moor and Offerton Moor are particularly rich in holloways, but further north Kinder and Bleaklow were formidable barriers that few cared to cross. [2]

Once the commons and wastes had been enclosed, choice of route was restricted to the roads and lanes authorised by enclosure surveyors. Such routes are mostly still in use, their former appearance concealed by metalled surfaces. William Marshall, writing about the Vale of Pickering in 1788, remarked that within his lifetime all the roads of his district 'lay in their natural form; that is, in a state of flatness, in flat situations; or in hollow-ways, on the acclivities of hills. Now, there is scarce a flat road or a hollow-way left'. [3] Sunken tracks survive only where they were ignored by the enclosure commissioners and turnpike trustees or where a

Above: Side Lane, Cordwell valley. Long disused as a through route, this deep holloway was used by wheeled traffic during the reign of Elizabeth I, no doubt in connection with the lead-smelting works in the valley bottom. **Below:** Hob Lane, Holmesfield. The route from Totley into the Cordwell valley followed the western edge of Holmesfield's medieval deer park. Carts still used this holloway in the early twentieth century, making it deeper and deeper. *Sheila Edwards.*

country bridleway has fallen into disuse since the horse was replaced by the motor car. A holloway through Kitchen Wood was once the direct route from Holmesfield to Dronfield; on the opposite side of the valley a bridleway up to Summerley has the same distinctive appearance. One of the best examples of an abandoned track is Judd Field Lane, which descends the southern slope of the great ridge which separates Penistone from Midhopestones. Once, this was the direct route for traffic heading out of Derbyshire via the Strines to the West Riding textile towns, but the turnpike road which replaced it in the 1770s sought an easier climb (though still 1:4) past Sheephouse Farm to Penistone. Judd Field Lane survived as a path, but its flagstones are now overgrown and even the sunken appearance of this ancient way is obscured by trees, bushes, grass and rosebay willow-herb.

Packhorses were capable of wearing down shallow holloways and of creating deeper tracks in the soft peat. The numerous ramblers who walked along the southern stretch of the Pennine Way before a mat surface was provided have shown how easily the peat is eroded. Once the surface vegetation was worn away the peat was susceptible to natural erosion, especially by water. Some holloways now carry semi-permanent water courses which have altered their flat-bottomed profile, while others have partly silted up or have been converted into drains by the water authority. The deepest holloways on the moors have cut right through the peat to the original sub-soil and they can be readily distinguished by the lighter-coloured vegetation in the bottom. A good example of this phenomenon is the track from Hope to Chesterfield which passes just to the east of the Lady Cross on the Big Moor. But as we shall see, these deep moorland holloways are not the natural result of centuries of traffic. Some were deliberately constructed to facilitate the movement of millstones, others were the turf-gates by which winter fuel was brought down on sledges from communal or private turbaries. The older inhabitants of Edale remember that the sunken track up to Grindslow Knoll was once their Peat Way. A group of holloways that climb from Owler Bar to Totley Moss come to a sudden end where the peat covering has been completely cleared. Every settlement in the Dark Peak had turf-gates like these.

Away from the peat moors. the deepest roads must have been created not by trains of packhorses and travellers on foot but by horse-drawn carts, waggons and wains. William Marshall was of the opinion that;

> *although a horse path may be poached in wet weather, yet in dry it is, in the nature of the tread of horses, trodden level again, to receive with benefit the water of heavy showers; but not one soil in a hundred is capable of affording materials sufficient to bear the wheels of laden carriages; which, in the action of wheeled carriages, tend, not to fill up and level, but to deepen the holes and gutters made by running water; and of course act in concert with it to render the road impassable.* [4]

The 'Cart Way' from Wortley to Wharncliffe Lodge was no doubt being damaged in this way in 1734, when a note in the Wharncliffe papers tells us that the circumference of a wheel with dirt on it was 8ft 3¼ins whereas without dirt it was only 8ft 2ins. In earlier times wheeled vehicles had been even more destructive to the roads, for they had fixed wheels both fore and aft and were therefore difficult to steer out of a rut once they were in.

The deepest holloways in the region are in the Cordwell valley. That signposted at Ewe Ford as a public bridleway to Horsleygate Lane is known as Side Lane and is a convenient short-cut down the hillside on the former highway which came from Totley, Woodthorpe Hall and Hob Lane to Fox Lane and so on to Curbar Gap. In places it is twelve to fifteen feet deep and about twenty-four feet wide at the top, tapering to its present width of only two feet at the bottom. Tall oaks grow in the banks and hinder the way and the bottom is often wet and muddy for it serves as a drain for the surrounding fields. Horses from nearby riding schools come this way and churn up the mud, but wheeled vehicles can no longer obtain a passage. That they could do so long ago is evident from the Holmesfield manor court rolls, which record that on 12 April 1588 Christopher Wood and Nicholas Wosenam were ordered to cut the wood that 'hangeth over' Side Lane 'by reason that it hyndreth Carryages which shall chaunce to passe through'.[5] The carriages of this period were probably horse-drawn carts or two-wheeled wains pulled by oxen. The Eyres had lead-smelting works by Smeekley Wood during the reign of Elizabeth and the traffic associated with this trade was no doubt largely responsible for the great depth of this holloway. Hob Lane, which is almost as deep and which can be followed for about six hundred yards, skirted the western edge of the medieval deer park at Holmesfield. Local people remembered carts churning up the mud in this lane, making it deeper and deeper.

Sunken lanes or holloways mark routes that were once well used, though their depth is not a clear indicator of age. A sunken lane could be formed quickly through intensive use by sledges or wheeled vehicles or by its conversion to a watercourse in winter. Many holloways are now V-shaped because of the movement of soil in their banks and because they are no longer used by vehicles; they were not constructed that way to allow space for packs, as is sometimes thought. Overgrown and abandoned as many are, they often provide a good starting point in identifying an old route, though map and documentary evidence is needed to determine their status. Many moorland holloways were not through-routes, but those that go past guide stoops or lead to bridges can sometimes be shown to have been so.

2 Causeys

The problem of worn and sunken surfaces was tackled by laying down a single or double line of flagstones known as a causey. Derived from the French *caucie* and ultimately from the Latin for 'trodden', the word was frequently lengthened to causeway, but it is still used in

left: Cat Hill causey. This well-preserved series of flagstones formed a single causey that linked the hamlets of Gunthwaite and Cat Hill with the parish church and the market at Penistone. *Sheila Edwards.*

local speech in the sense of 'causey edge' to mean a slightly-raised pavement. Few surviving features of the packhorse era as as evocative as the moorland or woodland causey, now often overgrown and difficult to follow, but occasionally still forming a delightful track for travellers. Causeys were not needed on firm surfaces and therefore are rarely found in the White Peak, but they were a great help on moors made soggy by heavy rain and on the sides of hills where holloways were commonly formed. Sometimes they were even laid at the bottom of existing holloways to prevent further wear and tear. According to an Act of 1691 and an order of the Derbyshire quarter sessions of 1709, the flagstones were supposed to be at least three feet wide, but in practice about two feet was the usual width. [6] In some places a different technique was used, as for example on the track down from Woodthorpe Hall to Totley and on the route over the hill from Brightholmlee to Glen Howe, where a lot of small stones were placed sideways on and packed closely together. But the characteristic causey consisted of a line of thick, massive slabs of sandstone. In recent years the National Trust has brought hundreds of flagstones by helicopter from Lancashire mills to Lost Lad and Back Tor on the Derwent moors to form paths that look pleasingly like the causeys of the packhorse era.

Existing causeys are impossible to date; they could have been lad down at any time from the Middle Ages to the nineteenth century. Causeys are recorded at Barnsley in 1467 and at Wombwell in 1516 and others are known from references in medieval deeds. [7] Joseph Kenworthy suggested that 'the staircase of Midhope' *(scalarium de Mitthop)*, which formed a boundary of the Broomhead estate about the year 1280, is to be identified with Stocks Lane at Upper Midhope, where a causey's graceful descent of the hillside has the appearance of a staircase. [8] It is an attractive theory, but the present stones are not worn enough to have supported seven centuries of traffic and the Broomhead estate probably did not extend that far in the thirteenth century. The resemblance of another stepped causeway to a staircase seemingly accounts for the name of Stairfoot, where roads descend steeply from Barnsley and Darfield and from Monk Bretton priory. There, the causey has been obliterated by a modern surface, but a couple of miles further west another long staircase winds down from Kingstone Hill to Gilroyd along the western boundary of the old township of Worsbrough. The best known of all the local causeys, however, is that which picks its way through the boulders and bracken from North Lees, Hathersage, over the cliff to Stanedge Pole and along the Long Causeway towards Sheffield. Near the pole the causey becomes a double track capable of bearing carts, but wheeled vehicles could have climbed the edge only by a less direct route from Bamford via Bole Hill; even a packhorse would have had difficulty in reaching the summit by the narrow, winding causey. Perhaps the carts only went as far as the edge to collect the millstones that were manufactured there.

Double lines of flagstones sometimes served as major highways. In central Yorkshire Hambleton Causey was described in 1640 as 'the high roade way from Halifax, Bradford, Leedes, and Wakefield unto the markett towne of Selby and the towne of Kingston upon Hull, which causey is two miles in length, and soe extraordinarilye broken and decayed with cartes and cariages that the inhabitantes theraboutes are not able to repaire and maintaine itt'. [9] More usually, a major highway consisted of a sunken carriage way and of a flagged causey on the bank high above. When Celia Fiennes made a journey from Prescott to Wigan in south Lancashire in 1698, she travelled 'mostly in lanes and some hollow wayes, and some pretty deep stony way so forced us upon the high Causey many [times]'. [10] Oliver Heywood, the famous Nonconformist preacher from Coley near Halifax, has provided a vivid description of a similar highway in his account of a misadventure near Brighouse on 1 November 1680. He wrote:

Opposite page: The Moorland causey that climbs up toStanedge Pole from near North Lees.
D. Hey.

I met a man riding on an horse and driving two horses before him with pack-saddles, yet empty. He had tied them together with an halter. Now just as I met him there was a deep hollow way below and an high Causey above, and the one of the horses took the higher, and the other the lower way. It was impossible that the lower should leap up to the other and there was great hazzard of the higher falling, and both ways they could not go for the distance was beyond the reach of the halter ... At last the man fearing the issue light off his horse and run towards the lower horse to pull off the halter; but as he ran the horse in the hollow way leapt up with his fore feet to mount the Causey, but not being able, fell down and pulled the other backwards after him. With the fall was a crashing noise. I made account that the horse's back or neck had been broken, for there lay the horse with his feet upwards and stirred not ... However there was no hurt except for two bakestones on the horse that fell which were masht to pieces and the man made great lamentation for the breach of the Baking Stones. [11]

T. D. Whitaker wrote in 1816 that:

As late as 1753 the roads near Leeds consisted of a narrow hollow way little wider than a ditch, barely allowing of the passage of a vehicle drawn in a single line; this deep narrow road being flanked by an elevated causeway covered with flags or boulder stones. When travellers encountered each other on this narrow track, they often tried to wear out each other's patience rather than descend into the dirt alongside. The raw wool and bale goods of the district were nearly all carried along these flagged ways on the backs of single horses. [12]

John Farey observed that in Derbyshire:

A very commendable spirit prevails, throughout most of the Coal and Shale districts ... for providing very solidly paved Paths by the sides of the Road, from two to three feet wide, that are used by persons on foot and on horseback; these Paths are mostly laid with thick flat paviers of Millstone Grit, which is excellently adapted to this purpose, for wear, and as not apt to occasion the feet of Horses and Men to slip, as Limestone is dangerously liable to do: but owing to the constant use of these Paths by Horses, where in many cases the same is quite unnecessary, these paths are too commonly worn quite hollow in the middle, holding puddles in wet weather, and being extremely unpleasant to walk on, the feet constantly tilting towards each other, unless by straddling, they are placed on the edges; these edges are in some places frequently dressed down, and the path made flat again, by the rough tool of the Mason. [13]

Short stretches of flagstones alongside our country lanes are still a familiar sight. A less common but more intriguing survival from the packhorse era is the single track across lonely moors or down woodland slopes or perhaps along the edge of a field. Some causeys consist of no more than a few rough stones placed in a line over a wet patch of shale, but others are formed from a series of well-shaped flags and continue for hundreds of yards. In the delightfully wooded countryside to the north of Penistone, the finest causey in the region takes the rambler up a long flight of steps to Gunthwaite and its glorious sixteenth-century barn. The hall has long since gone, but there is little doubt that the causey was built by one of the Bosvilles, the ancient gentry family that resided there, for the route heads from Gunthwaite towards the parish church and the market place that Godfrey Bosville was instrumental in founding at Penistone in 1699. For half a mile or so it drops steeply from the hamlet to the stream at Gunthwaite Bottom, so steeply in part that some of the steps have been cut with a chisel to stop

The causeway on Stanage Edge, looking towards Stanedge Pole. *C.L.M. Porter.*

the horses slipping. A deep, gloomy holloway, much obscured by trees and brambles, descends alongside it. At the other side of the valley a steep cartway climbs the hill to the seventeenth-century gabled hall at Cat Hill, and beyond, another perfect length of causey heads towards Wellhouse farm and so on by lane, track and path for another mile to Penistone. Few routes are so redolent of a bygone age when men travelled on horseback or on foot.

Nowadays, these causeys are used only as footpaths, but originally they were frequently referred to as 'horse causeys'. [14] William Marshall wrote in 1808 that:

> *These flag pavements were formed for horse paths, not foot paths. Before carriage roads were formed of hard materials, these horse paths were common in the north of England, and, necessarily, on the sides of public lanes, in every deep soiled district of the kingdom; — for the use of pack horses and travellers on horseback, in the winter season; when clayey lanes were otherwise impassable. Where broad stones were not to be procured narrow causeways of pebbles were the packways.* [15]

With the advent of motor traffic these packways have either been widened and covered with a modern surface or else they have continued in use as footpaths or have been abandoned altogether. But many are still known to ramblers and some can still be recognised under a modern disguise. The path from Penistone to Thurlstone over Stottercliffe, for instance, has a new surface but can be recognised as a former causey by its narrow width between two long walls, and former causeys are commemorated in street names at Matlock and Crich.

Many causeys were the result of private initiative as lords and freeholders improved the ways across their land. In 1566 Mr George Barley of Barlow 'paved the way between [Barlow] Hall and Sudbrook, and all about the north barn door, and so unto the stable door' and on 3 December 1745 John Wilson of Broomhead Hall 'Lead out of the Nether Cow pasture 24 load of small stone and two load of scaplings, out of the Broad Leys with which I made a causway up to the great barn doors'. The agent to the fourth Duke of Devonshire explained how the previous duke diverted the road that came over the hill to Chatsworth, when he wrote in 1757, 'My late Lord Duke ...[made] a causeway all along the top of the flat part of the Parke by the Firs and turned the Packhorses down the Hill thro' the Coppice by the mill to the bridge ... this is no carriage-road, only a packhorse way'. [16]

Manorial courts also sometimes assumed responsibility, as in 1659 when the Wath upon Dearne court ordered, 'That Ralfe Smith doe make the Cawsey in the Skitrigg at his Wall Side' and 'That the Cawsey in and about the Holme and Holme-Lane and to the Gee-flatt Close be mended that Passengers may pass'. [17] But the majority of causeys were the responsibility of the overseers of the parish highways under the supervision of the justices of the peace at the quarter sessions. Unfortunately, the accounts of such overseers are extremely rare before the late eighteenth century and even then they are not particularly informative. However, entries such as '3 Days leveling and forming Ground for Causway' at Worsbrough on 30 March 1800 suggest that new causeys were being laid at a relatively late date and other accounts show that older causeys were being repaired regularly. The overseer at Dore, for instance, spent £2 in 1773 on flagstones leading to Old Hay cupola and the overseers of Ecclesfield lower division spent 1s.3d. in 1815 on 'Causway Repairing'. [18]

The former importance of the moorland causey over Holme Moss is brought home vividly by the diary of Arthur Jessop of Underbank, near Holmfirth. Much of the last months of the diary were taken up with the threat of invasion from Bonnie Prince Charlie's Highlanders. The arrival of the Scotsmen in Manchester caused consternation amongst the people of Holmfirth, who felt that the prince would not march immediately on the capital but would cross the Pennines and attack them. Amidst tremendous excitement, the Revd William Eden, the minister of the Unitarian chapel at Lydgate, organised an army of volunteers to defend the route over Holme Moss. Jessop wrote on 29 November 1745, 'It is reported this day that the Rebels are leaving Lancashire and are coming into Yorkshire and so come by Woodhead, and they are for pulling up Holm Causeway to hinder any of them from coming over Holm moss, and some say they have pulled it up'. The following day an invasion seemed certain and all sorts of wild rumours were flying about. Jessop wrote:

> *We heard soon this morning that a very great Mob was risen and plundering all before them, and was got to Marsden and would be in Huddersfield this day, and they sent from Huddersfield in the night to the Clothiers to fetch away their Peices, and they are gone for them soon this morning. They are in a terrible consternation in Huddersfield, Holmfirth, Wooldale, Scholes and all places hereabouts and are securing their best effects. And in Holmfirth they are getting their Guns ready and Iron forks, etc. and they are coming into Holmfirth from every side with what weapons they can get.*

Mr Eden's men were never called upon to defend their homes, for the Highlanders continued south to Derby, but nineteen months later the inhabitants of Holmfirth were presented at the quarter sessions for allowing 2,000 yards of their causey at Holme Moss to fall into 'great ruin and decay'. [19]

Bakewell bridge. One of the finest of the medieval stone bridges across the River Derwent — good visual evidence that wheeled traffic used Pennine routes in the Middle Ages. *C.L.M. Porter.*

3 Bridges

Many riverside settlements were founded at key fording or ferrying points, or in the lower reaches of rivers as small inland ports. In either case, they were placed where ancient roads crossed or approached a river. Some of these settlements became known by the name of their ford and a few of them had acquired their names before the Norman Conquest. Ashford was recorded in 926 and Bamford ('the ford marked by a tree') appears in Domesday Book. [20] In south Yorkshire the ancient Ricknield Street crossed the Don at its confluence with the Dearne by the meeting-place of the wapentake at Strafford Sands, and Domesday Book records Keresforth ('Cenfrith's ford'), near Barnsley, also Wath, a less obvious ford name which was in common usage much further north. [21] The early appearance of these names, especially in the case of Wath, which was the focal point of a large parish, suggests that the routes across these fords were of considerable antiquity. Other ford names may also be ancient, for although they were first recorded in the later Middle Ages they may have been in existence long before they were written down. Lumford ('the ford in a woody valley'), near Bakewell, is recorded in the thirteenth century and Stoke Ford, Abney, which lies on an old route across the moors from Hope and Castleton to the bridge over the Derwent between Stoke Hall and Froggatt, was mentioned in a document of 1319. This ford is almost three miles from Stoke but the use of the same name indicates a direct connection. [22]

A few miles further south, at Alport, near Youlgreave, a ford over the River Lathkill on one of the important highways from Manchester and Stockport to Derby and London remained in use until 1718 when the J.P.s meeting in quarter sessions accepted a petition for a horse-bridge.

Conkesbury Bridge, an eighteenth-century stone bridge that replaced an earlier one that was first referred to in 1269. *C.L.M. Porter.*

soe Narrow that the King's Subjects could not passe and repasse over the same with Carts and Carryages without great danger of their Lives and Goods'; they therefore voted £20 towards the repair of the bridge and a further £30 to widen it. [34] The new work can be seen underneath the bridge, upstream from the old.

County bridges spanned the Derwent at regular intervals of between one and two miles. A great deal of money was spent by the J.P.s in widening, repairing or rebuilding these bridges in the late seventeenth and eighteenth centuries. In 1687 £120 was spent on Grindleford bridge and in 1708 the old ford south of Hathersage, known as Hazelford, was spanned for the first time. The original intention was to have a wooden bridge carried by stone abutments and two stone pillars, but after £50.5s.6d. had been spent and the work was almost complete, it was 'unfortunately taken down by a flood before the wood was laid over'. Having decided to cut their losses, the Justices appointed a Hallamshire mason, Ezra Moreton, to erect a stone bridge of three arches and later they asked him to add another arch and to lay a causey at each end. [35] A similar decision had previously been reached over Yorkshire bridge, which led towards the county boundary. £40 was spent on it by the county in 1692 and in the following year the J.P.s resolved that 'beinge a Wood Bridge [it] Stood in frequent need of such large Summes to repair it And that it was much more for the Countys Interest to Convert it into a Stone Bridge there beinge plenty of Stone neare at Hand'. The masons were ordered to build a bridge of three turned arches, at the cost of £130. The present bridge looks as if it could be of that date, but it has only two arches.

Finally, the bridge which has stood at Slippery Stones near the head of the Derwent since 1959 originally spanned the river four miles downstream, but was removed in 1942 upon the construction of the reservoir. It had served an ancient route described in a fourteenth-century charter as 'the common way which leads from Sheffield towards Derwent'. The bridge appears to date from 1683 when the county awarded £100 towards its construction, and a further £34 was granted in April 1684 when Simon Holt, the county mason, reported that 'the foundacion thereof proves much worse than expected and the carriage of Stone very deare'. Although a county bridge, it is not wide enough to take wheeled traffic and in any case the steep hills on either side of the valley would have restricted travel to horseback and foot. [36] A similar narrow county bridge of seven arches, which spans the River Wye at Holme Hall north of Bakewell, was built in 1664-65. [37]

Though none of the original structures survives, it is evident from the records of the Derbyshire quarter sessions that the Rother was spanned by county bridges at Beighton, Killamarsh, Renishaw, Tapton and Hasland. The bridge at Ashford was marked on Saxton's map and other county bridges include those at Staveley, Wormhill, Whaley, Hayfield and Smithy bridge at Chapel en le Frith. [38] The 1531 Statute of Bridges gave J.P.s the power to levy a county rate towards the upkeep of bridges and to appoint surveyors. The number of bridges taken over from boroughs, rural manors and parishes grew as their importance to the county as a whole was gradually acknowledged, but local officers had to plead a convincing case to get a bridge taken off their hands. In July 1714 the Derbyshire J.P.s felt obliged to order

that Isaac Kirkbridge Master [sic] of this County to demolish deface or pull down all manner of Inscriptions carved or engraven in posts or Stones set upon any bridges in this County purporting the same to be County bridges Except on those that actually are so.

Unfortunately, the records of the Derbyshire quarter sessions for the years before 1682 do not survive, nor is there an extant survey of the county's bridges.

Early in 1602 the West Riding J.P.s named forty-eight of 'the most considerable' bridges which were to be kept in repair by the county. [39] Some which did not achieve this status were made the responsibility of one or more wapentakes, for it was judged that a single parish could

Willow bridge, Oxspring. This picturesque bridge over the River Don appears to date from about 1734. It lay on an old through route from Bradfield to Wakefield. Most packhorse bridges date from 1660-1740. *Sheila Edwards.*

not reasonably be expected to provide for the upkeep. For example, in 1611 Darfield bridge on the important highway from Saltersbrook to Doncaster was made the responsibility of the three southern wapentakes of Strafforth & Tickhill, Osgoldcross, and Staincross. [40] The county authority was sometimes willing to assist parishes in difficulty; for example, at the quarter sessions held at Pontefract in May 1698, a £30 gratuity was awarded to the parish of Ecclesfield towards the repair of Wadsley bridge on the road from Sheffield to Huddersfield and Halifax. The way that an influential J.P. could get a bridge upgraded is illustrated by the *Memoirs of Sir John Reresby* of Thrybergh, who wrote on 12 October 1686:

> *The sessions were held at Barnsley, wher I assisted. I gott ther an order for 10£ to be raised upon the weapontack of Strafford and Tickil, for the repair of Saddle Brige or New Brige, being that which parts the lordships of Rotherham and Brinsford or Ickles in the way from Rotherham to Sheffield. This brige was built about 100 years before by the family for their own conveniency, and was a publique brige and a highway only since Sir George Reresby's time, that suffered it to be lost, for till then the highway to Sheffield was by Knouck Brige. And though the use of it was now publique, yet the charge of repairs was still the families bycaus we built it, till by this 10£ being given or raised upon the weapontack it will now be entitled to be soe repaired for the future. I gott also ten pounds to make Dern Brige passable for coach and carriage, which was only before used for horses.* [41]

In 1752 a complete survey of the West Riding's bridges was made by the county surveyors, Westerman and Gott, and the architects, Robert Carr and John Watson. Plans and elevations to a uniform scale of twenty feet to one inch were made and brief descriptions added. This 'Book of the Bridges belonging in Whole or Part to the West Riding of the County of York' is invaluable for describing all the major bridges not long before many of them were widened or replaced in order to cope with the increasing volume of traffic. [42] The most notable fact to

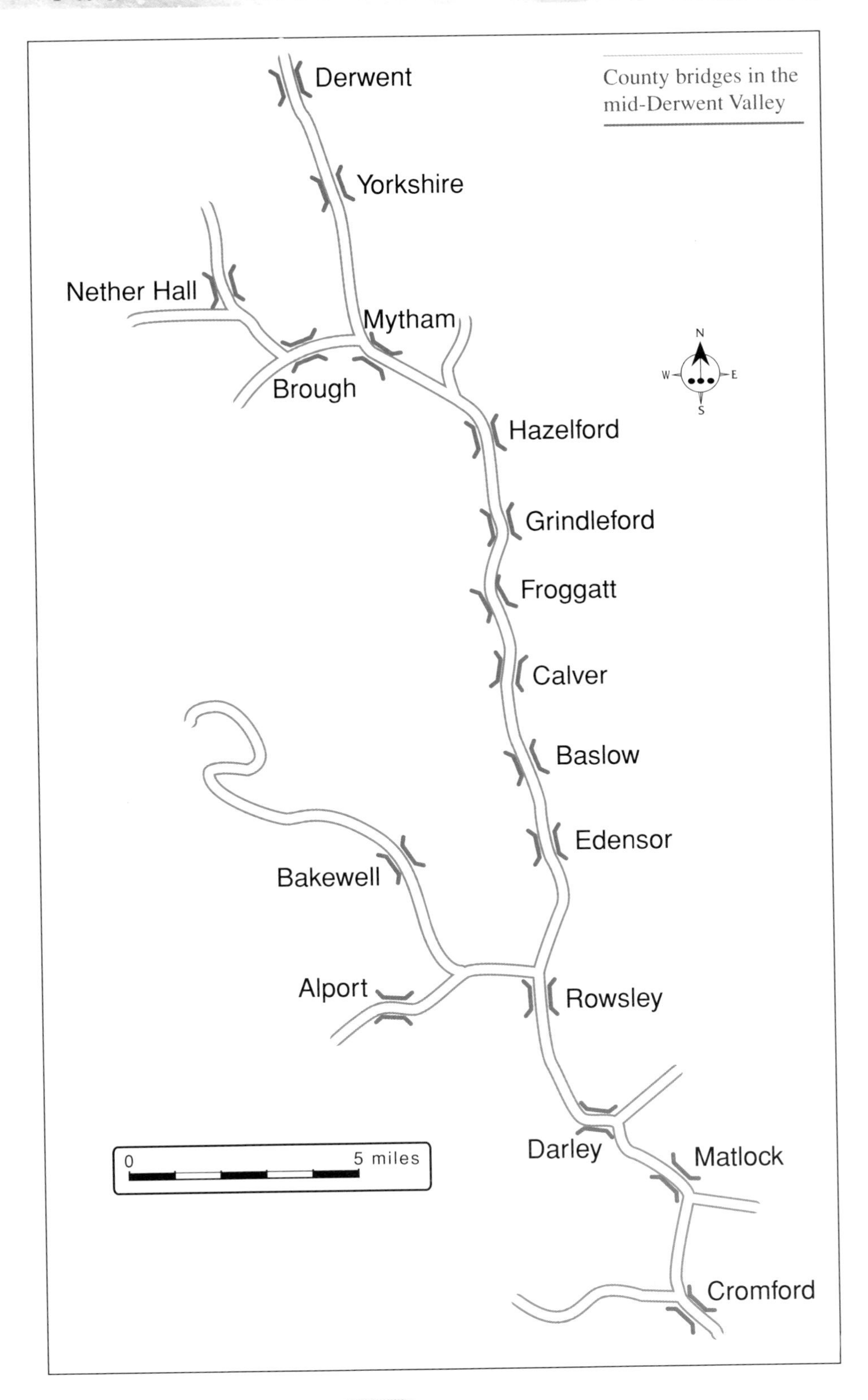
County bridges in the mid-Derwent Valley
Derwent
Yorkshire
Nether Hall
Mytham
Brough
Hazelford
Grindleford
Froggatt
Calver
Baslow
Edensor
Bakewell
Alport
Rowsley
Darley
Matlock
Cromford
N
W
E
S
0
5 miles

Glen Howe Park bridge. Moved here upon the construction of Ewden reservoir, it was originally known as New Mill bridge. It was built in 1734 on the site of a wooden bridge. *Sheila Edwards.*

emerge from these notes and drawings is that the largest bridges in the county were no more than eleven to sixteen feet wide. The medieval bridge at Rotherham was the broadest bridge in south Yorkshire, being 114 feet long and fifteen feet wide. Thurgoland bridge over the River Don was only twelve feet wide and the width of Aldham bridge over the River Dove in Darfield parish was a mere eleven feet. The survey shows that the Dearne was spanned by county bridges at Darton, Barugh, Burton Grange and the two Marl bridges near Darfield, and the Don by bridges at Sheffield, Attercliffe, Rotherham and the Bow or Saddle bridge whose predecessor had been erected by the Reresbys. [43]

Until the middle and later years of the seventeenth century only the major bridges were built of stone. Indeed, Leland's *Itinerary* reveals that in parts of the country where no suitable building stone was at hand, all the bridges were wooden ones. As late as 1738 a new wooden bridge was erected across the Idle at Bawtry at the joint expense of the counties of Yorkshire and Nottinghamshire, and this was not replaced by a stone structure until 1810. [44] The small stone bridges that occasionally appear in early records, like that at Dronfield in 1330 or that which marked the boundary of Hassop in 1432, were probably simple stone slabs. That the term 'bridge' covered any spanning structure is obvious from Thomas Woolhouse's statement in 1715 that the Little Sheffield bridge was 'only a single plank laid across the river'. [45]

During the seventeenth and eighteenth centuries wooden bridges were deemed inadequate as waggons got heavier and the volume of traffic increased. In 1641 the West Riding J.P.s decided that the two Marl bridges which took 'the High Rode way from the markett towne of Pontefracte and other Northern Parts unto the markett towne of Rotheram, and soe upp to the Cittye of London and other Southern Partes' across the Dearne and the Dove by Darfield were in 'great ruin and decay'. They therefore voted that £100 should be spent on replacing the wooden structures by new stone bridges, measuring 25½ft long and 14ft wide and 6ft long by twelve feet wide. [46] We have already noted how in Derbyshire the wooden Yorkshire bridge was replaced by a stone one in 1693 and how, in 1709, initial plans to build Hazelford bridge of timber and stone were discarded in favour of a bridge built entirely of stone. The whole process of gradual improvement is illustrated by the bridge which once crossed the Don at the western edge of the township of Attercliffe. At first, this was simply the West ford, but by the reign of Henry VIII a bridge had replaced the stepping stones. George Moore of Sheffield left a bequest of 3s.4d. to 'Westforthe Bridge' in 1535 and by 1607 the name had been corrupted by some to Washford bridge (the dialect pronunciation of wash being wesh). At that time it was described as being on 'the common passage between Sheffield and Rotherham' and was badly in need of repair. A new name first appears in 1647 when it was called 'Westforth, alias Attercliffe Bridge'. Finally, in 1672 the wooden bridge was replaced by that described in 1752 as being of 'good hewn Stone', measuring 92½ feet in length and thirteen feet in width. [47]

Other Bridges

Other substantial bridges were also rebuilt in stone during this period. Ralph Hunter, a Sheffield husbandman, aged sixty, stated in 1693 that he could remember that the lord of Sheffield rebuilt Sheaf bridge (which led from the town to the park) in stone about thirty years previously. [48] Not only was the volume of traffic increasing, good quality building timber was becoming scarce. It had become more economical to build bridges, houses and public buildings in stone. In the northern part of the West Riding, beyond Skipton, Gargrave bridge stood on 'the high roade way betweene the citye of London and the counties of Westmorland and Cumberland'; in 1641 the J.P.s judged that £300 was 'sufficient to rebuild that bridge of stone, which must of necessitie be soe, because there is no tymber in that part of the country fitt for the worke'. It is most unlikely that parishes went to the expense of building in stone earlier than this. The delightfully picturesque packhorse bridges that lie on abandoned routes in the upper reaches of streams and rivers are often said to be medieval, but in fact they appear to date from the century between the restoration of Charles II and the accession of George III. In Glen Howe park near Wharncliffe Side is an 'An Ancient Pack Horse Bridge' which was re-erected by Joseph Dixon, a local paper manufacturer, when the original site was submerged under Ewden reservoir. Originally known as New Mill bridge, it lay on the route from Bolsterstone to Bradfield and Sheffield, and its predecessor is referred to in a charter that dates before 1270. The present structure is a perfect example of a packhorse bridge, but it is no earlier in date than 1734. John Wilson, the eighteenth-century antiquary of nearby Broomhead Hall, tells us that the inhabitants of Bolsterstone employed Benjamin Milnes in that year to take down the old wooden bridge and to replace it by a new stone one. The same mason was employed to rebuild the bridge over the Don at Oughtibridge about the same time. [49]

John Wilson also noted 'a new stone bridge built over the river Uden by one Thomas Garlick a mason in 1735 in room of the old wooden one'. He had in his possession a copy of part of a bond by which Garlick was paid £14 for this work by the inhabitants of Westnall and Waldershelf, two of the divisions of the chapelry of Bradfield, also the agreement of 28 June 1735 by which Thomas Garlick of Hunshelf, mason, was bound to Thomas Hawksworth of Dwarriden and Samuel Ellis of Midhope Hall, to 'build a new stone bridge over Uden'. This was 'enlarged for a caryage bridge' in 1775-76, when the Strines route was turnpiked. Wilson also had a record of another bond, dated 11 November 1735, by which George Wood of Newland and Joseph Beever of Peckhall, both in the chapelry of Bradfield, masons, agreed to build a new stone bridge over the river Steyne (or Loxley) a little below the mill in Nether Bradfield and to uphold the same for seven years for the sum of £19. [50]

Quite a few bridges in these Pennine foothills appear to have been rebuilt in stone at this time. Unsliven bridge, which was described in a pre-1290 as Unshriven bridge on the road leading from Midhope and which also served the road from Bradfield and Bolsterstone across the grain of the land to Silkstone and Cawthorne, and so to Wakefield, is shown in a painting of about 1730 to have been of wood. A few years later a new stone bridge similar in width to the one now standing in Glen Howe park was erected in its place. This was widened later, and widened again in 1796, as the date on the parapet and an examination of the underside of the arches testifies. [51]

The most attractive of these bridges is Willow bridge which spans the wooded valley of the upper Don between Penistone and Oxspring. Neglected since the turnpike era, it stood on the same route as Unsliven bridge and the re-erected New Mill bridge and appears to be contemporary. Guide stoops that can be dated between 1733 and 1738 mark this forgotten route; indeed, that at Dyson Cote bears the date 1734, the year that the New Mill bridge was built. Apparently, an effort was made at this time to improve facilities along the whole of this ancient route. Other packhorse bridges of a similar style may be found in secluded places at Clayton West, Bradford by Youlgreave, at the end of Coppice Road in the Rivelin valley, and at the foot of Jacob's Ladder in Edale. Boulder bridge, a mile or so upstream from Willow bridge, is mentioned in the will of William Wordsworth, the vicar of Penistone, in 1495, but the name refers to the profusion of boulders in the stream, not to the construction of the present bridge which is evidently of eighteenth-century date. The packhorse bridges of county status at Holme Hall (1664-65) and Slippery Stones (1683), mentioned above, are a little earlier, though by no more than a generation or two.

In some places simple slab bridges were still thought sufficient for crossing the smaller streams. That across Bar Brook, a mile to the east of Curbar Gap, consists of two slabs resting on firm foundations; it is inscribed 1742 and also 1777H as it forms the boundary of

The former Derwent village packhorse bridge, re-erected at Slippery Stones, at the upper end of Howden Reservoir on the River Derwent. *C.L.M. Porter.*

Bar Brook slab bridge. Two slabs resting on secure foundations bridge the stream on the Big Moor on a track formerly much used by packhorses carrying lead ore. The earliest inscription on the bridge is '1742'. *Sheila Edwards.*

Holmesfield manor and township and was marked upon a perambulation. Such bridges were all that were needed on routes frequented only by packhorses and travellers on foot. As Charles Cotton's Viator exclaimed when he caught sight of a bridge near Alsop en le Dale, 'What's here, a bridge? Do you travel in wheelbarrows in this country? This bridge was made for nothing else — 'tis not two fingers broad'. When Edward and Thomas Browne reached Ashford in the autumn of 1662 they had to choose 'Whether wee would swim our horses through an overflown ditch or ride over an extream narrow bridge'. One of the brothers wrote, 'I had heard that elephants had danc'd upon ropes and so ventur'd my horse on the latter'. [52]

Such bridges had to make way for new ones capable of taking wheeled traffic on the many routes which were improved in the second half of the eighteenth century. At the Michaelmas sessions in 1776, Derbyshire J.P.s heard that Ashford county bridge 'is so extreme narrow that it is dangerous for Carriages to pass over the same, and that the Battlements are very frequently knocked off by carriages which renders the Bridge dangerous for Passengers'. [53] Many of the new bridges were associated with turnpike roads, indeed the improvement of the Strines highway in the 1770s was largely a matter of replacing the packhorse bridges by wider ones. [54] Only where a route was not improved, especially in the upper reaches of the rivers, do packhorse bridges survive. The name Packman bridge is still attached to the main London road south of Rotherham, near Ulley, but a much wider bridge takes the modern traffic across the valley. To find the packhorses bridges we have to turn to the Pennines, but even there we will will not find any that are earlier in date than the reign of Charles II. Old and quaint they may now appear, but they were the product of an age which was concerned to improve its highways in response to the growing demands of the traders who used them.

4 Packhorses and Wheeled Vehicles

1 Packhorses

It is surprisingly difficult to obtain a clear picture of what a packhorse looked like. Local artists have left no illustrations and writers did not describe the animal in detail. Even John Farey, who had as good an eye as anyone, was merely content to observe (in 1817) that packhorses were still used in north Derbyshire, 'each muzzled, to prevent their stopping to graze by the Road sides'. [1] The earliest local usage that has come to light dates from the reign of Henry VIII, to 1522 to be precise, when Henry Swift of Sheffield bequeathed forty shillings to the repair of the highways between Sheffield and Heeley and left his brother Alexander 'a pakehors with all things belonging'. [2] The word was obviously a familiar one, providing the names of inns which still stand at Chapel en le Frith, Hayfield, Mortomley and Little Longstone and others that are now gone, of farms near Matlock and Wirksworth and of features such as the Packhorse Weir, which in the eighteenth century crossed the Don near the Sheffield Silk Mill, [3] but accurate descriptions of the horses have not been passed down to us. The probable reason is that any horse which carried a pack was called a packhorse and that several breeds and crosses were used by packmen and carriers.

When John Aikin described the district forty miles around Manchester in 1795 he noted that lime was carried from Chapel en le Frith to Mottram, 'on the backs of small Welsh horses, which run up and down the hills with as sure a foot as goats', but no other information has been found to suggest that Welsh horses were commonly used in the Peak District. It is much more likely that local breeds were used, for notable horse fairs were held at Ashbourne, Derby and Doncaster, and to this day Thorne has its Horse Fair Green. Horses could also be obtained from the famous breeding districts of Staffordshire, Northamptonshire and the North Riding of Yorkshire. [4]

The sturdy Galloway, originally bred in Scotland, may well have been the favourite type, for it was ideal for pack carriage. W. B. Crump spoke of 'gals' or Galloways as if they were the normal means of transport in the West Riding before the age of the motor car and the clothmakers depicted by George Walker in his *Costume of Yorkshire* (1814) carried their cloth to market on the backs of Galloways 'which are always overloaded [and] have a manner of going peculiarly their own'. Documentary evidence for earlier periods is hard to come by, but when Rowland Challoner of Sheffield died in 1713 he had in his stable 'Four Little Gallowaies with four old Pack saddles sursingles Wanties and Panyers For Coale Carriage', worth in all £6.2s. and in 1729 John Grisedale, a Dore yeoman, left 'four Galloways & gear for them', together with '20 dozen pots & pot crates'. [5] Unfortunately, such detailed information is rare and the two to three thousand Yorkshire and Derbyshire inventories that have been examined normally speak only of horses, mares, geldings, foals and fillies. Most carrying was undertaken as a part-time occupation, so the horses that worked on the farms were also employed on the roads.

The packman with a single horse or a small group such as Challoner's Galloways formed the most common sight on the highways, but country people on certain routes must also have been familiar with long trains of pack animals heading for the ports and the great regional fairs. At the West Riding quarter sessions in 1707 the J.P.s received a petition from the townships of

Packhorse and cart ways across the Big Moor

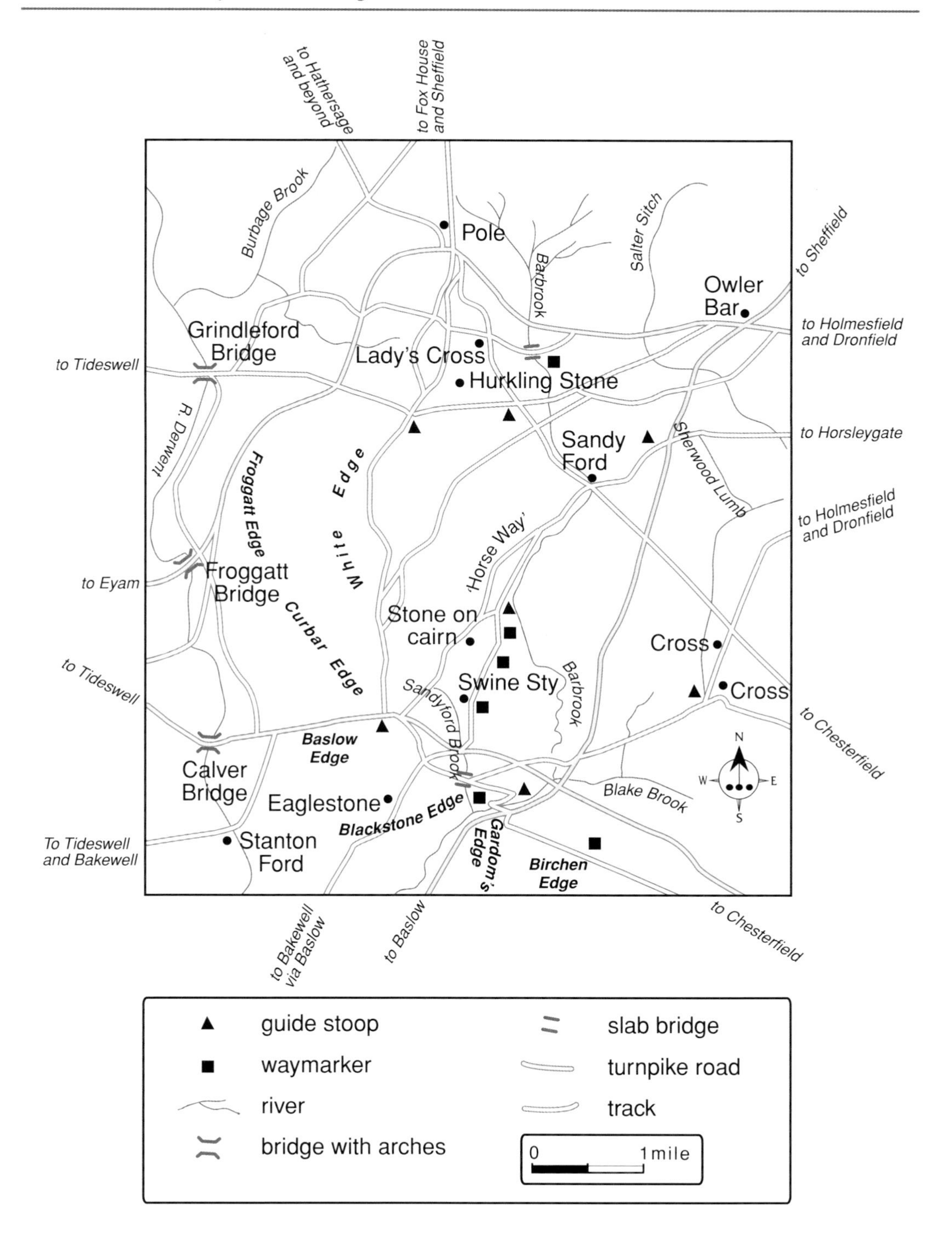

together comprised the 72,000 acres of the lordship of Hallamshire. Such vehicles were emphatically not confined to the lowland zone of medieval England.

When Richard Johnson, alias Edmondson, of Chesterfield made his will in 1557 he bequeathed 13s.4d. 'towards mending Tapton Bridge to make it as low as they can for the ease of weyns'. Wains were recorded in forty-three of the 215 probate inventories which were drawn up in the parish of Chesterfield between 1521 and 1603, but the sturdier cart was a rarity. Agnes Holme had a cart as early as 1535, but only two others were mentioned in the Chesterfield inventories. [23] In his *Essays on the Farming of Cumberland* (1853), William Dickinson wrote that in the mid eighteenth century, 'Only yeomen and the larger occupiers could boast of carts; the produce of the farms, hay, corn and peat being brought in on railed sledges and the more portable articles on pack horses'. [24]

In the hilly parts of Yorkshire and Derbyshire smallholders continued to use such horse-drawn sleds within living memory. In 1817 it was the opinion of John Farey that, 'The use of Wains, drawn by Oxen, succeeded the Pack-Horses pretty generally, in the Hilly Districts ... but have now almost entirely given place to Carts and Waggons, with nothing very peculiar in their construction; a Gentleman in Ashover told me that he remembered there being neither Cart or Waggon in that Parish'. [25] This statement needs modifying on two counts; in the first place, as we have seen, wains had not replaced packhorses recently but had been used since the Middle Ages; and secondly, although carts were much rarer than wains they were found occasionally in some of the remoter parts of the Peak District during the reigns of Elizabeth and the Stuarts. For instance, in 1598 Henry Bocking of Eyam had a cart and William Booth, a Charlesworth husbandman, had both a cart and a wain; in 1632 Francis Drabble of Abney Grange, husbandman, owned a cart and a wain; the probate records of the parish of Peak Forest reveal that Nicholas Hall had a cart in 1637, that Thomas Peake owned a corn cart in 1688, and in 1712 Francis Vernon of Sparrowpit Gate, husbandman, had 'Two Carts and one pair of Wheels' worth £2.10s. as well as 'Three Mares and their Carrying Geers' valued at £10.2s.6d. Farm waggons came later and may well have been introduced into the region by Dutch settlers after the draining of Hatfield Chase.

South Yorkshire probate inventories, which survive in bulk from the 1690s onwards, show that in 1696 William Millman, a Dikesmarsh husbandman, had an old waggon and a Dutch plough in his yard and that about the same time waggons could be found amongst the possessions of Thomas Mapplewell, a Campsall dyer, Richard Hawood, a Sykehouse yeoman, and William Fretwell, a yeoman of Thorpe in Balne. On the Coal Measure sandstones further west, William Winter, a Silkstone blacksmith, also had a waggon, but here and on the edges of the Pennines wains were still considered more suitable. Even a gentleman like Samuel Sanderson, of Sheffield Park, preferred wains. [26]

The point that wheeled vehicles, though no doubt of a primitive kind, were in common use in this region before the eighteenth century is worth labouring, for it is widely believed that the highland parts of Britain were limited to packhorse traffic. [27] The fine medieval bridges over the Derwent, Don and Wye are sufficient in themselves to refute this view and to show that loads much wider than those carried by packhorses were brought regularly across the rivers. Information gleaned from manorial court rolls and estate papers confirms that wains and carts were normally used for conveying heavy, bulky loads, particularly stone. In 1549, for instance, three men were presented at the Oxspring manor court for carrying away eight wain loads of stone slates and walling stones and the Stainborough manorial court rolls of 1614 mention the use of oxen and wains for leading stones towards the repair of the highways. [28] Building accounts for Hardwick Hall in 1594 include a payment for the overnight grazing of oxen that had brought blackstone to the site and in the following year a letter written from Sheffield spoke of the need for more oxen to carry ironstone and charcoal and to bring ironstone from Tankersley. [29] In 1575 an Oxspring man was charged with the illegal crossing of two closes with a wain and carts, in 1603 a 'cartway or road' at Stony Royd, Brightholmlee, along which hay, seeds, corn and manure were carted, was said to have been obstructed, and at another court six years later four Sheffield people were ordered to 'cutt ther hedges in Brockhill layne that a wayne may goe with a topp loade'. [30] Similarly, in 1639 the inhabitants of Northowram and of Shelley within the manor of Wakefield were ordered to clear and repair their wain ways. [31]

Today, it is natural to think of moorland routes simply as packhorse tracks, but quite clearly some, particularly those serving the quarries, were also used by wheeled vehicles. A fieldbook sketch made in 1769 by William Fairbank, the Sheffield surveyor, reveals that the packhorse way between two different points could have been quite different from the cart way between the same points. His sketch shows that the Big Moor, east of the River Derwent, could be crossed 'From Curbar Bar Head along the Cart Way which goes through Lidget, or Lidyate to the Smithy in Holmesfield', a distance of five miles, one furlong, ten yards. Alternatively, the traveller could go 'From the same place along the Pack Horse Road till it joins the aforementioned Road and from thence the same way to the said Smithy', a shorter journey of four miles, four furlongs, 176 yards. As usual, the packhorse track took the most direct line.

The use of carts and wains was largely restricted to the summer months. In particular, coal was normally carted during slack periods on the farm immediately before or after the hay harvest. In the exceptionally wet summer of 1725 Nicholas Blundell of Crosby, near Liverpool, was unable to obtain coal and had to buy it by the pack load in winter, a thing 'never known before'. Heavy summer rains posed equal problems in parts of south Yorkshire. On 10 October 1724 Thomas Simpson, a Doncaster merchant, wrote to Mrs Copley of Sprotbrough Hall, asking permission to hale boats through her land, because 'by reason of the great rain that have happened this summer the roads have been and still are almost impossible for Carts and Carriages which have occasioned a great Scarcity of Coals at and below Doncaster'. Then in August 1735 Richard Dalton, a Sheffield timber merchant, wrote to his business connections in Hull, asking them to forward deals 'before the roads grow bad', as difficult roads meant higher transport costs. Even on relatively firm land on the Yorkshire Wolds, Henry Best of Elmswell laid up his waggon in the autumn of 1641 and sent his corn to market during the winter months on a string of eight packhorses with a couple of men to guide them. [32]

About 1564, according to John Stow, 'began long waggons to come in use, such as now com to London from Canterbury, Norwich, Ipswich, Gloucester, &c with passengers and commodities'. Waggon was a Dutch word, for this heavy, four-wheeled vehicle was introduced from the Low Countries. For a long time its use was confined to southern England, where it was employed to carry loads up to seventy hundredweight. The carriers who protested against the royal proclamation of 1618, which ascribed the decay of highways and bridges to the use of these waggons and thus limited draughts to five horses, came from Sussex, Hampshire, Wiltshire, Berkshire, Oxfordshire and Northamptonshire and those who were subsequently brought before the J.P.s for infringing this new regulation came from the same or adjoining counties. The earliest reference to waggons in our region comes from the parliamentary survey of Tickhill in 1649. New legislation in 1662 increased the legal draught for a wheeled vehicle to seven horses or eight oxen, but limited loads to thirty hundredweight in summer and twenty hundredweight in winter. In 1696 a further change in the law allowed an extra horse to be added to the team, which is why, four years later, Oliver Heywood of Coley, near Halifax, was able to observe eight oxen and a horse bringing him a load of timber. A little later, in 1708, J.P.s were authorised to issue licences allowing the use of greater numbers of horses or beats to draw vehicles uphill. [33]

William Marshall, that acute observer of rural affairs, explained why oxen were still used in the Vale of Pickering in the late eighteenth century: 'In stiff pulls of every kind', he wrote, 'most especially in going up steep hills, a pair of oxen are considered as a sheet anchor. Indeed oxen seem to be considered as essentially necessary in an awkward hilly country'. [34] Revd J. C.

Atkinson has written of his astonishment when, upon his first visit to the parish of Danby on the North York Moors in the mid-1840s, he met a team of ten horses and ten oxen:

> *drawing a huge block of fine freestone up the terribly steep 'bank' or hill-side road, which runs like a house-roof on the eastern side of Stonegate Gill. At the foot of the bank, on the limited level space available, there were standing four other waggons similarly loaded. The full complement of animals dragging each of these 'carries' was a pair of horses and a yoke of oxen; and when they reached the foot of one of these stupendous hills, the full force of animal power was attached to each of the carriages in succession, and so the ponderous loads — five tons' weight on the average — were hauled to the top; and then, when all were up, the cavalcade proceeded on its slow march again.* [35]

Marshall noted that oxen could be worked every day for longer hours than horses and that 'Even the timber-carriers (an industrious, wary set of men) continue to use them; tho' their sole employment be upon the road'. [36] The invention of lighter ploughs and the new, stony road surfaces, which were unkind to cloven hoofs, hastened their decline, but probate inventories show that oxen were used in south Yorkshire and Derbyshire well into the eighteenth century and in some places much later still.

Farey has left us with an interesting account of how horse-drawn carts negotiated steep hills in Derbyshire. Considerable lengths of strong drag-chain were fastened to the top of the rear part of the cart, and the horses (up to four per cart) were fitted with strong breechings and belly-bands. At the top of a steep hill the carter would take off his trace horses and hook them to the drag-chains. 'It is surprising to see', wrote Farey, 'with what safety, and ease, after a little training, the Horses thus succeed in letting loaded Carts down most tremendous steep and long hills: on which I think it would be very unsafe to trust a one-horse Cart with an adequate Load'. [37] Farey observed nothing distinctive in the construction of Derbyshire carts, but the authors of the *General View of the Agriculture of the West Riding of Yorkshire* (1799) reported that about Rotherham and Sheffield carts were led by three horses, had narrow wheels, were 7ft long, 3ft 6ins wide, 1ft 8ins deep, and could carry up to a ton. The reporters considered them too narrow and long and 'in the highest degree destructive to the roads'. [38]

Mr Joseph Willis told a House of Commons committee in 1758 that broad-wheeled waggons drawn by eight horses carried thirty packs, each weighing 240 pounds, from Halifax to London. This load was 3.75 times heavier than the equivalent number of horses could carry by packs strapped on to their backs. He claimed that the recent use of waggons on the improved turnpike roads had reduced transport costs to the capital from fourteen shillings a pack to 7s.6d. [39] But as J. A. Chartres has shown, waggons could be used profitably only where roads were passable both in winter and summer and where demand for carriage and back-carriage was substantial and regular. [40] Before the major highways were improved in the eighteenth century waggons were the appropriate means of conveying heavy and bulky goods over short and middle distances, both in terms of cost and of quality of service, but packhorses offered sterner competition as the distance increased. Until the roads were turnpiked few goods were taken all the way from Yorkshire to the capital by waggon or cart, though it was profitable to transport goods from parts of Derbyshire to London in this manner. Packhorses could cross difficult terrain and were much faster than horses drawing waggons. Moreover, whereas each waggon needed a driver, one or two men could manage a large team of packhorses, so that which was lost in provender was more than recouped in wages. Packhorse trains were also more flexible in that horses could be added to the team or taken away according to demand.

The larger stage-waggon, with a swivelling front axle, had been introduced by the middle of the seventeenth century, but local information is hard to come by until another two or three generations had passed. [41] When James Fretwell of Thorpe in Balne near Barnby Dun returned

Peat Cart. When George Walker painted this scene in Langstrothdale in 1814, he believed that this cart was 'the only one now remaining of this original construction'.

home from London on Monday, 29 February 1720 he 'set forward for Yorkshire in the Mansfield waggon, which came only to Nottingham, and thither they sent horses to bring their passengers to Mansfield, where we arrived on Saturday'. That same year, Ralph Skampton and Thomas Litchfield, 'common Waggoners, or Carriers' on the Derby to London route, petitioned Parliament against the restriction of six horses to a waggon or three horses to a cart, saying that they needed an extra horse to operate efficiently. In 1734 two regular services to the capital were operated each week by Derby carriers, setting off on Tuesdays and arriving on Saturdays, with an extra day needed in winter. By 1742, however, the *Derby Mercury* was able to advertise that;

> *The Derby Flying Waggon sets out from the Wheat Sheaf, Derby, early every Wednesday morning and will be at the Bell Inn in Wood Street early on the Saturday following and sets out again from the said Bell Inn every Monday morning and will be at the Wheat Sheaf Inn in Derby every Thursday Evening and carries Goods and Passengers to and from London.* [42]

3 Coach Travel

Richer people could travel by coach. Even though coaches did not have steel springs until 1754, for a long time this method of travelling was considered rather unmanly. After Ralph Thoresby had been seriously ill in 1678, his father brought him from Hull to York in a coach, but, said Ralph, 'it proved a mortification to us both, that he was as little able to endure the effeminancy of that way of travelling, as I was at present to ride on horseback'. His father persuaded him to ride the last part of his journey from York to Leeds on horseback, 'weak and crazy' though he was. [43] John Stow informs us that, 'In the year 1564 Gwylliem Boonan, a Dutchman, became the queen's coachmanne and was the first that brought the use of coaches into England ... within twenty years began a great trade of coach making'. At first the use of coaches was confined to the London area, though as early as 26 February 1599 a letter in the Talbot correspondence refers to the Earl of Shrewsbury's coach coming from London to Sheffield. By the reign of Charles I the fashion for private coaches had begun to spread and soon a number of towns were linked with the capital by public stage-coaches.

John Taylor's *Carriers' Cosmographie* shows that in 1637 the use of stage-coaches was still restricted to an area thirty miles around London, but by the Restoration, if not before, south Yorkshire was connected with the capital in this way. An advertisement in 1658 claimed that coaches from London reached Stamford in two days, Newark in 2$^1/_2$ days, and Bawtry in three days. It cost £1.10s. to travel to Bawtry and a further five shillings to Doncaster and Ferrybridge. Wakefield could be reached in four days for £2. [44] The *Memoirs* of Sir John Reresby record that on 10 October 1660, 'I returned for Thriberge, and soon after to London in the stage coach' and on 5 February 1679, 'I took room in a hackney coach' from London to York, arriving there on the 11th. Reresby made several journeys to and from the capital and eventually acquired his own coach. On 3 June 1680 he records, 'I began my journey for Yorkshire in my own coach ... I gott home to Thriberge the 8th', and on 29 July 1685 he 'sett forward for Yorkshire. I gott to Thriberge in my own coach the first of August'. On at least two occasions he was accompanied by his family. [45]

The stage-coach used by Reresby came either along the Great North Road or along the other principal highway from the capital via Mansfield and Rotherham. Travellers to Wakefield certainly came via the Great North Road, for James Fretwell noted on 19 January 1719, 'My aunt Woodhouse set out from London, in the Wakefield coach, for Doncaster', and on 20 May 1726 John Hobson of Dodworth Green near Barnsley travelled ten or eleven miles to the north to meet his sister, 'who came down from London in the stage coach'. [46] Another generation passed before Sheffield acquired regular stage-coach services to the capital. As in many other towns, it was an innkeeper who took the initiative. Samuel Glanville, an Exeter man who came to Sheffield with a recruiting party in 1741, married his landlady and afterwards kept the *Angel*, the principal inn of the town. In 1760 he started stage-coach services to Wakefield and Leeds, to Mansfield and Nottingham, and to Derby, where he and three other innkeepers provided a twice-weekly service to London by a 'flying machine' that took only two days. This machine needed an extra day to come from Manchester via Stockport, Buxton and Ashbourne. By 1787 it was possible to reach the capital from Sheffield by continuous travel in a 'flying machine' in as little as twenty-six hours. Moreover, in 1774 six innkeepers began a twice-weekly service by a post coach, which left Birmingham at four o'clock in the morning and arrived at Sheffield the same day. Links were provided at Birmingham with Bristol machines and at Sheffield with a daily post coach to Wakefield, Leeds and Harrogate, and so on even to Carlisle. [47]

The Great North Road was, of course, one of the main post-roads of the country. As early as 26 June 1588 Doncaster corporation had ordered that John Parker, William Hayforth and Alexander Moore should each keep two sufficient and able post horses for one year and 'shall serve and dyschrage the said poste well, honestlie, and orderlye, and take the profetts of the two post cloases and the Holmes, as they have been accustomed to do'; in other words, the rents of some lands owned by the corporation had been set aside to pay for the postal service. [48] When Daniel Defoe visited this 'noble, large spacious town' in the early eighteenth century, he observed that as Doncaster stood upon the great northern post-road it was full of good inns; 'and here we found our landlord at the post-house was mayor of the town as well as post-master, that he kept a pack of hounds, was company for the best gentlemen in town or in the neighbourhood, and lived as great as any gentleman ordinarily did'. [49] The first direct service to western parts of south Yorkshire was established during the reign of Charles II. A royal proclamation of 1663 forbade anyone except Daniel O'Neale or his deputies to carry or deliver letters for hire and ordered searches to be made for the discovery of unlicensed letter carriers. One of the official post routes under O'Neale's care was from London to Sheffield by way of Northampton, Market Harborough, Leicester, Loughborough, Derby and Chesterfield. Packets from London arrived at Sheffield on Mondays and Thursdays at 2 p.m. and were dispatched from Sheffield on Wednesdays and Saturdays at 9 a.m. In 1691 the service was increased to three deliveries a week and the route changed so as to come via Kettering, Melton Mowbray and Mansfield. [50]

The new turnpike roads were designed to cater for wheeled traffic and though the early ones merely followed the old routes, the steeper gradients were eventually avoided and bridges widened or rebuilt. In 1730, five years after they had obtained their powers, the trustees of the Manchester to Buxton turnpike road claimed that, 'Whereas carriage was usually by horses, by the great amendment and widening of the said road it is of late changed to wheel carriage. [51] Improved roads no doubt facilitated the spread of the new fashion for private chaises. John Hobson of Dodworth Green noted in his diary on 14 August 1731 the novelty of 'a two-wheeled chaze come down from London'. [52] Three or four decades later, such vehicles were seen on occasion even in the remote Pennine hamlets. John Wilson, who lived at Broomhead Hall, high above the Ewden valley, wrote in his notebook on 5 June 1767, 'Mr & Mrs Oates came in a Post Chaise from Barnsley to Bolsterstone being the first chaise ever seen there', and on 26 August 1776 that, 'Mr Francis Scott, Grace Scott & Mrs Armitage came here down Uden from Wakefield by Bullhouse; being the first chaise that ever came that way'. Furthermore, in 1770 'Mr Edmund of Worsbro & Captn Winn came from Penistone down Uden to Bradfield in a whisky the latter end of [the] shooting season, Thomas Hattersley being their guide'. [53]

One of the bridges built on the Strines route in the mid 1770s, once the road had been improved to take wheeled traffic. *D. Hey.*

5 River Transport

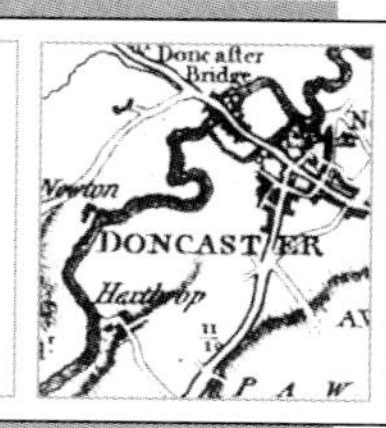

Until the coming of the railways the carriage of goods over land was far more expensive than the carriage of goods by water. Whereas the normal load for a packhorse was about 240 pounds, a single horse could tow up to thirty tons along a navigable river. Weighty and bulky goods of low value had to be taken by river and sea for they could not stand the cost of land carriage over long distances. In the sixteenth century it was profitable to take coal from Newcastle to London because it could go all the way by sea, but the south Yorkshire and Derbyshire coalfield could not be developed in any significant way until the age of canals and railways. On the other hand, goods of high value, such as woollen cloth, could absorb greater transport costs and could be taken all the way to the capital or to provincial fairs and markets by packhorses or wheeled vehicles. In the Middle Ages Derbyshire lead was taken many miles overland to the ports of Boston and Southampton. Though water transport was cheaper, its risks were greater, for certain types of goods, notably wool, were easily damaged and the sea trade was subject to delays and losses through storms and war. Moreover, purchasers often lived at considerable distances from the sea or a river port, whereas the inland carrier could provide a door-to-door service. [1]

Water transport and land transport were not just competitive systems, they were complementary to each other. A petition in favour of turnpiking the road from Saltersbrook to the Don navigation at Doncaster and Rotherham claimed that:

> *The Towns of Manchester and Stockport are very large, and considerable Trading Towns, and send weekly great Quantities of Goods, Merchandizes, and Manufactures to Doncaster in the County of York; which are carried from thence by Water to Hull, in order to be shipped to London, and foreign Parts; and bring back considerable Quantities of Flax, Yarn and other Commodities, which are manufactured in the said Towns of Manchester and Stockport.*

Few parts of England are more landlocked than south-west Yorkshire and north Derbyshire, but the region was able to export a high proportion of its minerals and manufactured goods via the nearest inland ports, principally Bawtry and Doncaster. A network of tracks near the centres of production in the west gradually merged into a few principal highways leading towards the east. [2] In summer time in particular these roads must have been very busy as lead, millstones, metalware and other goods were carted to the wharfs and a great variety of consumer goods were brought back the other way as back carriage.

T. S. Willan has written that, 'The more commercially important river-boats appear to have been sailing-barges of every shape and size. They were usually square rigged with a single square sail ... Boats appear to have been largely open with goods piled up without covering'. With vessels such as these the boatmen of Thorne took loads of turf down the river to Hull or up the Ouse to York. [3] During the seventeenth and eighteenth centuries, and probably long before, Thorne boatmen were part-time farmers enjoying generous common rights on the turf moors. Some were of the poorer or middling ranks, like John Watson (1697), who had 'turfes on the moores' worth £5 and an old boat valued at £1, together with farm stock and equipment worth £17 and other personal estate priced at £16, or Thomas Sutton (1727), who had merely

'2 Cows an old boat and riggin, £8.10s.0d, 2 small heiffers, £2, Turves on the Moors, £2.10s.0d', and other goods worth £6. On the other hand, William Middlebrooke (1726), who was described alternatively as sailor and mariner, was more prosperous and ventured further afield. Upon his death his personal estate was valued at £198, he had £280 out at interest and he was owed £66 by various people. His farm stock and equipment alone were valued at £78 and he had "Turves paid for Deliver'd and undelivered' worth another £10. His inventory records his share in 'Loppingtons Keel' and his will refers to shares in his eldest son's ship and in the keels of his two younger sons. [4]

The Don was navigable for much of the year as far inland as Doncaster, and some of the small settlements in the lower reaches of the river acted as small ports and ferrying points. Stainforth had once flourished in this role and in 1348 had acquired the right to hold a weekly market and an annual fair. In the late 1690s Abraham de la Pryme, the Hatfield antiquary, observed that traders in the lowlands in times past had loaded their goods here and carried them by horse to Doncaster market, and that 'all sorts of mill stones, grind stones, Iron ware, Lead, etc. in great Quantitys' had been exported down the river from Stainforth. However, by 1686 this trade had disappeared entirely and Stainforth had but two guest beds and stabling facilities for only three horses. Meanwhile, Thorne had started to flourish and in 1659 had obtained a market charter; by 1686 this little town had seventeen guest beds and stables for thirty-two horses. [5] Nevertheless, Bawtry remained the principal port of the region until it was by-passed by the Don navigation and the Chesterfield canal.

1 Bawtry

Bawtry's history as a river port probably goes back to the Roman period, for here was an important crossroads and a fort that guarded the banks of the River Idle. Bawtry was possibly the outlet for pigs of lead such as those with Roman inscriptions that have been found near Matlock and Cromford. Throughout eastern England the rivers were navigable as far inland as the Great North Road and both Bawtry and Doncaster fitted into this pattern in the Middle Ages. At Bawtry a new market town was grafted on to the little riverside settlement in the late twelfth or early thirteenth century, at a time when many new towns were being founded up and down the country. About a third of these plantations were planned on a regular grid pattern, and this design can still be traced on the ground at Bawtry. The church, however, stands just outside the block of streets that is arranged in this way and it obviously served as a focal point for the original river port; significantly, it is dedicated to St Nicholas, the patron saint of seafarers, who has many churches in his honour in the eastern ports.

In 1857, long after the decline of the wharf, the Great Northern Railway Company diverted the water away from the church and from the foundations of their viaduct along a new, straight channel, but the course of the old river can still be traced on the ground and the map and in fact still acts as the boundary between Yorkshire and Nottinghamshire. Amongst the curious collection of re-used twelfth-century and later material in the north aisle of the church are pieces of ironstone and Jurassic limestone which are not found in a natural state locally and presumably came up the river as ballast. Bawtry was described as a port in the Hundred Rolls of 1276 and lead is known to have been taken down the Idle from here during the reign of Edward II (1307-27). Another surviving records speaks of sacks of wool which were exported from Nottinghamshire in 1337 via Bawtry and Hull to Dordrecht. [6]

The townsmen never achieved complete independence from the lord of the manor, nevertheless they were called burgesses and Bawtry was governed as a small borough. During the later Middle Ages the town suffered from the great decay of trade which affected urban and rural settlements all over the country and nothing more is heard of the borough. When John

An aerial view of Bawtry showing the planned layout of the medieval town, the site of the former wharf, and the River Idle, whose course was altered upon the coming of the railways (by courtesy of Meridian Airmaps Ltd).

Leland came this way about 1540 he described the place as 'very bare and poore, a poore market towne'. [7] But as the national economy revived during the reign of Queen Elizabeth, Bawtry's fortunes improved and it soon became the major export centre for the minerals and manufactured goods of north Derbyshire and south-west Yorkshire and an important avenue for imported goods. The memorandum book of William Dickenson, the Earl of Shrewbury's steward in Sheffield, records the safe delivery of six barrels of (Spanish) 'steele' on 8 October 1574 and as early as 1537 Henry Reynshaw of Chesterfield had a considerable quantity of Spanish iron valued in his probate inventory. Richard Johnson of Chesterfield had a smaller amount in 1559 and this import trade was possibly a regular one. [8]

The lord of Bawtry had a wharf or staith by the riverside, but for a long time he was faced with competition from the burgesses. A 1567 agreement referred to 'the common stay ... called the burgess stay' and in 1641 Katherine Morton, a Bawtry widow, aged sixty-six, told the court of exchequer that she 'hath heard that there is a Stath in Bawtry called by the name of Burgesse Stath placed by the water side ... [which] Butted upon the Churchyard Wall'. [9] The townspeople had to struggle hard to preserve their privileges against the determined Elizabethan and early-Stuart lords. George, the sixth Earl of Shrewsbury, and lord of Sheffield, Rotherham and Chesterfield, took a lease of the manor of Bawtry from the Crown and built a warehouse there to store the lead which he was exporting from Derbyshire to London and Hamburg. Lord George was the largest lead smelter in England and by the late 1570s he was sending forty to fifty tons per annum through Bawtry; by 1585 his exports had risen to over 100 tons a year and Hull merchants were soon complaining that business was being transacted at Bawtry so that lead was shipped directly to London, by-passing Hull. Gilbert, the seventh earl, who succeeded his father in 1590, was equally determined to benefit from this lucrative trade and to override local opposition. [10]

A prolonged dispute over the wharfage of 'Leade, Millstones or other wares or stuffe' was resolved in 1599 when the earl's agent agreed not to demand wharfage and tolls from the inhabitants of Bawtry in respect of their own goods, in return for pledges that they would not encourage others to load or unload at any wharfs except the earl's wharf, that they would try to obtain him a lease of the burgess staith, and that they would agree to a by-law of the manorial court leet which would forbid the stacking of goods on the side of the highways leading to the river. [11] Other points at issue could not be agreed upon and the dispute dragged on for another half-century. Three years after Lord Gilbert's death in 1616, the dowager Countess of Shrewsbury claimed the tolls and sole profit and benefit of the River Idle and of 'all the boats Catches and other Vessells wherewith any manner of traffique hath been used or any goods chattells or merchandize transported or conveyed upon the said River'. The local inhabitants resisted this claim, saying that as the river was tidal they had 'free and common passage [for] Ketches and Keeles and other Vesselles'.

Godfrey Platts of Whittington near Chesterfield, a seventy-three year old yeoman, said in evidence that boats of ten or twelve tons burden used the river, that for thirty-five years he had traded without restraint and had regularly sold lead in Hull, and that although he had paid the earl's labourers to weigh his lead he had not paid any tolls. [12] The countess also claimed that anyone selling lead through Bawtry was obliged to use her warehouse and weigh-beam. In the court of exchequer in 1622-23 witnesses such as John Staniforth, a fifty-four year old Darnall yeoman, and Nicholas Turton, an Attercliffe yeoman, aged seventy, said that a moveable beam for weighing lead had been set up about thirty years previously by Lord Gilbert by the warehouse at Bawtry Hall and that this had been replaced about five years later by a fixed weigh-beam. [13] Lord George had bought the 'wharfe warehouse or storehouse sometymes Stephen Bartholomew', which adjoined the burgess staith by the churchyard wall, and had enlarged the wharf; later, Lord Gilbert built a new warehouse there for his lead. [14] This appears to be the 'warehouse in the New Shore' that was recorded in 1650. [15]

The dispute dragged on until 1648 and possibly beyond. When the manor of Bawtry was sold in 1623 the manorial perquisites were said to include profits of boats on the Idle, the weighing of lead and the tolls, the lord's wharf or staith, the former burgess or St Nicholas staith, two warehouses and two weighing houses. However, in 1641 Katherine Morton claimed before the court of exchequer that 'the Inhabitants or Burgesses have had free liberty to carry all their goods, wares and Marchandizes upon the River of Idle at their wills and pleasures without the payment of any Tole or other Duties whatsoever for the same, and that shee ... hath knowne the same by the space of fifty years or there aboutes'. Seven years later the local defendants were still insisting that the inhabitants of Bawtry were anciently called burgesses and as such had the right time out of mind to use warehouses and to be free of tolls, but the judge's verdict was in favour of the lord until the inhabitants could prove their claims at common law. [16] Nothing more is heard of the dispute, so presumably the defendants finally admitted defeat.

In 1633 Sir John Lister, a wealthy Hull merchant, purchased the manor. His son, Thomas, headed the Bawtry hearth tax returns in 1672 with fourteen hearths, but unfortunately few family papers survive for the seventeenth and early eighteenth centuries, when Bawtry's fortunes were at their highest point. [17] Navigation along the Idle had recently been improved by Cornelius Vermuyden's drainage scheme for Hatfield Chase and a greatly increased national and international demand for lead, millstones, metalware, coal and other industrial goods was soon to be reflected in the volume of trade through Bawtry. For instance, in 1640 Stephen and John Bright of Carbrook Hall, Sheffield, shipped 1,969 pigs of lead from Bawtry to Stockwith and the following year they shipped 2,416 pigs; they dealt not only with Hull merchants but directly with merchants of Amsterdam. The parish register of Edwinstowe records that in

September 1664 a man was killed in Birkland Wood 'with a piece of shipp-timber as he was with his carriage and had taken it up to go to Bawtrie'. So much timber was sent through Bawtry that the wharf was said to be 'clogged' with it. Evidently, West Riding clothiers also used Bawtry as an outlet, for a letter written during the civil war refers to the garrison at Tickhill castle, which 'did much interrupt the trade and transportation of cloth from Leeds, Halifax, and other parts, to Bawtree; their horse also bringing in frequently 20, 30, 40 horses at a time loaden with cloth; which oftentimes upon payment of twenty shillings the horse-load, they were released again'. [18] The lack of later information about this trade suggests that the clothiers normally went all the way by land or that they preferred the river ports on the Aire and Calder, especially after the navigation of these waterways had been improved under the terms of a private Act of Parliament of 1699. Corn was also exported from Thomas Lister's staithes by means of his 'boats, catches or other vessells' and in 1652 he made an agreement with Tickhill men on a fourpence toll for every quarter of barley or grain sent from Bawtry to Stockwith or Gainsborough, or in the reverse direction. [19]

Little is known about imports through Bawtry at this period, but one important item of back-carriage was the great quantity of hides that the tanners of the West Riding and north Derbyshire brought from London. By the late 1620s Yorkshire tanners were importing 4,000 hides per annum and about one-sixth of these went to Sheffield. Upon their arrival in the coastal vessels at Hull, the hides were taken 'upp Humber and the fresh rivers there to Turnbridge and Bawtrey, and hence by land'. The probate inventory of William Aldam of Upperthorpe, Sheffield (1696) refers to 'Hides bought and shipt, £20' and that of John Brook of Dodworth, gentleman (1694) records 'Money return'd to London for buying Hides, £20'. A little further north at Kirkheaton, in the mid-1640s, Thomas Pickles had 'Eleven score hides bought at London, £220, 120 hides bought at London and not yet at Hull, £150'. Tanning remained an important local trade until the nineteenth century. [20]

In 1686 Bawtry was a flourishing small market town and river port with fifty-seven guest beds and facilities for stabling sixty-nine horses. [21] In 1704 the local merchants were said to 'chiefly subsist by the Navigation of the River Idle, which, by Boats, conveys into the Trent, Lead, Millstones, Corn, and other Commodities, which come out of Derbyshire and Nottinghamshire' and eight years later two Bawtry merchants, John Goodwin and Christopher Dempster, agreed to pay the lord of the manor £22 per annum for the right to collect 'all dues for lead, iron, millstones, wood [and] corn which shall be brought to the wharf or stored in the warehouse, and all dues for lead weighed at the beam'. [22] Daniel Defoe was greatly impressed by the vigour of the trade in Bawtry when he visited the town in the early eighteenth century. He wrote that it was:

> *bless'd with two great conveniences which assists to its support, and makes it a very well frequented place.*
>
> 1. *That it stands upon the great post highway or road from London to Scotland; and this makes it be full of very good inns and houses of entertainment.*
> 2. *That the little but pleasant River Idle runs through, or rather just by, the side of it, which contrary to the import of its name, is a full and quick, though not rapid and unsafe stream, with a deep channel, which carries hoys, lighters, barges, or flat-bottom'd vessels, out of its channel into the Trent, which comes within seven miles of it, to a place called Stockwith, and from thence to Burton, and from thence, in fair weather, quite to Hull; but if not, 'tis sufficient to go to Stockwith, where vessels of 200 ton burthen may come up to the town loaden as well as empty.*
>
> *By this navigation, this town of Bawtry becomes the center of all the exportation of this part of the country, especially for heavy goods, which they bring down hither from all the adjacent countries, such as lead, from the lead mines and smelting-houses in*

Derbyshire, wrought iron and edge-tools, of all sorts, from the forges at Sheffield, and from the country call'd Hallamshire, being adjacent to the towns of Sheffield and Rotherham, where an innumerable number of people are employed ...
Also millstones and grindstones, in very great quantities, are brought down and shipped off here, and so carry'd by sea to Hull, and so to London, and even to Holland also. This makes Bautry Wharf be famous all over the south part of the West Riding of Yorkshire, for it is the place whither all their heavy goods are carted, to be embarked and shipped off. [23]

Little is known of individual Bawtry merchants other than Aquila and Samuel Dawson. Aquila's receipt book for 1693-94 shows that he was exporting wrought iron wares for Francis Sitwell of Renishaw and that he was importing deals and miscellaneous goods such as brandy, ginger, oil, whalebone and gunpowder. When he died in 1696 he left personal estate valued at just over £400, including debts of £100 that were owed to him and goods in the shop and warehouses worth £154.15s.8d. [24] The size of his house suggests that he was far from being the leading merchant in Bawtry. Samuel Dawson's business papers for 1715-21 reveal that his main concern was the importation of deals, spars, pipe staves and other fir timber from Norway. He dealt directly with the Oslo firm of Colletts and Leuch and employed John Dickinson, the master of the 'Milkmaide', to ship his timber. On one occasion, on 9 July 1715, he paid Dickinson £777 for the safe delivery of an order. Later, he seems to have concentrated on importing wainscot-boarding. [25]

Trade through Bawtry was largely restricted to the summer months for the highways were often impassable after heavy rain. On 27 February 1586 Richard Torre wrote from Worksop Lodge to the sixth earl of Shrewsbury in London, promising to send a number of provisions as soon as the foulness of the way to Bawtry allowed, and during the winter of 1735-36 Richard Dalton (who had worked for Samuel Dawson before setting up as an independent raff merchant, i.e. one who imported foreign timber, especially deals) had to arrange for his incoming goods to be left at Bawtry until the following summer. [26]

2 The Don navigation

Doncaster was Bawtry's chief rival as a river port for south Yorkshire, though it lay too far north to benefit from the trade in Derbyshire lead and millstones. In the early eighteenth century the town could be reached by small boats coming up the river for nine months a year and larger vessels could get that far 'in times of rises and freshes'. Further progress up the river was prevented by the corporation's mills and beyond the town by rocks, shallows, and banks of sand and gravel. Nevertheless, some traders preferred to take their goods overland to Doncaster

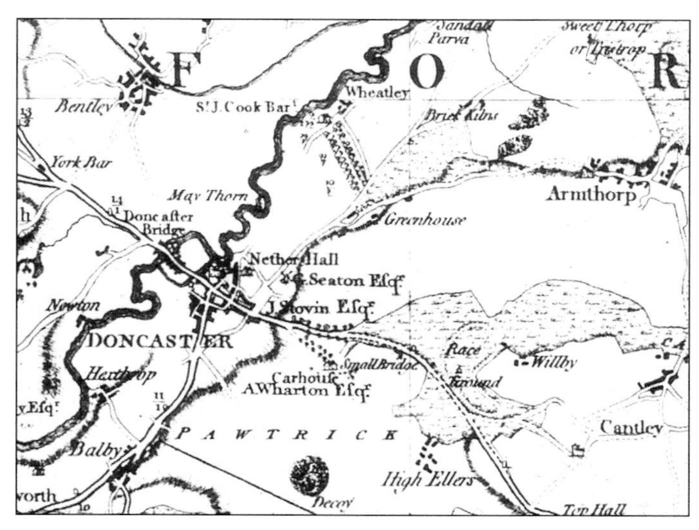

Doncaster and the navigable River Don, shown on Thomas Jeffrey's map of Yorkshire, 1772.

rather than to Bawtry. We find, for instance, that about 1701 Thomas Patten of Warrington was proposing to send tobacco by cart to Stockport, thence by packhorse to Doncaster, and from Doncaster to Hull by water, and attempts to improve the navigability of the Don were supported by London cheesemongers who claimed that the moorland route to Doncaster and thence by water was 'the easiest and readiest way' to send Cheshire cheese to the capital. [27] Furthermore, ironware was brought through Doncaster occasionally, if not regularly; in 1667, for instance, a corporation rental records the ten shillings paid by Lionel Copley for the right to land iron in the Chapel garth, and during the first decade of the eighteenth century William Ambler, a Doncaster keelman, bought considerable quantities of ironware from Sheffield ironmasters. [28]

Doncaster occupied a favourable site where the Great North Road crossed the Don at the highest point of navigation. River-borne goods were unloaded at Docken Hill right alongside the large market place. During the seventeenth and eighteenth centuries Doncaster's corn market and livestock fairs enjoyed wide fame and the wool market was undoubtedly one of the largest in the kingdom. Sometimes as many as 6,000 fleeces were sold here each Saturday during summer and the West Riding clothiers obtained much of their supplies from the midland and eastern counties in this way. One of the local men who benefited from this trade was William Rowbotham, a stapler whose inventory in 1702 included 'In the Woole Chamber over the Hall: Woole £100, Woole in the gate-house shop £100, Woole in the Shop in the Maudlens £150'. When the War Office made enquiries about spare accommodation in 1686, Doncaster had no less than 206 guest beds and stabling facilities for 453 horses, compared with 119/270 at Sheffield, 64/109 at Barnsley and 63/72 at Rotherham. Doncaster was the only corporate town in south Yorkshire and Daniel Defoe found it noble, large and spacious. [29]

A great number of private Acts of Parliament were obtained in the late seventeenth and early eighteenth centuries to improve the navigability of English rivers and much was done to improve inland water transport long before the age of canals. As T. S. Willan has written, these schemes were inspired not by any great advances in technical knowledge but by the growing importance of industry. A private Act of Parliament was necessary to obtain compulsory purchase powers in order to widen or straighten stretches of the river and the battle to obtain such an Act was often fought over many years against determined opposition from landowners and from merchants in rival ports who felt their interests threatened. When Sir Godfrey Copley of Sprotbrough and the leading inhabitants of Rotherham petitioned Parliament to improve the Don in 1697, landowners to the east of Doncaster (who feared floods on the scale of those which had followed Vermuyden's drainage scheme in the late 1620s) combined effectively with merchants from Bawtry, Gainsborough and Pontefract to crush the scheme. [30]

Doncaster corporation offered no support in 1697 for they had recently spent £1,000 on the repair of their mills and dams alongside the river, but in 1704 they came round to the view that it was to their advantage to make the river 'more navigable'. A new petition was sent to Parliament stressing the need for cheaper carriage and emphasising Doncaster's role as a great corn market. London factors were said to buy great quantities of corn, especially red wheat, in the region, but expensive land carriage forced up the price. The bill was suppressed by rival interests and for many years the scheme was abandoned. Then in 1721 the Hallamshire Cutlers' Company took the initiative. They claimed, no doubt with considerable exaggeration, that 'not less than 6,000 workmen, besides smiths, anvil-makers, edge-tool makers, naylors and several thousands of other manufacturers in iron not incorporated' together produced goods worth £100,000 per annum, more than half of which were exported.

Exports included 4,500 tons of lead per annum and millstones, coal, Derbyshire marble, salt, cheese, butter, hewn stone, lime, wood and bark, 'which abounded in the countrey, lying up this River'. Doncaster corporation gave its official support, but was considerably embarrassed to find that nine aldermen, seven common councillors and other inhabitants with estates on the river produced a counter petition. The aldermen and councillors were called singly to give an account of their actions and the leaders' behaviour was voted 'scandalous, vexatious and malicious'. More formidable opposition came from the merchants of Bawtry, who cunningly played on Sheffield fears that improved navigation would mean that the cutlery trades would become centred on Doncaster and Doncaster fears that Sheffield would become a rival market centre. But the most effective opposition came from the Duke of Norfolk who, as lord of Hallamshire, feared that the proposed navigation would draw off vital water supplies from the ironworks and cutlers' wheels immediately east of Sheffield. The bill was defeated in committee and no progress was possible until a compromise was made with the duke.

That compromise came in 1726 when the cutlers agreed to stop the navigation at Tinsley, three miles from Sheffield. The initiative again came from the Cutlers' Company, who were concerned about the cost of land carriage. George Steer, their representative, claimed that recently the cost of carriage from Sheffield to Doncaster had doubled from fifteen shillings to £1.10s. a ton. An Act was passed without much trouble authorising the Cutlers' Company to improve the navigation between Doncaster and Tinsley for boats of up to twenty tons and to keep the road between Tinsley and Sheffield in good repair; they were allowed to levy a toll of a penny a ton on water-borne goods carried on this road. The following year Doncaster corporation encountered no opposition to a bill authorising them to improve the navigation downstream as far as Wilsick House in the parish of Barnby Dun, from where the river was tidal.

By 1733 the river had been made navigable as far upstream as Aldwark, 1½ miles from Rotherham, and two years later Richard Dalton (who had now moved from Bawtry to Sheffield) was able to import some deals which 'never landed since they were put aboard at Stockholme until they came to Aldwork'. His other imports included Hamburg pipe-staves, horn for the cutlery trade, German linen, Dutch oats, wainscot-boards, and 'Iron of all styles and German steel'. [31] By 1739-40 a wharf had been established at Rotherham and in 1751 the river was finally made navigable all the way to Tinsley. [32] Bawtry obviously suffered from the success of this rival enterprise, but Derbyshire lead and millstones still came her way, so all was not yet lost. Richard Dalton, for instance, still received some of his goods through Bawtry and in 1738, when the 'antient Wooden Bridge' at Bawtry was replaced by a new one, it was described at the quarter sessions as being on:

the great road from Leeds Wakefield Halllifax Sheffield and other Trading Towns in this Riding to Lincoln Norwich and other places of considerable Trade ... great numbers of heavy Carriages and Horses loaden with Wool Coals Bricks Tyles etc. are frequently passing and repassing for the greater part of the year.[33]

Bawtry survived as a port until the canal age. Its death knell was sounded in 1777 when the Chesterfield canal by-passed the town and provided a direct link between Derbyshire and the Trent at Stockwith. In any case, the great days of the lead trade were soon to be over. Bawtry survived for many years as a small local port, but in 1822 Edward Baines wrote in the first commercial directory of the West Riding, 'Notwithstanding its advantageous situation, Bawtry has little or no trade'; Thomas Parkinson of Shore Lane still found employment as a wharfinger and two men were still timber and raff merchants, but the great era of the river trade was over. Bawtry continued to flourish as a thoroughfare town and market centre and was largely rebuilt during the period 1780-1840, but there is now little sign of its former prosperity as a river port. [34]

NB: The rivers are shown on the map on page 5.

6 THE CARRIAGE OF MINERALS AND MANUFACTURED GOODS

From very early times Man has exploited the physical resources of the Peak District and of the area overlying the Coal Measure sandstones. During the Middle Ages and the early-modern period a high proportion of the inhabitants of this region combined farming with an industrial occupation. In the rural settlements, earning a living as a weaver-farmer, miner-farmer or metalworker-farmer was the normal way of life and all sections of society from great aristocratic landlords and rural gentry downwards benefited from local industry. Derbyshire lead and millstones, Hallamshire cutlery, edge-tools, nails and wrought-iron were exported to many parts of the country and abroad and the local highways were used principally for the carriage of minerals and manufactured goods and for importing flour, meal, malt, miscellaneous consumer goods and high quality iron and steel for Hallamshire craftsmen to work upon. In 1720 a petition against the proposed Derwent navigation was signed by the inhabitants of Tickhill, Firbeck and Letwell in south Yorkshire and Harworth, Styrrup and Oldcotes in Nottinghamshire, most of whom were 'maintained by the Land-carriage of Lead, Millstones, and several other Commodities to Bawtry ... bringing back Raff, foreign Iron, Groceries, and several other Sorts of Goods, to supply themselves, and the Towns adjacent'. As Philip Kinder wrote in his manuscript *Historie of Darby-Shire* in 1656, 'Thus we see Lincolne Nottingham Darby and Cheshire men to follow transportation of Corne, lead, making of Cheese, York-sh[ire] and Lancaster making of Clothes'. [1] The history of the development of each of these industries is basic to an understanding of the nature of the road system within the region.

1 Lead

Inscriptions on the pigs of lead that have been found in and around Cromford and Matlock show that the Derbyshire lead mining and smelting industry was well established in Roman times. The subsequent history of the industry is obscure for many centuries, but it is certain that the Anglo-Saxons worked some mines in the Wirksworth area and scraps of information that survive from the Middle Ages suggest that the trade was extensive in at least some periods. In the twelfth century, for instance, 265 cartloads of Derbyshire lead were sent via Boston and London to Waltham Abbey (Essex) and in 1184 Derbyshire and North Country lead was shipped from Boston and the Humber estuary to Rouen. In the middle of the fifteenth century Derby and Chesterfield men carried lead in wains all the way to the port of Southampton and returned with foreign dyes for local clothiers. English lead production slumped badly in the second quarter of the sixteenth century, but recovered during the reign of Elizabeth. Improved smelting technology and increased demand both at home and overseas made the Derbyshire lead fields the most important in Europe between 1580 and 1680. They remained productive until well into the nineteenth century. [2]

The early lead miners were independent men, the free miners who worked in gangs of two or three and who clung tenaciously to their privileges. Often they were smallholders with the right to graze animals on the extensive wastes and commons, but undoubtedly many of them

Lead rake, Tideslow. The grassy hillocks and hollows formed by waste material mark the long, straight line of a typical Derbyshire lead rake, near Tideswell and Great Hucklow. *Sheila Edwards.*

A Saxon or Medieval carving of a miner with a pick and a whisket, Wirksworth Church. *P. Deakin.*

were very poor. The ore was mined in long *rakes* on the Carboniferous Limestone, mostly to the west of the Derwent but with two important inliers further east at Ashover and Crich. However, lack of fuel in the White Peak meant that most smelting was undertaken east of the river where wood was abundant. The earliest forms of smelting hearths were sited on the brows of the windy gritstone scarps, such as those on Beeley Moor, along Froggatt Edge and north of Hathersage. Few physical remains survive, but Bole Hill is a common place-name wherever lead or iron was smelted and Boler is one of Derbyshire's distinctive surnames.

In 1817 John Farey, wrote that lead ore, when cleaned and dressed, was moved across country to the smelting mills by strings of packhorses in the charge of a man known as a jagger. Thomas le Jager of Little Longstone was alive in 1316 and the occupation has given rise to a West Riding surname. The 'Jagger waye' recorded at Carsington in 1592, the well-known Jaggers' Lane at Hathersage (which had acquired its name by 1688 and possibly long before, and which was the original route from Castleton and Hope), the Jaggers' Gate which acted as one of the boundaries of the Forest of the Peak between the rivers Wye and Goit, and the present Jagger Lanes in Ashover and Darley, all appear to have their origins in the lead trade. But this is not the whole story, for the name was certainly not restricted to areas where lead was mined or smelted. Jaggers Clough on Edale Moor has no apparent connection with a smelting site, nor has a field in Thrybergh which was known in 1764 as Jaggers Close, and much further north, well away from any place connected with the lead trade, Jagger Wood at Thurgoland stands near the old highway from Oxspring to Barnsley, and the ridgeway that passes Emley Moor television station is known as Jaggers' Lane.

Some of these minor place-names may have been derived from the surname. W. B. Crump's intimate knowledge of West Riding lore and topography led him to suggest that a jagger was simply a man who travelled with a load or jag, while in 1857 Thomas Wright defined jagger as 'one who works draught horses for hire'. Crump wrote, 'The name never seems to have been applied to regular pack-horse carriers making long journeys with miscellaneous goods, or common carriers. It is restricted to men and horses carrying specific goods, either fish or lead ore or coal from the place where it was produced to the place where it was consumed'. Sixteenth-century probate inventories from the parish of Chesterfield support the idea that a jag was simply a northern or north-midlands dialect word for a load. In 1602 Ralph Maunsoldale had 'one Jage of haye' worth twelve shillings and in 1587 Widow Tatesall had '2 Jayges of haye and 2 cartes full'. *The English Dialect Dictionary* found that by the end of the nineteenth century the word jagger had a great variety of meanings. Nevertheless, a Derbyshire jagger was more likely to have carried lead ore than anything else. [3]

During the reigns of Elizabeth and the Stuart kings the number of lead miners increased considerably, indeed it was claimed in 1614 that twenty times as many miners were working within the county than fifty years previously. As Andy Wood has written, 'In the High Peak what had been thinly settled hamlets in 1563 had become heavily populated industrial villages by 1664'. The free miners were now accompanied by large numbers of 'hirelings and cavers', the labourers and very poor individuals who scratched a tenuous living from the lead trade. All these groups were in frequent conflict with the Cavendishes of Chatsworth, the Manners of Haddon Hall and the wealthy gentry families that owned royalties and other rights in mining and who invested heavily in smelting furnaces. [4]

The increased demand for lead was met by improved smelting technology from about 1570 and by expensive schemes to drain the mines. By the early seventeenth century most of the larger veins had been worked down to, or were rapidly approaching, the water table. The earliest known drainage sough was constructed in the 1630s and by 1717 a Newcomen pumping engine had been installed in a Winster mine. The necessary capital investment could be provided only by large companies or by the local aristocracy and richer gentry. From the 1570s onwards, the new water-powered smelting furnaces were fired by white coal, that is small chopped wood that had been dried in a kiln. The new smelting mills were sited in the wooded river valleys on the gritstone shales of the eastern Peak and were more scattered and more numerous than before. [5]

All the old deciduous woods west of a line drawn from Sheffield to Chesterfield and east of the River Derwent contain small, Q-shaped pits where the white coal was prepared. In the hundred of Scarsdale alone twenty-one smelting mills were in operation in 1652. Derbyshire gentry families such as the Bagshawes, Burtons, Eyres and Gells made a lot of money out of smelting during the sixteenth and seventeenth centuries and sometimes they owned mines as well. The Eyres, for instance, had lead mines at Calver, Hassop, Priestcliffe and Taddington and smelting mills at Dore and Totley and on the Barlow Brook. Not all the smelters were county gentry, but most of them were rich; a list of 'Persons fitt to lend the Kinge Money' in 1662 included ten lead merchants from Ashgate, Bakewell (and Beeley), Chesterfield, Hemsworth, Holmesfield, Litton, Great Longstone, Stoney Middleton, Tapton and Tideswell. [6] After the introduction of the cupola or reverberatory furnace in 1737 the smelting process was concentrated in even fewer wealthy hands. About thirty cupola sites have been recognised, mainly on the gritstone moors, and many of these were associated with large concerns such as the London Lead Company or the Barker-Wilkinson partnership. But no more fortunes were made after the late eighteenth century when severe drainage problems and the exhaustion of some seams caused a rapid decline of the industry.

Except in the case of lead mined in Ashover and Crich, the movement of ore to the smelting mills was fraught with difficulty. First the often-turbulent Derwent had to be crossed, then the steep edge overlooking the river had to be climbed, and even then the jaggers and their horses were faced with a weary trek across the moor. Arthur Raistrick and Bernard Jennings have written that in the Yorkshire Dales 'in almost every mining field the ore was carried from the mines to the smelt mills by pack animals'. Alston Moor was crossed by a number of 'galloway roads' by which trains of twelve to fifteen horses, working on behalf of the larger companies, carried ore to the mills or lead between the mills for refining. Most of the packhorses were kept by local farmers, with often as many as twenty or thirty a farm. Ore was sent to the Dukesfield smelt mill from the Allenhead mines only at stated intervals so that farmers could combine carriage with their normal work on the land. [7]

In Derbyshire packhorses were often used to carry ore, but on occasion wains or carts were preferred. In 1551 James Rigge was paid at the rate of twopence a horse for carrying sixty-four loads of ore from Bonsall Dale to Haddon Hall six hilly miles away. The account speaks of 132 horses, but this probably refers to animals used on several journeys rather than a single lengthy train. Over two centuries later, the 1759 Act authorising the turnpike road from Nottingham to Newhaven provided for a special toll on one section of the road 'for the passage of any ... beast, being only loaden with Lead Ore'. Oral tradition at Chelmorton preserves the memory of long trains of packhorses standing in the village street and stretching back to the mine, waiting to take their panniers full of ore to the smelters. On the other hand, as early as 1505, when Roger and John Eyre took a lease of a bole hill at High Wood in the manor of Holmesfield they were allowed access to their property with carts or carriages. Perhaps in this case carts were used just to take away the finished lead and not to bring the ore, but there can be no doubt about the wording of Rowland Eyre's lease of the Barlow smelting mills in 1586, when free passage was given to his 'servants workmen cariers and jaggers with horses oxen waynes carts and cariedges ... for bringing and carieng of lead ore'. [8]

The smelting mills were conveniently situated on the way to the inland ports and the terrain at this stage of the journey was less difficult than at the first stage further west. Raistrick and Jennings write that when the mines in the Yorkshire Dales were worked through a large number of shafts it was usually uneconomical, as well as in some cases physically difficult, to make and maintain adequate roads for wheeled vehicles to all of them. The replacement of these

Chelmorton village where packhorses used to wait in long trains down the street loaded with lead ore; presumably while the Jaggerman was in the inn! *C.L.M. Porter.*

numerous shafts by a few main ones in the late eighteenth and early nineteenth centuries brought about a radical change. Until then, packhorses had been used in Swaledale and Arkengarthdale to carry lead from the smelt mills as far as Richmond, where another set of carriers took over with waggons for the rest of the journey to Stockton. [9] In Derbyshire, however, it seems clear that lead was taken directly from the smelting mills to the ports by carts or wains.

We have already seen that wain loads of lead were referred to in the Domesday survey of Hope and that cart-loads of Derbyshire lead were exported from Boston in the twelfth century. Lead was also taken from southern parts of the Peak to Nottingham by medieval carters and sent by boat up the Trent or by road to Leicester, Northampton and other great midland towns. Henry Foljambe's lead was in 'weynes' when it was distrained at Nottingham in 1498 upon his refusal to pay tolls and when Robert Gamylston was ordered by the king in 1394 to buy forty fodders of lead in Nottinghamshire and Derbyshire, he was empowered to arrest sufficient horses and carts for its carriage to Westminster. [10] The will of Anthony Bright of Woodthorpe (1625) mentions two lead wains, in 1650 the inhabitants of Calow protested that 'the many carriages of Coale, leade, and milne stones' were destroying their roads, and in 1722 Thomas Lister of Bawtry referred in a letter to 'the carts which bring lead this way'. [11]

John Houghton, writing in London in the last decade of the seventeenth century, claimed that lead smelted at Derby went via the Trent to Hull, that lead from Crich and 'the mills about Wirksworth' was taken to Nottingham and sent up the Trent, that lead from more northerly mills near Chesterfield went to Bawtry, and finally that lead smelted near 'Sheffield and all those parts' was taken overland to Doncaster and down the Don and the Humber. [12] There can be little doubt, however, that the lead merchants near Sheffield preferred Bawtry to Doncaster. In 1585, for instance, John Booth wrote to the sixth Earl of Shrewsbury: 'At Totley lead is ready to convey to Bawtry', where the earl had a weigh-beam and a warehouse. The Brights of

Carbrook shipped their lead from Bawtry in the 1640s and Barlborough carriers are known to have taken lead from Horsleygate to Bawtry a decade or two earlier. [13] Certainly, Bawtry was the principal outlet for lead when Defoe visited the town in the early eighteenth century.

Though many aspects of the lead trade are very well documented, few records shed light on the transport system. The steward of Haddon Hall noted the expenses of 'my selfe & James Ragge & my Man' when they visited Hull for seven days in the summer of 1550 'for dyvers Matters ther to be done as Consernynge my Masters leayde' and on the way back he paid Roger Gregorey of Stockwith nine shillings for 'the Caryege of xviij pyssis of leade by watter from stockwythe to hulle'. The accounts of Lawrence Oxley, a Chesterfield lead merchant, for 1672-78, show that his lead was taken overland to Bawtry, then down the River Idle to Stockwith on the Trent, and so on to Hull and London. An entry on 4 August 1677 reads, 'Recd yn advice from Bawtry that had sent 40 pigs bought of mr Leonard Cowleys to Stockwith to bee shipt for London'.

Earlier entries show that Oxley was exporting lead from the smelting mill at Wessington Hay and that on 8 May 1673 he 'paid George Hodgkinson & John Purslove for carriage of 3 loads 8 dish from Overton to Chesterfield'. The accounts are not sufficiently detailed to enable us to analyse the cost of carriage either overland or by water, but the frequent references to Bawtry, Stockwith and London clearly show that Oxley's major market was the capital and that the cheapest way to send his lead was by water. Many other merchants must have used the same route, for in 1719 a petition against making the Derwent navigable as far as Derby claimed that 'abundance of Families in the several Hundreds of Scarsdale and High Peak are chiefly employed in getting Lead-ore, and carrying the same to the Smelting Mills, and making it into Lead, which is carried to Bawtry'. [14]

One of the places that lay on the route from the smelting mills to Bawtry and whose inhabitants therefore benefited from the opportunities for carrying lead was Killamarsh. The probate inventories for this township contain eight references to lead wains between 1621 and 1671, three mentions of 'lead horses' between 1669 and 1706 and many other references to packhorses, work-horses or 'horses and their furniture'. In her will of 1703 Mary Atkin, widow, left to her son-in-law 'all my part of the horses, geldings and mares which wee two use in carrying lead with the pack saddles and furniture belonging to them'. [15] A 'Particular of certaine tenurments in Killamarshe' in 1632 stressed the high rents that could be obtained 'in regard it lyeth in the best place for lettinge grounds in all this parte of the Cuntrye, the place consisting most of Lead carriers'. [16] In 1711 John Morton, a Killamarsh husbandman, 'did by misfortune in the ordering a cart loaden with Lead cause one pigg of Lead to fall on him which did soe wound and bruise the said John Morton that hee did languish thereon until the 13th of the said month, when he dyed thereof'. [17] Perhaps he was transferring lead into his cart when the accident happened?

2 Coal

The south Yorkshire and Derbyshire coal mining industry is undoubtedly older than the first surviving records, which date from the late thirteenth century, though most of the coal that was mined before the improvement of the River Don navigation was consumed locally. When John Leland visited the area about 1540 he was surprised to find that, 'Though betwixt Cawood and Rotheram be good plenti of wood, yet the people burne much yerth [earth] cole, bycawse hit is plentifully found ther, and sold good chepe. A mile from Rotheram be veri good pittes of cole ... Hallamshire hath plenti of woodde, and yet ther is burned much se cole'. [18] Numerous small mines were worked by miner-farmers and by the seventeenth century coal pits were a common sight both on the thin 'gannister coal' seams in the west and on the richer Silkstone and Barnsley (or Top Hard) seams further east. By 1598 Hewett Osborne's miners in Waleswood were producing about 2,000 tons per annum, 'towardes the furnishinge of the countries next adjoynynge' and by 1652 twenty-three mines were in operation in the north-east Derbyshire hundred of Scarsdale. [19] The largest mines in the region were naturally on the estates of the great landlords, who were keen to exploit the potential of their minerals; in particular, George, the sixth Earl of Shrewsbury, developed collieries in his park at Sheffield during the Elizabethan era and by the eve of the civil war the annual rent from these mines amounted to £200. The lessees of such mines were often gentry and yeoman farmers who also had mines of their own, but later on ironmasters and lead merchants also became involved. [20]

Early eighteenth-century visitors were surprised at the cheapness of coal and the amount that was burned in domestic fires. Home-brewing and a variety of crafts such as glass-making and the manufacture of pots also ensured a steady demand for fuel and so much coal was consumed in the cutlers' smithies that pollution was already a problem in Sheffield when Defoe described the houses as 'dark and black, occasioned by the continued smoke of the forges, which are always at work'. [21] Coal was also taken westward into the Peak District. When William Furness took a lease of some property in Calver from Rowland Eyre of Hassop in 1583, he agreed not only to pay an annual rent of 12s.4d, but each year to deliver 'one wayne load of sea coles' to Eyre's house. That a wain load amounted to a ton is evident from a lease of Sir George Wentworth's pits on Staincross moor in 1652, when the lessee agreed to pay £20 a year together with six wain loads or roughly as many tons of well-dressed slack. [22] Later evidence of regular journeys into the western hills is provided by Titus Wheatcroft's observation in 1722 that one of the great highways through the parish of Ashover was 'by a place called Knoe Cross, betwixt the coal pits and the Peak' and by William Bray, who in 1783 saw carts loaded with coal slack going from about Sheffield and Chesterfield to Stoney Middleton and returning with lime. [23]

In earlier times, before the turnpike road was completed, this arduous journey across the moors was undertaken by packhorses rather than carts; the Duke of Devonshire was told in 1762 that 'all the Coals that come from Brampton and Chesterfield as well as Baslow that come on Horseback' were brought across Beeley Moor. [24] No doubt the use of packhorses for carrying coal was abandoned once the road had been turnpiked. Certainly a turnpike road was the scene of an accident reported in the *Derby Mercury* on 22 May 1839:

> *As Mr. Bower of Chesterfield was returning from Chesterfield on Monday, his horse came into contact with several coal carts from Foolow betwixt Baslow and Robin Hood Bar. Owing to the drivers being a very considerable distance from the carts, the horses were taking the wrong side of the road and the wheel of the first cart came suddenly upon Mr. Bower's horse, knocked it down, and consequently overthrew the rider.* [25]

Carts and waggons for carrying coal are recorded in much earlier periods, in fact as far back as 1290 William of Nayleston was killed at Breaston in south Derbyshire by a cart laden with sea-coal and drawn by three horses. [26] The coal-carrying trade was largely confined to the few weeks in the summer before and after hay making, for not only were the roads normally at their driest and firmest at that time of year, but the carriers were part-time farmers who took advantage of this slack period before they returned in autumn to the tilling of their land. In 1692 John Houghton reported that Derbyshire pits in the Smalley-Heanor-Denby area supplied places as far afield as Northamptonshire in the summer time. [27] No local road seems to have acquired the name Coal Way or Coal Lane, presumably because a variety of traffic used the same highways. In the White Peak, Chelmorton has an Old Coalpit Lane, which is presumably the same track as 'the Cole Pitt Road' recorded in 1690, but this is merely a minor lane leading to a small pit; the region's highways are not named after its major minerals and manufactures in the manner of the saltways leading out of Cheshire. [28]

The improvement of river navigation led to a significant expansion of the export trade in coal. The probate inventory of John Foster, taken early in 1721, shows that he had taken advantage of the Aire and Calder navigation to export coals from his pits at Woolley and Darton. The size of the pits is suggested by references to two gins, twenty-four picks and seventeen sledges, to 'coales unsold at Bimshaw Pitts, £30', and 'For Darton Coale Mine and the coales got there, £110'. His 'Debts for Coales sold to York, Lincolnshire, and several other places' amounted to over £260 and the 'Coales unsold and now being upon the Stennard at Wakefield' (i.e. land near the wharf) were valued at £110. [29] Coal was also to become the principal commodity transported along the Don navigation and its branch canals. Mining on a larger scale than hitherto began on the Greasbrough portion of the Wentworth estates, where in 1735 John Hirst of Ginnhouse installed the first steam engine that was employed to drain a local mine. He also constructed a wooden railway on the Newcastle model to enable his horses to take coal down the navigation. A report in the *Gentleman's Magazine* in 1763 noted that Greasbrough had three large collieries and that 'the coals are conveyed from hence chiefly by carriages upon Newcastle roads'. [30] The Marquis of Rockingham improved the transport facilities in 1780 by opening the Greasbrough cut, a new link with the Don navigation. The famous Barnsley and Silkstone seams, however, were not greatly exploited until after the opening of the Dearne-and-Dove and Barnsley canals in 1799 and the branches to Elsecar and Worsbrough Dale five years later. The full potential of the coalfield was not realised until the age of the railways.

3 Iron

The Tankersley seam of ironstone, which ran through south Yorkshire and north Derbyshire, was mined well before the first surviving deeds refer specifically to the industry. The village of Orgreave, meaning 'the pit from which ore was dug', had acquired its name by the time that Domesday Book was compiled in 1086. Firm evidence not only of shallow bell pits but of bloomeries and smithies is provided by an agreement of 1161 whereby Cistercian monks from the Lincolnshire abbey of Kirkstead were allowed to establish an ironworks on the borders of the townships of Kimberworth and Ecclesfield. During the same century monks from Louth Park (Lincolnshire) and Lenton Priory (Nottinghamshire) obtained similar rights in the township of Barlow.

By the later Middle Ages several primitive furnaces and forges were at work; their sites are often commemorated by the place-names Cinder Hill or Smithies. [31] Charcoal blast furnaces were introduced into the region during the reign of Elizabeth by the sixth Earl of Shrewsbury, the lord of Sheffield, Rotherham and Chesterfield. Within the next hundred years the local industry expanded considerably, so that by 1652 in the north Derbyshire hundred of Scarsdale eight townships had ironworks. The investment and organisational flair necessary for this expansion came from well-to-do local gentlemen, notably Lionel Copley of Wadworth and George Sitwell of Renishaw. During the later decades of the seventeenth century and the first half of the following century a gentry syndicate led by the Spencers of Cannon Hall, Cawthorne, dominated the Derbyshire and West Riding iron industry. By 1720 no less than twenty-nine undertakings were financed by a complicated system of partnerships which were to last until the end of the charcoal era. [32]

Charcoal blast furnaces were sited alongside streams within a mile or so of the ironstone pits. They often stood in isolation in the countryside, in the present manner of Rockley furnace, a remarkable survival from this era. Despite this isolation, only Chapel furnace (and that

Cannon Hall, Cawthorne, the home of the Spencers, gentry ironmasters and organisers of the nailmaking trade.

obliquely) is commemorated in the name of a local lane. This furnace stood on the site of the later Izal factory in what used to be called the White Field after an outcrop of a light or 'white' seam of ironstone, which was so named to distinguish it from the two darker seams that lay below. The name White Lane was applied originally to the whole stretch of road from the centre of Chapeltown past this field to the parish boundary at White Lane Head Farm (now the *Norfolk Arms*), but with the coming of the railways the lower part was re-named Station Road. [33]

The furnaces produced on average 300-400 tons of pig iron per annum and required 1,000 to 1,200 horse loads of charcoal a year. Two-thirds of this fuel came from within a five-mile radius, but for the rest the ironmasters had to go up to fifteen miles away on to the Magnesian Limestone belt. Between 1699 and 1705 Rockley furnace was supplied with charcoal from forty-three different places, mainly from a north-easterly direction. All the old deciduous woods of south Yorkshire and north Derbyshire were managed carefully and coppiced on a regular rotation. In 1602, for instance, a servant of the seventh Earl of Shrewsbury was concerned with 'the preservation of the springs'. The distinctive place-name, Springwood, is still found in various parts of the region. In many of these old woods flat areas of burnt soil mark the places where charcoal was made. [34]

John Hobson's description of the panniers used by seventeenth-century charcoal burners has already been quoted in Chapter 4. Arthur Raistrick has written that practically the whole of the carrying of charcoal was done by packhorse, but local evidence suggests that wheeled vehicles were used more frequently than has been thought. Anthony Roberts, the Earl of Shrewsbury's steward in Sheffield, wrote on 19 May 1595 of the need for more oxen to carry ironstone and charcoal, and on 1 September 1683 eight men paid Mrs Elizabeth Bowden of Barnby Hall for passes for the 'carying of Charckcole ... with our waines & Carts from Cawthorne Parke' to the furnace at Rockley. [35]

During the charcoal era pig iron had to be taken several miles overland from the furnaces to the river-valley forges. The surviving accounts do not specify the nature of this carriage, nor the way in which foreign iron was imported and finished goods exported, but presumably such loads were brought to and from the river ports by carts or wains. In the 1660s George Sitwell, the Renishaw ironmaster, exported goods via his agents at Bawtry and Hull or sent them to London by a private carrier or the Nottingham waggon. The 'venerable and sturdy' iron wain at Wortley forge was still in use at the beginning of the twentieth century, though it had long ceased to make two regular journeys a week over the moors to Manchester with finished goods. Wortley forge accounts for the year ending 30 September 1696 refer to a warehouse at Woodhead and to a payment of £2.10s. to 'Mr Francis Cartwright for houseing and Selling Iron att Manchester and receiving money'. Rod iron was taken the fourteen miles to Woodhead at the rate of ten shillings per ton and the thirty-two miles to Manchester at £1.5s. a ton, which was about ³/₄d. per ton/mile. Rod for the local nailers and bar iron were charged at a variety of rates, ranging from a little over to just under ¹/₂d. per ton/mile. Rod iron cost five shillings a ton regardless of whether it was carried only four miles to Mortomley or nine miles to Staincross, and bars were taken six miles to Barnsley at 8s.4d. per ton or over similar terrain to Sheffield, ten miles away, for the same price. Rod and bar iron had identical transport charges when taken to Sheffield, but the inhabitants of Doncaster, twenty-two miles away, paid twelve shillings a ton for rod and fourteen shillings a ton for bar iron. [36]

The Attercliffe group

The contemporary accounts of the 'Attercliffe group' of ironmasters, centred on Attercliffe forge, indicate not only the local places which were supplied with iron to be worked into shape by the secondary metalworkers, but demonstrate the wide area in which metal goods were sold in the regional markets during the last decade of the seventeenth century. The accounts refer to 'Iron sent to Barnsley for Wire-drawers', to 'Steele sent into Lancashire' and to nails, pans and the plating trade (which probably included tools such as chisels and saws). During the first fifteen years of the eighteenth century goods were sold in the Lancashire and Cheshire market towns of Chester, Knutsford, Liverpool, Nantwich and Warrington, and by the late 1730s the group was also trading in Kendal, Nottingham, Scarborough and Whitehaven. A decade or two later the branch of the partnership that was centred on Staveley forge was selling goods as far afield as Cambridge, Colchester, Hull, Ipswich, London, Newcastle, Norwich, Nottingham, Stockton and Yarmouth. [37]

Much of the iron produced locally during the charcoal era was made into nails. About 100 of the 600 or so smithies recorded in south Yorkshire and north Derbyshire in the hearth tax returns of 1672 belonged to nailers in the villages and hamlets that lay both to the north and the south of the Hallamshire cutlery district. The nailers worked within a few miles of the slitting mills at Wortley, Masborough and Renishaw and were supplied with rod iron by local chapmen. These middlemen sprang from local stock, usually from families of peasant-craftsmen who had long been occupied in the trade. They were often of yeomen rank and were sometimes rich enough to be described as gentlemen. George Guest of Thorpe, for instance, had capital invested in three local farms at the time of his death in 1698 and farm stock valued at £319: the personal goods within his house were valued at £108, he was owed a total of £234, and he had 'Stock in Trade att New Castle and Hull and other places, £217' and 'The Sixteenth parte of a Hull pinke called the Southend Society, £30'.

The chapmen not only provided rods but collected and sold the nails. The probate inventory of William Gilley of Barrow (1718) noted that Mr Wilson of Wortley forge was owed £60.5s. for iron, but this was more than balanced by 'Iron not wrought up, £9.7s.6d., Nailes which lyeth in the Countrey unsold, £29.12s.3d. [and debts] Due in the Countrey according to my debt Book, £38.17s.6d.'. A generation later, Matthew Booth died at White Lane Head,

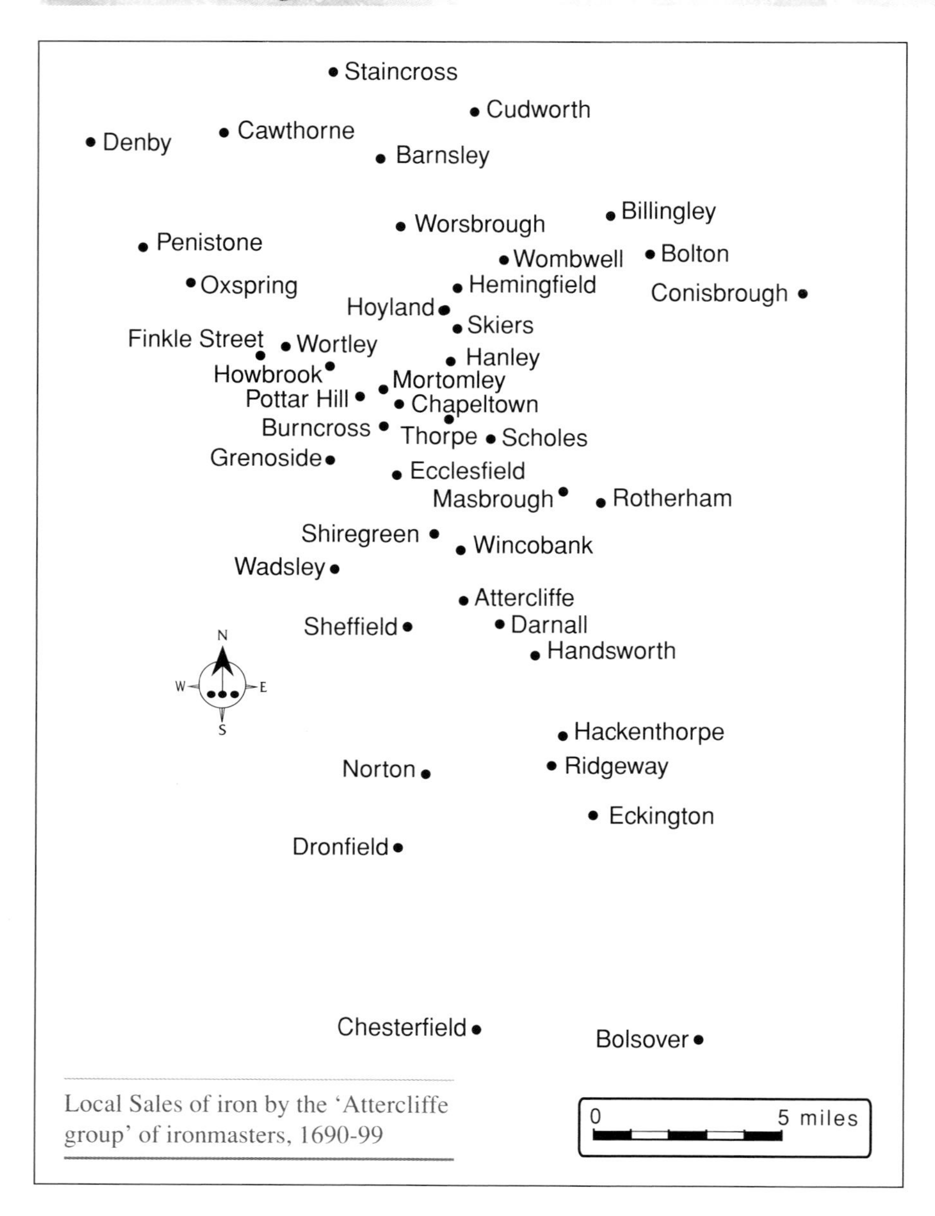

Local Sales of iron by the 'Attercliffe group' of ironmasters, 1690-99

Chapeltown, with 'Nails and iron in the Warehouse' worth £154 and 'Bills, Bonds, and Book Debts' to his credit amounting to £647. A nailchapman was often a large-scale creditor and in the case of Nicholas Gills of Chapeltown (1736) the debts and bonds that were due to him amounted to £1,800. [38]

All the iron produced at Wortley in the 1690s was sold in fairly small quantities to local customers, but from 1725 onwards the gentlemen in charge of the charcoal woods, furnaces, forges and slitting mills became directly involved in the nail trade. The diary and letter-books of William Spencer of Cannon Hall make it clear that great quantities of nails were exported to London and from there to America. During the 1740s local nails were sold in Virginia, Jamaica, the Leeward Isles, Newfoundland and Philadelphia and production expanded rapidly. In vain did 210 masters sign the Ecclesfield Nailers' Agreement of 1733 which tried

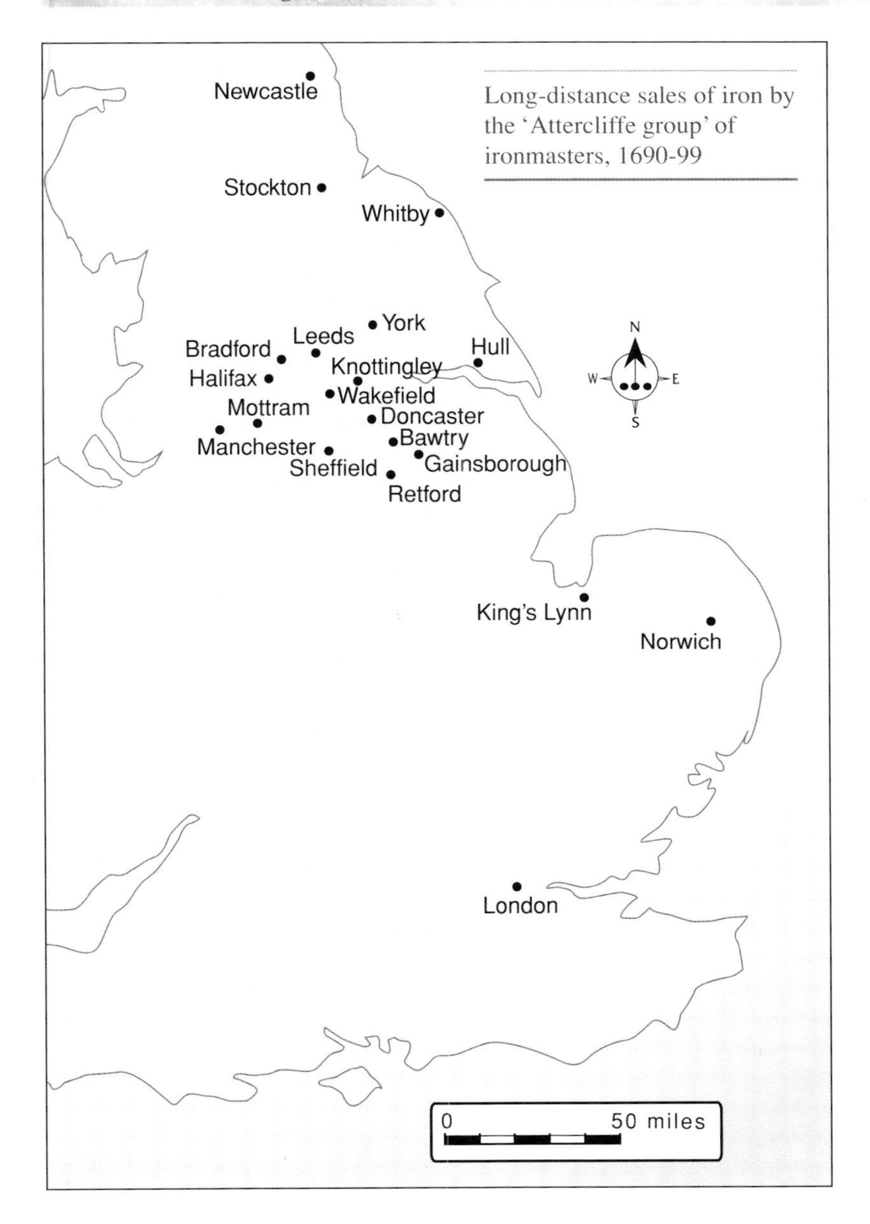

Long-distance sales of iron by the 'Attercliffe group' of ironmasters, 1690-99

to insist that apprentices should serve a full term instead of leaving after only two years' service, for as in the Black Country demand exceeded supply. Spencer employed Jonathan Dearden of Howbrook as his 'taker-in of nails' responsible for their dispatch from Rotherham wharf on the River Don navigation and he also used the services of local chapmen. Between 1742 and 1748 John Booth of Ecclesfield parish, James Wigfield of Hoyland, and an unidentified Samuel Lockwood delivered 4,465 bags of nails to Rotherham wharf. Invoices mention at least ten different types of nails, worth in all nearly £10,307, at £2.6s.2d. a bag, or about £1.10s. a hundredweight. According to William Murgatroyd, the clerk of Wortley forge, in 1739 'The Charges of a Bag of Nails from the Warehouse [at Howbrook] to London is Computed at 1s.10d. on any Average'.

The Spencer papers demonstrate the importance of the London and American markets, but the pattern of internal trade is much more difficult to reconstruct. John Parkin, a Mortomley chapman, was selling nails at Boroughbridge fair in 1744 independently of the Spencer organisation and nearly two years previously Spencer had tried to persuade Francis Holmes of Rotherham, a rival in the field, to sign an agreement whereby Holmes could have used Wortley iron if he had been prepared to sell his nails principally in London and not in Hull, Beverley, Newcastle, York, Scarborough or anywhere in Lancashire, Lincolnshire, Yorkshire, Derbyshire or Cheshire. Holmes refused, presumably because this regional trade was a lucrative one, orientated towards the northern counties, away from the markets of the Black Country nailers.

4 The cutlery and allied trades

'Ther be many smithes and cuttelars in Halamshire', wrote John Leland when he visited Yorkshire about 1540. The first documentary reference to the trade was to Robert the Cutler, who was taxed in Sheffield in 1297, and during the following century Sheffield knives had gained a sufficient reputation for Chaucer to mention one carried by the miller in *The Reeves Tale*. The earliest surviving cutler's mark was granted by the court of the manor of Sheffield to William Ellis in 1554, but an entry in the court rolls eleven years later to 'the ancient customs and ordinances' suggests that manorial supervision of the trade was much older than that. After the death of Gilbert, seventh Earl of Shrewsbury, in 1616 the lord of Hallamshire no longer resided at Sheffield Manor Lodge and rarely set foot in the town, so the cutlers determined to form their own company.

Above: Three sixteenth or seventeenth century knives from the mud banks of the River Thames. Their Hallamshire origins are proved by their trade marks. *D. Hey.*

They claimed that 'the greatest part of the Inhabitants of the Lordship and Liberty of Hallamshire ... doe consist of cutlers' and in 1624 upon the foundation of the company 182 marks were enrolled by craftsmen who had been engaged in the trade previously. The scissorsmiths, shearsmiths and sicklesmiths joined the company immediately, followed in 1676 by the awlbladesmiths and in 1682 by the scythesmiths and filesmiths. During the seventeenth century nearly sixty per cent of the workforce in Sheffield worked in the cutlery and allied trades, an astonishing level of specialisation for the time. Judging by the hearth tax returns of 1672, these urban craftsmen formed thirty-eight per cent of the local metalworkers. High-class goods were made in the town, whereas 'common wares' and special products such as scythes, sickles, forks and nails were made in the countryside. [39]

Local specialisation had its roots deep in the past, particularly in the case of the Norton scythemakers. John Parker of Little Norton was described as a scythesmith in 1459. Amongst those whose occupations were recorded in the Norton parish register between October 1559 and September 1579 were eleven scythesmiths, a scythegrinder, and John Allen of Woodseats, who was described

The Eastern edges are littered with abandoned millstones. Those with a mushroom shape being the oldest. Here are two of them, with Longshaw just visible in the distance. *C.L.M. Porter.*

they decided to fine heavily anyone who brought millstones that way in future. [58]

It is difficult to gauge the importance of the export trade to other parts of the country during the Middle Ages, for millstones were also imported from the Continent through the east coast ports. The 1331 grant of pontage (the right to levy tolls on goods crossing bridges) in Boston, which specified millstones, implies an inland trade, and it is possible that millstones were brought along the same route as Derbyshire lead. Local stone was certainly carried long distances, for nine fourteenth-century bowls or stone mortars, made of Millstone Grit, have been found in various parts of southern England, including Essex, Gloucestershire and Oxfordshire. During the reign of Elizabeth the parish of Hathersage was the centre of production, with major quarries at Stanage and Millstone Edge. A tithe dispute of 1590 shows that about 300 millstones a year were being made there. [59]

Information from the late seventeenth century is just as fragmentary. In 1673 Richard Blome noted that Bawtry had 'great Quarries, out of which Mill-stones are got, also Grindstones, and Sythstones, which imploy many hands in working up, and are dispersed over great part of the Nation'. Ralph Thoresby, too, in 1683, described Bawtry as famous for the export of millstones and pigs of lead. [60] Local mills were supplied by carters who were prepared to travel many miles with a single order; in 1676 a pair of millstones for the windmill at North Elmsall cost £9.10s. and 7s.6d. was charged for bringing them the twenty-two miles or so from the quarry at Bradfield. [61] But many more carters headed for Bawtry. In 1692 John Houghton observed that Derbyshire had 'rich Quarries of Mill-stones and they served most parts of the Kingdom, and they are worth 8, 9, or 10 Pounds the Pair, and Grindstones of all sorts, from 5 or 6 Foot Diameter and under, and Scythe-stones in abundance, which serve all parts of the Kingdom'. [62]

In the early eighteenth century millstones were amongst the major exports mentioned by those who petitioned for an improved navigation of the Don and by Daniel Defoe in his eulogy of Bawtry. Nevertheless, demand was easily matched by supply. John Wilson, the eighteenth-century antiquary of Broomhead Hall, noted that, 'In Riveling has been got great quantitys of mill stones and many still remain. About the year 1710 the work was discontinued since when the Mill Stone Edge near Hathersedge has been in vogue. Mr Rotherham has taken this in Riveling and will not let it be worked lest it should damage the sale of the other'. [63]

The comments of Richard Blome and John Houghton show that by the second half of the seventeenth century grindstones also were exported. In fact, a little earlier in 1656, Philip Kinder had claimed that Derbyshire supplied all England with scythe stones and grindstones. However, the great majority were undoubtedly sold to local cutlers, using that term in its widest sense, and most quarries lay within a few miles of Sheffield on the Coal Measure sandstones. As far back as 1442 the steward of Hallamshire had noted the receipt of 13d. 'for the grinding-wheels in the lord's quarry this year' and in 1637 John Harrison observed that 'course grinding stones for knives & scithes, & alsoe very good Millnstones are hewn out in Rivelin or stone edge'. During the late seventeenth and eighteenth centuries the cutlery industry expanded rapidly and so did the demand for grindstones. By 1770 Hallamshire had 133 wheels, containing 896 grinding troughs on its rivers. [64]

Many of the quarries were small and ephemeral. Beeley Moor is pitted with shallow quarries twelve to twenty feet in diameter and up to two feet deep, and a number of discarded querns and scythe-stones litter the surface. Numerous minor tracks link these quarries with the few thoroughfares that strike across the moor. More famous were the quarries at Ashover. In 1722 Titus Wheatcroft wrote, 'There is a Delfe (or pitt) where men get abundance of scythe sand, and send it abroad into other countries for the use of husbandmen, but the quarry for grindlestones is far beyond it in bringing profit to the lords of the parish, and they are of special use to all who make scythes, hooks, and all kinds of hardware, as they do at Sheffield'. [65] But the most notable grindstone quarry of all was at Wickersley, where over 5,000 grindstones per annum were reputedly manufactured at the beginning of the nineteenth century; in 1826 'the principal part of the grindstones used in the cutlery manufactures of Sheffield' were obtained here. [66] Quarries such as these specialised in the type of stones they produced, but few could hope to achieve the monopoly obtained by a quarry at Saddleworth, near the Lancashire border, in the production of bakestones. John Hobson of Dodworth Green wrote in his diary on 3 July 1732 that 'John Bradbury of Sadleworth, having lately had his house and barn burnt, came to ask relief. He is an old man, aged 87, and has sold havercake backstones in this country upwards of 60 years'. Fifteen months later, on 8 October 1733, Hobson 'went to Delf in Friermere, in the parish of Saddleworth ... It is there where all the havercake bakestones are got out of a quarry, the only one I ever heard of in England. The mine lies on the side of a hill, about 8 yards thick, about 3 yards of earth to clear of on it'. [67]

During the Middle Ages the Magnesian Limestone belt immediately east of the Coal Measure sandstones was nationally famous as a source of good building stone. In 1395 Marr stone was used to heighten the walls of Westminster Hall and when porches were added to King's College chapel, Cambridge, in 1513, the masons used 'good sufficient and noble stone of Hampole quarryes in Yorkshier'. Local stones were used for the building of churches, castles and a few of the finest manor houses, but until the reign of Elizabeth or the following century nearly all domestic buildings were of timber. When John Leland visited south Yorkshire about 1540 he wrote, 'The hole toune of Doncaster is buildid of wodde, and the houses be slatid; yet is there great plenty of stone there about'. [68] Only when timber became scarce and expensive did it become economical to build in stone.

In 1649 parliamentary surveyors reported that the manor of Barnsley had 'noe wood within the manor worth the valueing', but there were 'Quarries of stone and slate in and uppon the wast or common'. When Celia Fiennes travelled between Hemsworth and Rotherham at the close of the century she was struck by the number of fine houses and walls newly built of freestone. Many local quarries must have been exploited for the first time during this period in order to cope with increased demand. The manor of Sheffield, for example, was said in 1637 to contain 'good stones for building, & slate stones for tyling or slateing'. [69] Much later, parliamentary enclosure of vast wastes and commons meant that great quantities of stone were needed and the age of canals and railways brought a new and profitable trade in flagstones to pave the streets of London.

Derelict quarries offer few clues to their age or to the date when they were abandoned and hardly any place-names have survived to enable us to distinguish quarry roads from other packhorse tracks. Nor is it certain how millstones, slates or other stones were transported from the quarries. Most of the building stone for Hardwick Hall seems to have been borne or dragged by horses; the accounts for 15 February 1593, for instance, record payments for pack saddles, for a dozen ropes for the stone horses, and for 'making a drudge to lead stone upon'. [70] Celia Fiennes noted that in Derby, as in Bristol and Southampton, 'they carry much of their carriages on sledges to secure their pitching in the streetes' and horse-drawn sledges were certainly used to transport slates in the Lake District, but there is little documentary evidence that this was the method used in local quarries. [71] When Daniel Defoe stood on the hill-top above Chatsworth, he idly wondered what would happen 'should they roll down a pair of these stones coupled with a wooden axis, as is the way of drawing them'. It seems unlikely that millstones were dragged very far by this method. Oral accounts suggest that millstones were taken along specially-constructed holloways on horse-drawn sledges. They were far too valuable to risk rolling them very far.

According to G. H. B. Ward, a late eighteenth- or early nineteenth-century drive along the edge above Baslow, Curbar and Froggatt was described as Millstone Road upon 'an old rudely drawn map'. [72] Many of the quarry-roads look similar to packhorse tracks, but some have obviously been artificially hollowed out in order to produce a graded incline for sledges or carts. They look very similar to abandoned wooden railways, except that they have bends, presumably to slow down the traffic. Several of these tracks can be found on the moors immediately north of Fox House. The best example leads from the top of Millstone Edge quarry, through the Surprise View car park and across the A625, and down the steep slope to a ford across Burbage Brook, at the upper end of Padley Gorge. One branch then heads towards Fox House and Sheffield and the other crosses Longshaw Park and Big Moor towards Chesterfield; as it passes to the east of the Lady Cross the track again seems to have been artificially deepened. The best preserved section is that which descends to the Burbage Brook, and here its artificial nature is most evident. No amount of traffic could have worn down solid rock in such a regular manner. On the other hand, it is likely that this was an old track which was improved, rather than an entirely new one.

Another holloway which is difficult to interpret is that at Midhope known as Stoney Croft Lane, which descends the hillside towards the hamlet and joins the present lane at a right-angled bend. It is aligned with Judd Field Lane, the packhorse track up the hill across the Little Don valley, heading for Penistone, and may be thought of as part of the same route over the Strines from Ladybower. Thomas Jeffreys's map of 1767-72 shows, however, that the present road a quarter of a mile to the east was the route in use even before the road was turnpiked, and upon close examination Stoney Croft Lane appears to have been artificially levelled. The walls have fallen and the soil has slipped, but the lane still appears straight and uniformly wide, and to have been dug out of solid rock. No traces of a quarry can now be found, but some thirty years ago broken millstones were found in the top field adjacent to the lane. Artificial roads leading to large and deep quarries such as that west of Ringinglow are perfectly obvious, but some of the smaller ones such as Stoney Croft Lane may easily be confused with holloways associated with other traffic, which have been worn down naturally.

One holloway that can be shown to have been created to ease the movement of millstones is that which descends towards Hathersage from a small delph on Offerton Moor that belonged to the Eyre family. An account dated 13 July 1722 allows a payment 'For making out of the Edge so as the mylnestones might pass'. [73] Another piece of firm documentary evidence has

The Burbage Brook millstone road; two views of a track that was levelled to ease the carriage of millstones from the famous quarry at Millstone Edge towards the inland port of Bawtry. It probably dates from the early eighteenth century, though the quarrymen may have deepened an even older track. *Sheila Edwards.*

been found to prove that quarry roads were deliberately cut out. The evidence is a note by John Wilson of Broomhead Hall and it relates to a quarry only two or three miles from his home. He wrote:

> *The road to the new blew slate delf at Cartledge was begun by Mr. George Smilter of Sheffield on Monday 28th May 1750 and cut thro: the moss in many places three yards deep [wide?] in twelve weeks time, seldom having under twelve and never more than twenty six men employed. The cut is about a mile and half long the deepest place about 100 yards long each. The first waggon that came for slate was Richard Wilson's of Castle Fould, Sheffield. A good deal of the slate was sent to London and other places, was very fine and light but would not stand the weather. There has been none got many years.* [74]

It is worth stressing that slates were taken along this moorland route by waggons. None of the surviving holloways matches Wilson's description adequately, for they have altered considerably over the last two-and-a-half centuries, but the road must have connected Cartledge with the Strines, either at Thornsett or along the track that was known later as the Duke of Norfolk's road.

The tolls charged by turnpike trusts in the second half of the eighteenth century speak of millstones drawn by horses but do not specify the form of carriage. Unfortunately, the transport of millstones was not a subject that attracted local artists, but in the foreground of William Ibbitt's *South-east View of Sheffield* (1854) a horse stands between the shafts of a primitive wain or cart on which grindstones of varying sizes are piled. It seems that millstones were probably trundled along from the quarries to the sledge-roads, but once they were off the moors they were transferred to wheeled vehicles and taken the shortest possible route to the nearest navigable river.

6 Lime

In the early modern period burnt lime was frequently used for whitening the walls of houses. The Hardwick Hall accounts for 1596, for instance, record the arrival of 'one horse load of Crich lyme to whyte with'. Gypsum plaster from the mid-Trent valley and the Isle of Axholme was used for ceilings in many parts of the region, so that by the end of the seventeenth century Abraham de la Pryme could describe the houses in Hatfield, to the east of Doncaster, as 'neat, well furnished, and most of them ceiled with the whitest plaster within'. [75]

Burnt lime was used increasingly on agricultural land where the soils were too acid. In 1628 the manor of Campsall on the Magnesian Limestone belt of central south Yorkshire was said to contain 'great store of Lymestone an excellent compost beinge burned to Manure cold grounds'. Nearly thirty years later William Jubb, a lime burner from Knottingley, entered an agreement with Sir John Bright of Badsworth to deliver sixty loads of lime at a cost of £16.10s. and in 1663

Burning lime in a kiln, from *Microcosm* by William Henry Pyne, 1806.

Sir Francis Chantrey's view of lime burning in Middleton Dale c.1820, from Rhodes' "Peak Scenery."

Lawrence Thompson, a lime burner of Ferry Fryston, agreed to deliver eighty waggon loads of lime from his Knottingley quarries. [76] However, the quarrying of limestone only developed on a large scale when first the rivers Aire and Calder and then the Don were made navigable into the heart of the coalfield. Barges full of coal went down the rivers (and later the canals) and returned with lime for the kilns at the head of the navigation. In 1804 James Hutchinson of Hiendley said that about thirty-five years previously, when he was servant to Mr Thwaites of Round Green in the township of Worsbrough, he had led many loads of lime there from the Don navigation at Kilnhurst; with the opening of a branch of the Dearne and Dove canal to Worsbrough Bridge the long journey by road was no longer necessary as lime kilns had been erected by the canal basin. [77]

On the Carboniferous Limestone of the White Peak, quarrying and lime-burning were undertaken on a large scale somewhat earlier. In 1650 a survey of the manor of High Peak noted fourteen kilns alongside the Dove Holes quarries and ten more at Bradwell Townend, and in 1722 Titus Wheatcroft claimed that Ashover was 'especially noted for limestone and lime kilns, which furnisheth all the country round about us with lime for land and building'. When the freeholders of Carsington agreed in 1652 to plough their lower, stinted pasture and to put it to tillage for seven years, each man was obliged to lay at least sixty horse loads of well-burned limestone per acre for the first four years. [78] Loads of limestone were frequently recorded in Derbyshire probate inventories, e.g. those of John Allsop of Somercoates (1659), John Marshall of Woodthorpe (1662), George Booth of West Handley (1667) and John Cowper of Ripley (1692). South Yorkshire inventories rarely survive before 1689, but Richard Shepard of Elsecar had a quantity of lime in 1673, Lewis Nawl, a cutler-farmer of Sheffield Park, had thirty loads of lime valued at £15 in 1692, and Timothy Ellis of Coates in the parish of Silkstone had eight loads of lime on his land in 1695.

Lime was transported both by packhorse and by cart or waggon. At the West Riding quarter sessions held at Doncaster in 1641, Richard Herring of Wath upon Dearne, husbandman, was charged with 'placing in the open street at Wombwell certain cartloads of lymestone, so that the king's subjects could not pass by that way'. We have already seen that in 1663 lime was taken by waggons from Knottingley to Badsworth, and late in the next century carts bringing coal to Stoney Middleton were said to return eastwards loaded with lime. On the other hand, in 1789 Pilkington wrote that burnt Derbyshire lime was carried by packhorses, and South Head farm at Hayfield is still reputed to have been a place where packhorses were kept for carrying lime from the Bradwell kilns to neighbouring farms. [79]

7 Textiles

Numerous sixteenth- and seventeenth-century wills show that the manufacture of woollen cloth was widespread in south Yorkshire and north Derbyshire before the industry became concentrated further north. Fulling mills had been established near Dore by 1280, at Hoyland before 1290 and at Oxspring by 1306, and no doubt in many other places, and although the Sheffield fulling mill had been converted into a forge by 1637, three years later the towns-men of Barnsley were still fighting to preserve their cloth market in face of competition from Wakefield. [80] Doncaster served not only as an importer of Lincolnshire wool for West Riding clothiers but as a small manufacturing centre with a fulling mill, its own dyers and drapers, and a guild of weavers, walkers and shearmen. In 1595 about 120 knitters of woollen stock-ings, caps and underwear found employment in and around Doncaster, and during the reign of Charles I two merchants from Doncaster and Rotherham were said to be supplying London with such goods. [91]

In Chesterfield the textile industry went back to at least the thirteenth century. The town's

1294 charter stipulated that only burgesses should be dyers and by 1309 the drapers had their own row in the market. The 215 probate inventories that survive for Tudor Chesterfield and some of the villages that lay within its parish suggest that one in every three or four families had equipment such as spinning wheels, cards or looms or small quantities of wool. During the seventeenth century probate inventories were appraised there for five websters, four clothworkers, four dyers, three weavers, three coverlet weavers, two woollen drapers, a draper, a hosier, and a shearman, and many other people, farmers and craftsmen alike, found that preparing wool for the weavers was a useful by-employment. Imported woad and alum had been brought overland from Southampton during the middle years of the fifteenth century; we do not know where Thomas Heathcote obtained his supplies but in 1558 his dyeing equipment and materials included vats and leads, wool, flax and hemp, and madder, copperas, galls and alum. The local clothiers produced narrow, coarse cloths known as kerseys or carseys, but Chesterfield drapers also offered imported cloths for sale. When Thomas Denyson died in 1588 part of his stock of variously coloured friezes and cottons was described as a Rochdale frieze, and he owed money to four Kendal men, three from Shrewsbury, two from Leeds, and one from Rochdale. His neighbour, Hugh Hall, was a woollen draper who owed money to two London men and to several others elsewhere. [82]

A little further north, Stephen Bamford, a 'poynter' of Heeley Bridgehouse (1610), sold knives at Chesterfield and points to 'Adlington of Tibshelfe ... which keepeth a Stalle in Chesterfeld market'. Bamford had a small farm and a packsaddle, pair of panniers and a wantow. He and his family made extra money from spinning yarn on a wool wheel and two little tow wheels. He dealt with a mercer named Gibson and sold laces to Henry Cocke, a Dronfield mercer, but also sold wares to pedlars, including one who 'sometime lodgeth at Robert Dowes'. The local textile industry was much more rural than urban, with weaver-farmers pursuing a typical dual occupation, though it was much more thinly spread than in the countryside further north. Kerseys were made throughout the region, but a 1595 survey tells us that in addition, 'At Penistone near Barnsley and some villages thereabouts are made about one thousand pieces of White Peny Stones'; that is, coarse, narrow cloths $1^1/_4$ yard wide and twelve to thirteen yards long.

Penistone Cloth Hall and Shambles. A livestock market was held in the central streets of the town between 1699 and 1910. A cloth market was established in the upper rooms of the grammar school in 1743, and twenty years later John Platt of Rotherham designed the Cloth Hall and Shambles, now a chemist's shop. The arched windows were formerly open entrances. *Sheila Edwards.*

'Ordinary Penistones' or 'Forest Whites' and 'Sorting Penistones' were referred to in Acts of Parliament between 1553 and 1607, and at London's famous weekly cloth market at Blackwell Hall in 1561-62 ten Yorkshire dealers who had inferior penistones were fined by the searchers of defective cloths. Defoe speaks of penistones being sold at the great Stourbridge fair in Cambridgeshire, and the small Pennine market town which had given the cloth its name established its own cloth market in 1743 in the

West Riding clothiers. George Walker's painting of 1814 shows pieces of cloth being taken to the Piece Halls of the market towns on the backs of galloways. Walker noted. 'These men have a decided provincial character; and their galloways also, which are always overloaded, have a manner of going peculiarly their own'.

upper storey of the grammar school. Twenty years later John Platt of Rotherham was engaged to build the Cloth Hall and Shambles, which still stands in the market place though its original purpose has long been abandoned. [83]

A great deal of packhorse traffic crossed the eastern part of the region as clothiers from Wakefield and Leeds headed for London via Doncaster and the Great North Road and their counterparts further west used the great highway from Richmond to London that John Ogilby outlined crossing the hills from Halifax and Huddersfield to Barnsley, Wombwell and Rotherham and thus up to the capital. The Almondbury burial register for 2 September 1587 notes the death of Thomas Crosland 'on journey to London to St. Bartholomew's Fair' (the great annual cloth fair) and in 1636, when several Halifax clothiers sent off thirty-three unstamped pieces of cloth to London, their carriers were apprehended twenty-seven miles away at Wombwell at their usual overnight lodging at the end of the first day's journey. Another glimpse of the London connection comes seventy years later when Joseph Holroyd, a cloth factor from Sowerby near Halifax, wrote to a Mr Henry Carter, 'Sir, I wrote you 26th last and then gave you Invoice of forty-two Longe Carsays and thirty bayes by the Carrier John Hall. Said Carrier disappointed me and hath not taken one packe butt hath gott John Law to Conviye them up butt it will be tomorrow sevennight before he can gett into London being 3 dayes behind them which I thought proper to advise you of'. [84]

The annual Stourbridge fair in Cambridgeshire was the outlet for 'vast quantities of Yorkshire cloths, kerseys, pennistons, cottons &c', when Defoe described it, 'with all sorts of Manchester ware, fustians, and things made of cotton wool; of which the quantity is so great, that they told me there were near a thousand horse-packs of such goods from that side of the country'. Many of these horse-packs must have come from Manchester through Derbyshire. An eighteenth-century traveller from Buxton to Matlock saw a 'vast number of packhorses travelling, of which we counted sixty in a drove; their chief loading is wool and malt, which they carry from Nottingham and Derby to Manchester'. On another occasion Defoe wrote:

There are ... a set of travelling merchants in Leeds, who go all over England with droves of pack horses, and to all the fairs and market towns over the whole island, I think I may say none excepted. Here they supply, not the common people by retail, which would denominate them pedlars indeed, but they supply the shops by wholesale or whole pieces, and not only so, but give large credit too, so that they are really travelling merchants, and as such they sell a very great quantity of goods, 'tis ordinary for one of these men to carry a thousand pounds value of cloth with them at a time, and having sold it at the fairs or towns where they go, they send their horses back for as much more, and is very often in a summer for they chuse to travel in the summer, and perhaps towards the winter time, tho' as little in winter as they can, because of the badness of the roads. [85]

The clothiers in our region were modest figures by comparison, but great trains of packhorses taking woollen cloth and other draperies from Lancashire and the West Riding either to the capital or to the great fairs and provincial market towns must once have been a common sight on certain local highways.

8 Salt

Salt was one of the most important commodities that was carried over the moors to the medieval and early-modern market towns of Yorkshire, Derbyshire and Nottinghamshire, for it was used to preserve food as well as flavour it. Some parts of the country obtained their salt from the coast, but the people of the midland counties were able to get their supplies from the natural brine springs of the Cheshire wiches (the salt works at Northwich, Middlewich and Nantwich), or further south from Droitwich, the *Salinae* of Roman times. A distinctive set of names were attached to the routes which radiate in all directions from the wiches, and though these tracks were used for conveying a variety of goods, names such as Salterway, Salter Hill or Salter Ford show that the carriage of salt was the most important of all. Domesday Book shows how vigorous was the trade in the late eleventh century, when it took fifteen boilings of a pan to make a packhorse load of salt. Tolls were levied at the rate of fourpence per cart load drawn by four or more oxen, twopence for a cart load led by two oxen, twopence for a horse load, and a farthing for a load carried on a man's back; local carriers were allowed cheaper rates. [86] The long-distance journeys into Yorkshire and Derbyshire would have been too difficult for a man to have carried a pack efficiently and as the hills were too steep for carts, salt was almost certainly brought here entirely by packhorse on a round trip of four to six days.

The most southerly saltway into our region can be traced accurately all the way from Congleton, which was within easy reach of all three Cheshire wiches. In 1749 the Staffordshire townships of Leek and Onecote were indicted at the quarter sessions for not repairing 'a great carriers' road ... chiefly used by packhorses who carry salt out of Cheshire into Derbyshire and Nottinghamshire and bring malt back into Cheshire'. It was claimed that 'upon a moderate calculation above 100 packhorses loaded with salt pass weekly through the road' via Meerbrook, Middle Hulme, Blackshaw Moor, Stoney Cliff and the steep ascent to Blackmere House (now the *Mermaid Inn*) on Morridge. The climb was so difficult that forty years previously some of the inhabitants of Tittesworth had 'made a stone causeway down the bank and several of the carriers contributed towards it ... to prevent their cattle and goods being damaged for the sake of having a tolerable road'. [87] The route then descended gradually into Warslow and, according to the indictment, proceeded towards Winster. With the aid of a map and with knowledge of the local topography, it is possible to trace the most likely course via

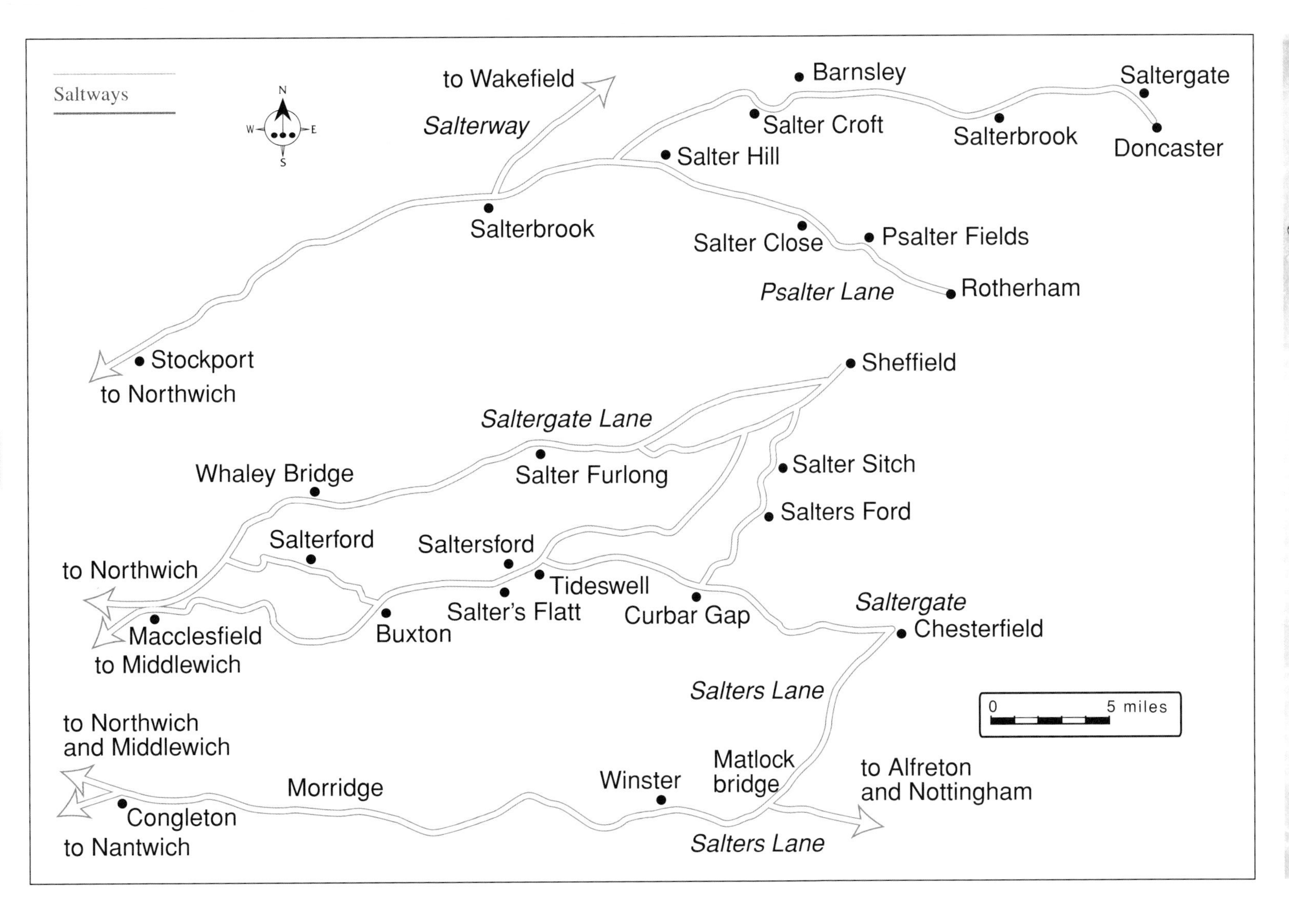

Saltways
N
W
E
S
to Wakefield
Salterway
Barnsley
Saltergate
Salter Croft
Salterbrook
Doncaster
Salter Hill
Salterbrook
Salter Close
Psalter Fields
Psalter Lane
Rotherham
Stockport
to Northwich
Sheffield
Saltergate Lane
Whaley Bridge
Salter Furlong
Salter Sitch
Salters Ford
Salterford
Saltersford
to Northwich
Tideswell
Salter's Flatt
Curbar Gap
Saltergate
Chesterfield
Macclesfield
Buxton
to Middlewich
Salters Lane
0
5 miles
to Northwich
and Middlewich
Morridge
Winster
Matlock
bridge
to Alfreton
and Nottingham
Congleton
to Nantwich
Salters Lane

Saltersbrook bridge. The county boundary stream has taken its name from the Cheshire salters who brought salt this way towards the Yorkshire market towns. The road was turnpiked in 1732-41 and the bridge probably dates from that time. It has now been restored. *Sheila Edwards.*

Hartington, then proceeding as directly east as possible. Nowadays the route is marked by a cart track to Dale End, a lane through Biggin, a path from Newhaven to Upperhouse farm and 3½ miles of modern road to Winster. From there, the salters could have gone towards Chesterfield via the medieval bridge over the Derwent at Darley, or they could have by-passed Winster by taking Bonsall Lane and Salters Lane to another medieval bridge over the Derwent at Matlock. The present A632 from Matlock was obviously used by salters heading for Chesterfield as, to the west of Ashover, it is known as Salters Lane. As the 1749 indictment referred to trade with Nottinghamshire, some salters may have continued in an easterly direction from Matlock to Mansfield or else have turned south-east towards the market towns of Alfreton and Nottingham.

Middlewich was the nearest source of supply for Derbyshire and the routes are well marked by salter names. First of all, the River Dane had to be crossed at Saltersford, which is obviously an old name, for a stone bridge was built to replace the ford in 1331. The approach to Siddington was along Salters Lane, where the Middlewich traders may have been joined on their way to Macclesfield by salters coming from Northwich. So far the going had been easy but at Macclesfield the difficulties began. W. B. Crump outlined three old hill routes across the Peak to the market towns of north Derbyshire and south Yorkshire. [88] The most northerly followed the course of the present road towards Whaley Bridge, crossed the River Goyt at Heybottom bridge, and continued towards Chapel en le Frith and the Winnats Pass down into Castleton. The salters may have rested overnight at Hope, for here was a Salter Barn and in 1688 a Salter Furlong [89] just to the south of the village; fields with salter names attached seem to have provided grazing stops for the horses. The following day men and horses proceeded along Saltergate Lane near Bamford before tackling the steep escarpment at Stanage. They then had another seven miles to go, either by the Long Causeway or by Ringinglow, before they reached Sheffield. A milestone which came to light when Redmires reservoir was drained a few years ago marked six customary miles to Sheffield and one to Stanage Pole. If the salters opted for the Ringinglow route they would have approached the town along Psalter Lane at Nether Edge. A deed of 1485 describes this way more prosaically as Salter lane; [90] the letter P was added later in the mistaken and romantic belief that this was a monastic route used by the canons of Beauchief abbey. (Psalter Lane at the Holmes, near Rotherham has also been mistaken for a monastic way.)

The second route from Macclesfield avoided the steeper hills and headed for the Saltersford (mentioned in 1452) near Goyt's Bridge before climbing the Long Hill to Buxton. Here it was joined by the third route, which had taken the most difficult line of all across the wild terrain by the *Cat and Fiddle Inn*, avoiding the headwaters of the Goyt to the north and the Dane to the south. The stretch was turnpiked in 1759 and is still a major crossing of the moors, but the old way from Buxton to Sheffield, which was turnpiked in the previous year, is now almost forgotten. Travellers leaving Buxton sought a lane that took them through Fairfield and on to a track which crossed the Saltersford that was recorded in 1272 and which has recently been located by Eric Heaf at the southern edge of Tideswell Townend. [91] The Wormhill tithe award also marks three closes named Salter's Flatt a few hundred yards south of this route, where no doubt salters' horses had stopped once to graze. [92] From Tideswell, traffic headed for the high ridge which stands so prominently on the skyline at Great Hucklow and then followed a direct line with clear views for miles around down the Sir William hill to an ancient crossing of the River Derwent at Grindleford. On the way to Sheffield the crossing of the Bar Brook was called Salters Ford on a 1614 perambulation of the Baslow boundary, and a stream that has to be crossed before descending into Totley is still known as Salter Sitch. It was recorded in a William Fairbank field-book of 1769 as Psalter Lumm. Another route from Tideswell went via Stoney Middleton and Calver bridge, or by Stanton Ford, to Curbar Gap, where a worn and almost illegible guide stoop points the way across the Big Moor to Chesterfield, Dronfield and Sheffield. [93]

The route through Curbar Gap was in fact the most direct way from the Cheshire salt wiches to Chesterfield market. Eighteenth-century guide stoops mark its continuation via Clod Hall and Old Brampton, along the road that was turnpiked in 1759, but which has since lost most of its traffic to the A619 from Baslow. The salters entered the town of Chesterfield along Saltergate, a main street which had acquired its name by 1285 but which was much older, for it led directly into the old market by the church and by-passed the present market place which was laid out in the twelfth century. A Salter Wood on the boundary of Brampton township near Oxton Rakes suggests another approach to the town and a Salterwelsick that was recorded near Staveley bridge in 1604 hints at a possible continuation of the route to Worksop. [94]

The most northerly of our region's salt tracks was that which came from Northwich via Saltersway to Altrincham and by Salters Hey to Stockport before ascending the Longdendale valley towards the market towns of Rotherham, Barnsley, Doncaster and Wakefield. We have already suggested that the long, narrow extension of the county of Cheshire to take in this valley demonstrated the crucial importance of this route in the Anglo-Saxon period. The boundary stream which separates Cheshire from Yorkshire is known as Saltersbrook. Having crossed this boundary, the salters soon parted ways, some leading in an easterly direction towards the market towns of south Yorkshire and others taking a north-easterly route into west Yorkshire. The Salterway or Saltergate to Wakefield formed part of the boundary between the Graveship of Holme and the township of Thurlstone on its way towards the great ridge at High Hoyland. [95]

Several salt names can be identified on the easterly route from Saltersbrook to Rotherham and Doncaster. When this road was turnpiked in 1741 it was claimed that 'great Quantities of manufactured Goods, Cheese, Salt and Potatoes, are carried from Manchester, Barnsley, and Parts adjacent, to Doncaster, on Horses, and return loaded with Hemp, Flax, and German

The saltway descending from Pym Chair into the Goyt Valley to Saltersford. *C.L.M. Porter.*

Yarn'. At Hartcliff, six miles into Yorkshire, the roads diverged. The salters who were heading for Barnsley and Doncaster descended the hill to the valley bottom at Hornthwaite and proceeded along the line of the present A628 and A635. Three salt names commemorate their ancient course. At Dodworth a house alongside the highway bears the name Salter Croft, a few miles further on another Saltersbrook is crossed at Goldthorpe, and near the junction with the Great North Road a school at Scawsby preserves the name Saltergate. The route from Hartcliff to Rotherham market is equally well supported by the evidence of place-names, by guide stoops at Hartcliff and Dyson Cote, and by several turnpike milestones. The salters continued along the great ridge which separates Penistone from Stocksbridge at about a thousand feet above sea level to Salter Hill and Green Moor.

The Don was apparently crossed not only by the present route down Well Hill and past Wortley forge but via Holly Lane further down the river. [96] A short climb up Finkle Street then led the way to Howbrook, High Green and Chapeltown and on via the present A629. In these latter stages the memory of the ancient salt trade is preserved only in the maps and field books of the Sheffield surveyors, the Fairbank family. In 1785 a field of nearly 3½ acres, which lay at the junction of Greengate Lane and the salt track as it passed through Mortomley, had the distinctive name of Salter Close. [97] No doubt it had once served as an overnight grazing stop for the salters' horses. Further on, a little to the north of the road at Thorpe Hesley, a Psalter Field of 10½ acres was included in a map of 1778 and a Psalter Close of less than three acres was marked on a 1760 map to the north of Psalter Lane, just before it reaches Holmes Green, having left the line of the present A629 to come through Kimberworth. [98] The name Psalter Lane is still used for this old bit of road, which headed for Rotherham's medieval bridge and market place.

Place-name evidence strongly supports the claim that the roads from Saltersbrook to Doncaster and Rotherham were ancient salt tracks. The existence of other routes is more uncertain for often only a single place-name suggests a possible line. For instance, a mile or so west of Bolsterstone is Salter Hill, with a Salt Springs beck, farm and cottage. The reference to Salt Spring must make this a dubious example, but looking at Salter Hill from Waldershaigh or Bolsterstone it is easy to believe that it took its name from salters' horses coming over the sky-line from Cheshire on their way to Sheffield. This was not the quickest route from the Cheshire wiches, but goods were certainly taken along these 'rugged, steep, narrow and circuitous lanes' before the Wadsley to Langsett turnpike road of 1805 opened up a new route along the valley of the Don and the Little Don. This Salter Hill may well have been on a southern branch of the salt track which entered the county at Saltersbrook. [99]

Other mysteries include the $5^1/_2$ acre Sauter Ing, meaning salter meadow, which appears on a 1785 map of Southey in the parish of Ecclesfield, [100] and the Salter Oak at Carlton, north of Barnsley, which is recorded in 1684. [101] Further east, a Salter Ford, which marked the boundary of the townships of Beighton and Killamarsh in 1777, lay between two county bridges but was apparently unrelated to either. [102] And a small stream at Wadworth, near Doncaster, still bears the name of Salter Sike. None of them can be fitted convincingly to an ancient salt route.

Finally, we must dismiss claims that have been put forward that houses known as Salt Pie are indicators of old saltways, [103] even when one such building stands alongside the highway from Saltersbrook to Doncaster at Hill Side, near Thurlstone. The word is commonly used in probate inventories for a salt box and was applied as a nickname to houses whose shape resembled the old wooden salt boxes that were fastened to mantelpieces. Salt Pie farm at Low Valley, Darfield, a demolished example at Monk Bretton, and houses known as Salt Box at Elsecar and at Hoyland Common (demolished 1968) acquired their names in this way. [104] Another demolished example at Grenoside has given its name to Salt Box Lane, which at first sight appears to be evidence of a salt track. Minor place-names have to be treated with proper caution before they can be accepted as evidence in tracing the pattern of ancient routes.

Though their routes can be located, the salters themselves remain shadowy figures and none has been identified by name. The transport costs were high, amounting to a quarter of the total cost in 1564 when the steward of Haddon Hall 'paid for iii crannocks of salt at xs. the crannocke xxxs, paid for carriage of the same salt xs'. [105] But then salt was a vital commodity and such costs could be absorbed in the price.

By concentrating on particular trades we are in danger of thinking that some of our roads were restricted to certain types of goods. That is true of the moorland millstone roads, but not of the rest, even the distinctive saltways. The variety of goods that were carried on our highways and byways is made clear by depositions in 1771 concerning a right of way from Hope to Sheffield. [106] William Simpson, a fifty-one year old labourer from Whiteley Wood, remembered 'that one Mr Cooper of Sheffield (now deceased) about 30 years ago travelled twice a year this way from Sheffield to Westchester Fairs (which were at Midsummer and Michaelmas) for five or six years with waggons loaded with hardware goods' and that he himself had 'conveyed many score cartloads of syckles from Sheffield to Hope this way for Mr Robert Bagshaw who resides near Sheffield'. He also recalled 'that John Fox of the Hills near Yatehouse (now deceased) brought small grinding stones in carriages from thence to Sheffield the same way for 40 years before the Turnpike Road was made'. Another deponent, William Ibbotson, a sixty-three year old farmer from Nether Hirst, 'carried lead via Gatehouse & Stannidge to Sheffield for Mr Rodgers' and brought back hardware. Between thirty and forty years ago he fetched tow, barrels of tar, hogsheads of treacle and other grocer's goods from Sheffield for several years. All these goods were transported along one of the most difficult, hilly routes in the Peak District.

7 The Transport of Livestock and Farm Produce

1 Markets and fairs

Doncaster's right to hold markets and fairs was based upon immemorial custom going back to the eleventh or twelfth century and possibly beyond. The market place occupied a key position within the town and was ideally situated at the point where the Great North Road crossed the limit of navigation up the River Don. Doncaster thrived as a great regional market centre. Rotherham and Sheffield also had markets and fairs based upon prescriptive rights which were confirmed or added to by medieval charters. Elsewhere in south Yorkshire the market place was of fundamental importance to the three new Norman towns of Barnsley, Bawtry and Tickhill.

The original settlement of Old Barnsley was merely a small village at the eastern end of the medieval parish of Silkstone, but in 1156 the manor was granted to the priory of St John at Pontefract and the monks created a new town half a mile away to the east, where the north-south route from Wakefield to Sheffield crossed the great highway that ran down the edge of the Pennines from Richmond to Halifax, Huddersfield and Rotherham, and so on to London. The choice of this site suggests that these highways were already important in the twelfth century. The fairs that were held in Fair Field to the west of the church and the markets on Market Hill were so successful that in 1249 the monks were encouraged to establish an additional weekly market and annual fair on the new site of May Day Green on the southern edge of the town, near to the major east-west road from Doncaster across the Pennines to Cheshire and Lancashire. Barnsley was not only situated alongside major highways but placed well away from rival centres. The presence in 1485 of two pewterers from York shows that Barnsley fair attracted traders from considerable distances. In the seventeenth century, in addition to its livestock and corn markets, Barnsley had special markets for malt and for cloth. The sixth edition of William Owen's *Book of Fairs* (1770) refers to the Wednesday market and to three great annual fairs for horned cattle and swine. The last fair of the year was also renowned for cheese and goose pies. [1]

The north Derbyshire towns of Bakewell and Chesterfield, and most likely Ashbourne, Tideswell and Wirksworth too, had markets and fairs based upon prescriptive rights. Trading was allowed by charter at the small medieval borough of Chapel en le Frith, at the little towns that nestled under the Norman castles at Bolsover and Castleton, and at the small, but thriving centres near the Nottinghamshire border at Alfreton and Ripley. Thirteenth- and fourteenth-century charters also exist for a number of villages, some of which still retain the outline of a market place or perhaps the stump of a butter cross, even though markets may not have been held there for centuries. Most of these smaller settlements declined in the later Middle Ages and ceased to hold their markets when the national economy decayed and the total population fell dramatically. The most spectacular casualty was Tickhill, which lost its urban status at the end of the Middle Ages. In an attempt to restore its fortunes, a splendid new market cross was erected in the late 1770s, but the place never recovered its former glory. Higham, Highburton and Pleasley managed to survive as minor centres and trading at Glossop and Wath was revived

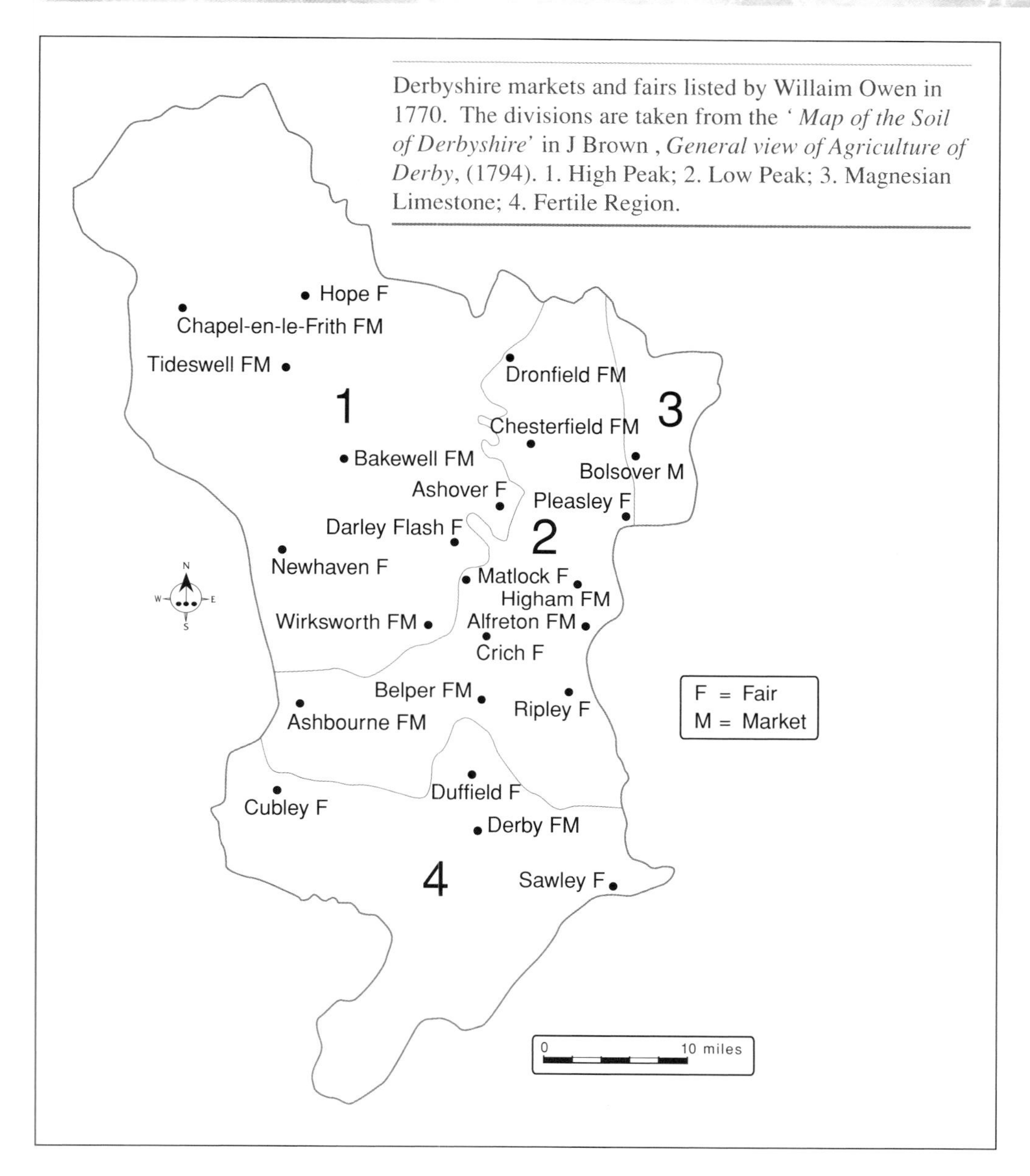

Derbyshire markets and fairs listed by Willaim Owen in 1770. The divisions are taken from the '*Map of the Soil of Derbyshire*' in J Brown , *General view of Agriculture of Derby*, (1794). 1. High Peak; 2. Low Peak; 3. Magnesian Limestone; 4. Fertile Region.

in the nineteenth century, but most of these village markets are heard of no more. In north Derbyshire they included Hartington (founded 1203), Charlesworth (1328), Denby (1334) and Monyash (1340) and in south Yorkshire Conisbrough (1201), Hooton Pagnell (1253), Braithwell (1289), Penisale (1290), Campsall (1294), Wortley (1307), Stainforth (1348) and an undated foundation at Scawsby, with two neighbouring markets just to the north at Emley (1253) and Almondbury (1294). [2] It is unlikely that all these markets were in existence at the same time, for a few had probably already vanished before others were created. Some of these places, notably Almondbury and Highburton, stood alongside ancient through roads, but others now appear to be well off the beaten track and to have had no permanent effect on the pattern of local highways. Even when they were sited at important crossroads, as at Wortley, they did not necessarily thrive.

The great revival in trade from the reign of Queen Elizabeth onwards restored the fortunes of some ailing towns and encouraged the growth of new trading centres. For many parts of the country the later Stuart period was a period of stagnation, but in the developing industrial centres such as ours this was a time when new markets and fairs were established. In 1659 the inhabitants of Thorne obtained a charter for a Wednesday market and for three-day fairs in June and October, and in 1662 Dronfield received a grant for a Thursday market and for four fairs each of one day's duration; they soon became prosperous little towns. The Saturday market at Winster was founded by 1690 and the curious little market hall that stands in the village street appears to date from the late seventeenth century. Winster was a thriving centre of the lead trade at that time and for much of the following century and as the district was predominantly pastoral, provisions for the lead miners had to be imported. Winster market was still a going concern in 1760 when Samuel Fox published his map of Derbyshire, but it was not mentioned in the sixth edition of Owen ten years later. However, it was flourishing in 1778, and nearly forty years later was still the main local supply of butcher's meat. Winster also had an annual fair on Easter Monday. Another venture in the Peak District was the weekly Saturday market and four annual fairs which John Balguy of Hope Hall established in his village in 1715. According to Fox and Owen, the market was defunct by 1760-70 but cattle fairs were still arranged for every May day and at Michaelmas. Other Pennine fairs established during this period include that held every 30 October at Holmfirth for horned cattle and those started by Joseph Swicket at Bradfield in 1714. Owen reported that the Bradfield fairs were held on 17 June and 9 December and were chiefly for swine. He also recorded new fairs at the periphery of the region, at Belper, Crich, Darley Flash, Matlock and Newhaven. [3] These small fairs did not attract customers from far afield, but together they made an important contribution to the Peak District economy.

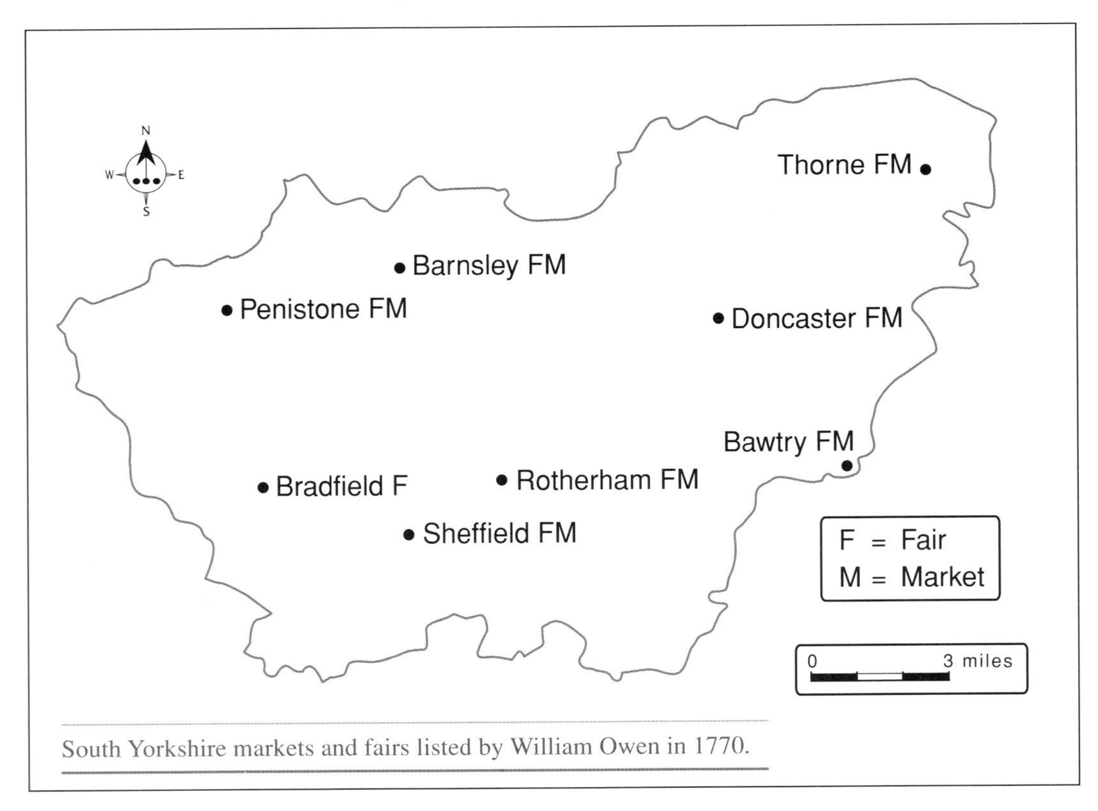

South Yorkshire markets and fairs listed by William Owen in 1770.

Horse drawn transport on market day in the nineteenth century at Ashbourne, continuing the weekly market established in the Middle Ages.

The inhabitants of Penistone had a more difficult time in establishing their village as a market centre. Led by Godfrey Bosville of Gunthwaite Hall, the parishioners tried the simple expedient of reviving the 1290 and 1307 charters which had allowed a Tuesday market and a three-day St Barnabas fair at Penisale, a lost manorial centre two miles away from Penistone, but within the parish. This move was thwarted by opposition from the townsmen of Barnsley and Huddersfield who feared that their own markets would be harmed. In 1699 Nathan Staniforth, Penistone's grammar school master, drew up several petitions which were taken round all the towns and villages in the neighbourhood. Beyond the Pennines, 171 signatures were obtained from Manchester and Salford, 125 from Stockport and Mottram, and nineteen from the rural parts of Cheshire. A further ninety-nine signatures came from Glossop and Glossop Dale, Hope Woodlands and Edale. The West Riding settlements were arranged into the following groups; Silkstone, Thurgoland, Dodworth, Stainborough and Hoylandswaine (150 signatures); Darton, Kexbrough, Barugh, High Hoyland, Clayton West, Skelmanthorpe and Cawthorne (105); Kirkburton, Shepley, Cumberworth, Shelley, Kirkheaton and Emley (224); Holmfirth and Saddleworth (240); Wakefield (35); Sandal Magna (21); Doncaster (28); Bolton, Barnburgh, Adwick upon Dearne and Goldthorpe (30); Tankersley, Wortley and Pilley (107); Wentworth, Hoyland, Thorpe Hesley, Scholes, Greasbrough, Morley, Haugh, Barrow and Cortworth (72); the Parish of Ecclesfield and the Chapelry of Bradfield (308); Sheffield (72); Attercliffe, Darnall, Brightside and Tinsley (104); and the various townships of Penistone parish (230).

In all, 2,140 people signed the petition. This impressive and comprehensive coverage, which included villages around and beyond Barnsley and others near Huddersfield, clearly gave tremendous support to Penistone's case. The claim in the petition to the Crown that such was the state of the country between Penistone and Barnsley, the nearest market, seven miles away, that persons had lost their lives returning home in winter time, is not supported by the evidence

Market day in Penistone in the first decade of the twentieth century. The view is down High Street into Market Street. *J. Biltcliffe.*

Winster market hall. A market was established in this Derbyshire lead-mining village by 1690, and the market hall appears to date from about then, judging by the style of the windows. The brick upper floor rests on stone arches that were originally open in the usual fashion of contemporary market halls. *Sheila Edwards.*

Places supporting the petition to establish a market at Penistone, 1699

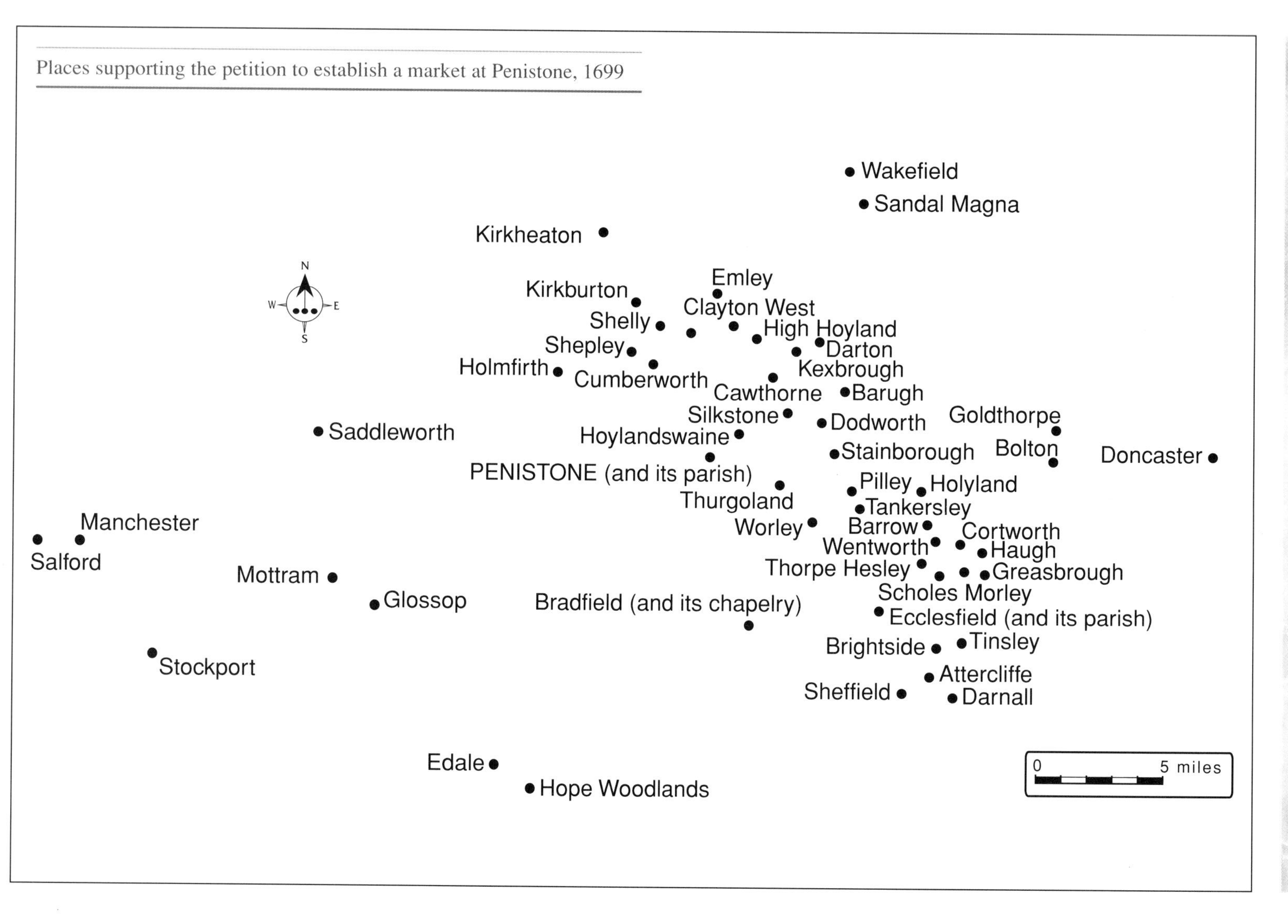

of the local burial registers but may well have been readily believed in London. The petition was granted and in 1699 Penistone held its first weekly market and annual fair. In order not to pre-empt the Wednesday market at Barnsley, it was agreed that Thursday, not Tuesday, should be Penistone's market day. In 1686, before the creation of the market, Penistone had been a small place with only five guest beds and stabling facilities for three horses, but during the eighteenth century it developed into a small town with several inns and even a coffee house. The whole lay-out of the town was affected by the market place, which was set out in front of the church, perhaps on an old village green; a plan of 1749 shows that here were the Beast Market, the Market Place, and the Market House and Sheds, which were replaced in 1763 by the Cloth Hall and Shambles. By 1770 four annual fairs for horned cattle and horses were held in Penistone and the livestock market remained in this central area until 1910 when it was removed to its present site away from the main streets of the town. [4]

Accommodation for Guests

The War Office returns of 1686, which record the country's available guest beds and spare stabling facilities, show that many small places had facilities that one normally associates only with market towns. [5] In Derbyshire no less than 257 places had at least one guest bed and 250 places had at least one spare stall in a stable. In the county as a whole, approximately two out of every five guest beds and about half the extra stabling facilities were to be found in villages and hamlets that did not possess the right to hold a market or fair. Some of these places were important crossing points on the Trent, such as Shardlow, Swarkestone and Weston, and others were recognised stopping points at junctions, such as Hilton, where the road from Uttoxeter to Derby was met by the highway from Nottingham. In south Yorkshire Wombwell and Wadsley Bridge were similar recognised stops. Some of these villages provided more facilities than did small market centres such as Bolsover and Dronfield. The comments of Abraham de la Pryme in the late 1690s show that it was not always necessary to visit market towns for supplies. Writing about his native village of Hatfield in the lowlands beyond Doncaster, he says:

> *Altho' this town be not dignifyd either with a market or faire, yet it stands so conveniently that it is not far off any, haveing Doncaster five miles distant to the west, Thorn two miles of on the east, and Bautry seaven miles on the south, so that if it stands in need of any thing, there is but a little way to fetch the same. But indeed the town of itself is so well furnished with one or two of almost every trade, as butchers, mercers, chandlers, joyners, cutlers, chirurgians, etc, that other places stands in more need of them than the latter of the former.* [6]

Villages and small market towns alike were completely overshadowed by the larger market towns, particularly Derby, which was an outstanding regional centre with 841 guest beds and 547 spaces in its stables. Over a third (34.8 per cent) of the available guest beds in Derbyshire were to be found in the county town. Derby was important not only for its market and for its role as the county capital but as a great thoroughfare town on the highway from London to Manchester. Ashbourne, which came second on the county's list of facilities in 1686, also lay on this route, together with the market town of Buxton and two smaller settlements, Brailsford and Brassington, which lacked market rights but which served as recognised stops on different branches of this highway. Ashbourne was well sited where the White Peak rises from the great Midland Plain and it had long been a natural market centre, but its generous provision of beds and stables (slightly more than at Sheffield) was due largely to its role as a thoroughfare town, the natural stopping point beyond Derby where travellers could refresh themselves before tackling the weary journey across the Pennines.

Ashbourne had the most guest beds available in the county (after Derby) in 1686. *C.L.M. Porter.*

Chesterfield was the natural centre of north-east Derbyshire. When Celia Fiennes came that way in 1697 'it was Satturday which is their market day and there was a great Market like some little faire, a greate deale of corne and all sorts of ware and fowles'. [7] Wirksworth had almost as many stables as did Ashbourne but significantly fewer guest beds. It did not cater so much for wheeled traffic and for the traveller on his way to distant places, but relied much more on packhorses. To a lesser extent so did Bakewell. Between them the big five towns had 51.8 per cent of Derbyshire's guest beds and 39.7 per cent of its stables. [8] Buxton, Tideswell, Alfreton, Crich and Chapel en le Frith formed a second group, smaller than the big five but distinguishable from the smaller market centres and the stopping places alongside the great highways, at ferrying points and road junctions. In the West Riding the leading towns were Leeds with 294 guest beds and 454 stables, Wakefield 242/543, Doncaster 206/453, Halifax 130/306, Sheffield 119/270 and Pontefract 92/235. In the second rank came Barnsley 64/109, Rotherham 63/72 and Bawtry 57/69.

In some of the towns the pressure of business was so great by the early seventeenth century that the market places were no longer able to accommodate all the stalls and livestock. In Sheffield extra market stalls were set out under the Town Hall at the top of High Street and in Doncaster the corporation agreed in 1605 'that the horse fair be held in Hallgate from the Pynfould to the Hall Crosse; that the beast fair be held in the market place; the sheep fair between the Butchers Cross and the Pynfould in Hallgate; and the swine fair in Sepulchre Gate within the bars'. A more permanent site for the Horse Fair was found in 1612 at Waterdale at the southern edge of the town. Meanwhile, the wool market had become one of the largest in the kingdom. The corporation benefited not only from this trade but from the tolls of through traffic at Doncaster bridge, which in 1614 were fixed at twopence for every score of beasts and horses, a halfpenny for every score of sheep, and a farthing for every laden packhorse. [9]

2 Drovers and butchers

The most distinctive of the long-distance travellers were the drovers who headed out of Scotland and Wales towards the rich grazing grounds of central England and on to the capital and other great market centres. The Peak District lay too far north to cause any inconvenience to the Welsh drovers, but the Scotsmen came along the eastern periphery of our region, following the general line of the Great North Road. Glimpses of the Scottish trade are provided by the records of an assault case in 1686 involving 'the tolls of drovers and carriers driving their cattle and packhorses over Doncaster Bridge', [10] and by the place-name Droversdale Wood, south-west of Bawtry, which suggests that once the drovers had crossed the Don they avoided further tolls wherever possible and looked for grazing stops away from the main road. Local people must have seen the same men and beasts as did young John Clare on the same route further south: [11]

Along the roads in passing crowds
Followed by dust like smoaking clouds
Scotch droves of beast a little breed
In sweltered weary mood proceed
A patient race from scottish hills
To fatten by our pasture rills
Lean wi the wants of mountain toil
Wi cocked up horns and curling crown
And dewlap bosom hanging down
Followed by slowly pacing swains
Wild to our rushy flats and plains
At whom the shepherds dog will rise
And shake himself and in supprise
Draw back and waffle in affright
Barking the traveller out of sight
And mowers oer their scythes will bear
Upon their uncouth dress to stare
And shepherds as they trample bye
Leaves oer their hooks a wondering eye
To witness men so oddly clad
In petticoats of banded plad
Wi blankets oer their shoulders slung
To camp at night the fields among
When they for rest on commons stop
And blue cap like a stocking top
Cockt oer their faces summer brown
Wi scarlet tazzeles on the crown
Rude patterns of the thistle flower
Untricked and open to the shower
And honest faces fresh and free
That breath of mountain liberty.

Few people were described as drovers in local records and the nearest inn with the name *Drovers Arms* lies on the other side of the Pennines on the road from Glossop to Hayfield. John Gastin, victualler and drover of Harthill, had a son baptised at his parish church in 1735, William Burnett of Wath upon Dearne was a drover with 201 sheep and a pack of wool upon his death in 1780, and Edward Buxton, a seventeenth-century Bakewell drover, was prosperous and respectable enough to be addressed as 'Mr'. The drovers who were licensed with the badgers and swailers at the Derbyshire quarter sessions were not very numerous. Of the thirty licences issued to dealers in the southern hundred of Appletree in 1729, for instance, only four were for drovers. [12]

Nevertheless, Scotch cows, bullocks, oxen and steers figure occasionally in estate records and probate inventories, [13] and herds of cattle and flocks of sheep that travelled much shorter distances than the Scottish and Welsh droves were a common sight on the highways leading to and from local markets and fairs. The tolls charged by the turnpike trusts show how some local roads were used by this sort of traffic; for example, the charges on the Sheffield-Leeds turnpike road (1758) included, 'For every drove of oxen and neat cattle per score, 10d, For every drove of calves, swine, sheep and lambs per score 5d.' [14] Yorkshire and Derbyshire families had little trouble in obtaining butcher's meat, for many local farmers concentrated upon rearing beef and mutton, and local fairs and markets brought in cattle sellers from miles around. In the early seventeenth century the beast fairs at Rotherham and Wakefield attracted sellers from as far as Middleton St George in County Durham. At the same time, buyers from other regions purchased stock reared locally or stock from further north which were offered for sale at local fairs. A York drover sold twenty cattle at Chesterfield fair to a gentleman from London, a Warwickshire drover travelled forty-five miles to Ashbourne to buy cattle which he subsequently sold in West Bromwich, and a gentleman from Norfolk regularly purchased sheep from farmers in Chapel en le Frith.

Though most sales were to local men, buyers were prepared to travel great distances. Late in the reign of Queen Elizabeth one purchaser at Rotherham came from Carlton (Lincolnshire), forty miles to the south-east and one seller came from Ellerburn in the Vale of Pickering, seventy miles to the north-east. [15] The accounts of William Dickenson, the bailiff of Hallamshire, for the year 1574 show that the Earl of Shrewsbury's employees travelled many miles to purchase cattle at northern fairs. During that year they bought thirty-two steers, thirty young beasts and a calf from Bedale fair in north Yorkshire, twenty-nine beats, twenty oxen and two fat heifers from Middleham fair, eighty miles to the north in Wensleydale, twenty steers from Leeds and seventy calves from the September fair at Chesterfield. Some of these beasts were eventually resold at Sheffield fair. That farmers were prepared to travel considerable distances to buy and sell at fairs with particular reputations is evident from the seventeenth-century farming and account books of Henry Best of Elmswell on the Yorkshire Wolds. In the first decade of the eighteenth century John Wasteney of Edlington Hall near Doncaster bought sainfoin seed from Doncaster market, attended Barnsley fair, and obtained wethers from Driffield and Market Weighton. [16]

Rotherham's reputation as a fat stock centre was greatly enhanced in the later eighteenth century when beasts fattened on the rich Leicestershire grazing lands were driven north to the butchers of the West Riding and Lancashire manufacturing towns. Lean beasts came in the opposite direction over the Pennines and several small farms alongside the route via Woodhead, Hartcliff and Green Moor were turned into beer houses until the railways provided a quicker and cheaper means of transport. Peck Pond farm at Hunshelf tried to attract the cattle-drovers by taking the name of the *Brown Cow.* When Edward Baines published his directory in 1822, Rotherham had 'an excellent market on Monday for corn, cattle and butcher's meat, and every second Monday there is a fair for fat cattle, sheep and hogs; and this, like the fortnight fairs at Wakefield, which it much resembles, is well attended by graziers and butchers from very distant parts of the country'. [17]

The probate inventory of Anthony Peace, a Rotherham butcher who died in 1696, reveals that he was fattening animals for slaughter in fields up to five miles away from Rotherham market and that 180 loads of hay, worth £107, had been laid in store for winter. His principal concern was mutton, for whereas he kept only nineteen head of cattle, he had 742 sheep at Firsby, Aldwark and in the 'Wood Closes'. In 1698 a Doncaster butcher, Mr William Cooke, had a slaughter house, three stalls and a shop, and livestock valued at over £505, comprising eighty-one beasts, thirty-three cows, a calf, over 200 sheep, five horses and a few pigs, most, if not all, awaiting slaughter. Butchers sold their meat in the shambles situated at the heart of the market place; Samuel Wortley of Crookesmoorside, for example, had the 'Tenant right of a Butchers Shop in Sheffield Shambles' until his death in 1697.

When the market facilities at Sheffield were rearranged in the 1780s, the slaughter houses adjacent to the shambles were said to be:

> *'in a very improper situation ... very offensive to all persons passing near the same, as well dangerous to the health of the inhabitants'.*

And the 1801 Act which improved the market arrangements at Rotherham claimed that:

> *'The present Market Place is inconvenient for the Purposes of the said Market, and the Passage along the publick Streets is greatly obstructed and rendered inconvenient to Passengers and Travellers by the Number of Stalls placed therein on Market Days, and great Nuisances are frequently committed by slaughtering Sheep and Cattle in the said publick Streets or in Places open thereto'.* [18]

Wills and probate inventories survive for thirty-one butchers in seventeenth-century Chesterfield and for a further fifty-six tanners, shoemakers and other leather craftsmen. [19] Tanning was an ancient industry in the town (the 1294 borough charter had insisted that only

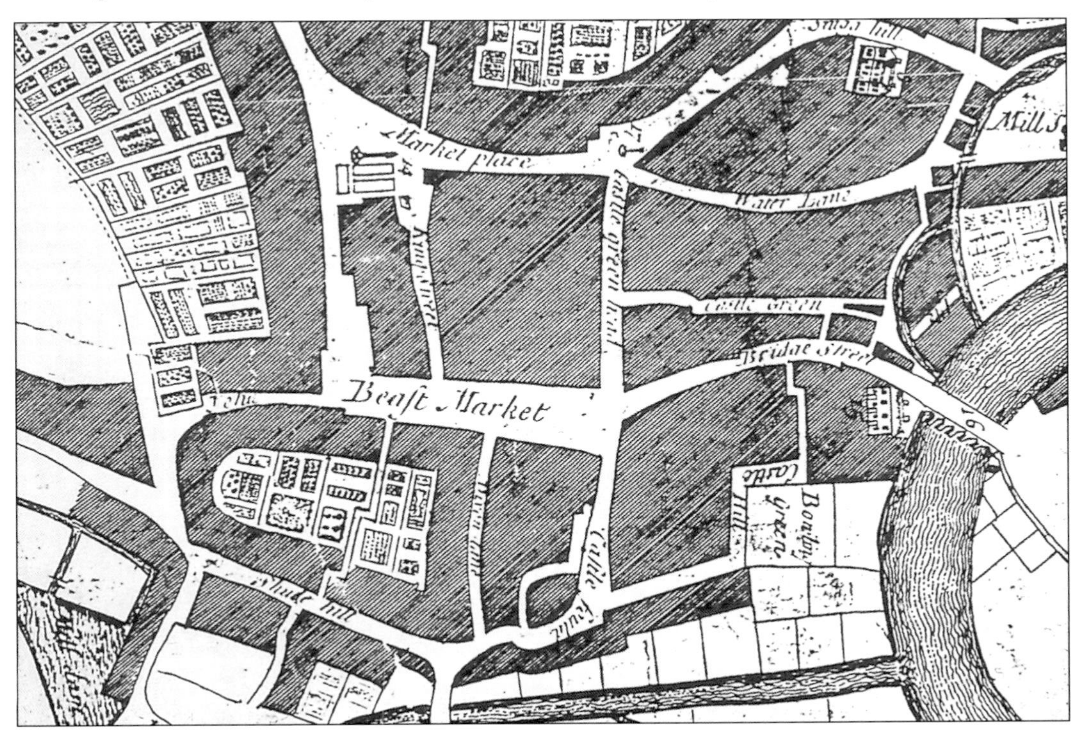

Sheffield market place, shown on Ralph Gosling's map of 1736.
The number 14 marks the cross and shambles.

burgesses should be tanners) and in the surrounding countryside, and it was equally as important in the urban and rural parts of south Yorkshire. Leather was need for footwear, garments, harness, horse collars, saddles, straps, bags and bottles, and in the Hallamshire district for bellows, grinders' beltings, and sheaths for knives. Oak bark for tanning was readily available at the springwoods which were coppiced regularly to provide charcoal for the blast furnaces, lime was obtained from the White Peak, and hides purchased from local butchers. We have already seen how extra hides were shipped as back carriage from London during the seventeenth and eighteenth centuries when the local industry was vigorous. John Hobson, a tanner of Dodworth Green, noted ruefully in his diary on 8 December 1731, 'There is now a certain account that wee have 46 hides sunk in John Dowson's ship'. The finished products appear to have been sold locally, usually directly from the tanyard to shoemakers and other craftsmen. [20]

3 Corn, malt and cheese

Pennine farmers had to import much of their bread corn and their brewing malt, for as Daniel Defoe remarked in typical journalistic fashion:

> *They scarce sow corn enough for their cocks and hens.*

A 1639 report on the food situation in the wapentakes of Agbrigg and Morley in the heart of the West Riding textile region pointed out that:

> *above two partes of the whole division doe consist of trading, and for the rest, the Corne that doth growe on itt is not able to sustaine itt ... for butter and cheese they are weekly supplied from Ripon, Knaresborough and other places 30 miles of.*

Eight years earlier the corn that was cultivated on the thin soils of the High Peak was said to be 'chiefly oats and oatmeal, little other grain growing in the said Hundred'. Brown's agricultural report of 1794 stated that in the Peak, 'About one fifth of the enclosures may be arable, and this part chiefly employed in growing oats; the remainder is in pasture, and the greatest part employed in dairying and breeding of stock'. [21] Although probate inventories show that other cereals were grown occasionally, the normal bread corn was oats, especially for the poorer inhabitants. Richard Dalton, a south Yorkshire merchant, observed in 1741 that a considerable quantity of oats was consumed in Sheffield, 'the lowest sort of people mostly using oatbread', and as late as 1819 a white loaf was still a rare commodity in Dovedale; 'oatcake was the chief food from day to day with black bread occasionally', and even gooseberry pie was made with an oatmeal crust. [22]

Corn was brought to the Pennine settlements by badgers operating from the market towns. The inhabitants of the adjoining Coal Measure sandstone region had less difficulty in obtaining supplies, for theirs was a mixed economy. Within the hundred of Scarsdale about fifty-four corn mills were in production in 1652. However, it is unlikely that the farmers there had much grain to spare and the bulk of the Peak District's imports must have come from the more fertile lands further east or from the great Midland Plain. A glimpse of the east-west trade is afforded in a letter written in 1592 by Sir Edward Stanhope of Edlington, in which he complained that the inhabitants of Barnby Dun had placed stepping stones across the Don for themselves and their sheep, thereby blocking the passage of boats carrying corn from Lincolnshire and the eastern parts of Yorkshire that was intended for Barnsley and the villages further west. Nor were the Pennines an insuperable barrier to the corn trade. The 1699 petition signed by 171 people from Manchester and Salford in favour of a proposed new market at Penistone claimed that 'these townes are very populous and usually are weekly supplied with wheat and other hard corne out of the West Riding'; the new market would be of great service and would save charges in carrying corn. An entry in John Hobson's diary on 25 October 1727 noted the death of an old man of ninety-two, who had 'often told me he could remember since wheat was £3 a load, and it cost 3s.4d. carriage to Woodhead'. [23] Unfortunately, no regular series of prices for carriage is available.

Malt

Brewing was a task for the housewife and the innkeeper. Large or 'common' breweries were unknown in the region before the late eighteenth century and for a long time afterwards they supplied only a small proportion of the total output. The malt consumed in the Peak District came as back carriage in the carts and wains that had taken lead or millstones to the Trent ports. Thomas Lister made this point when opposing the proposed River Don navigation: 'Mansfield and Worksop and other towns', he wrote on 28 November 1722, 'send great quantities of malt into Derbyshire, which trade will be entirely lost and all commerce between Nottinghamshire and Derbyshire, which is now commodious by the cheapness of sending goods back in carts which bring lead this way, will be at an end'. Likewise, in 1702 the mayor and burgesses of Nottingham opposed a bill to improve the navigation of the River Derwent as it would:

> *impoverish the Petitioners Families, by diverting their Trades, lessening their Tolls, lowering the Rents of Lands thereabouts, and will be the utter Ruin of many Families, whose only Support is to bring Lead, Salt, and other Commodities, from several parts to Nottingham, and carry back Malt, and other Goods, by Land-carriage.*

Earlier evidence of the east-west malt trade is contained in a bond of September 1621, by which Joseph Godfrey of Thonock in Lincolnshire and George Harrison of Bawtry promised Thomas Eyre of Hassop that they would deliver in the following spring twenty quarters of good, pure, sung and well dried malt by the usual measure of Warsop (Notts.) to Beth Grange in Derbyshire. Philip Kinder wrote in his manuscript *Historie of Darby-Shire* in 1656 that the inhabitants of the Peak District for the most part 'use noe tillage but live of milk and flesh ... Their Butterie for the most part is at Nottingham and Loughborough for from thence they fetch all their Mault and barley'. Two generations later, 'great drifts of Malt horses' came across the Pennines via Alport on their way to Manchester. [24]

According to William Woolley, writing in 1712, Derby supplied malt to a great part of Cheshire, Staffordshire and Lancashire. A few years earlier, in 1696, John Houghton reported that Derby contained 694 houses or families and no less than seventy-six malthouses, an average of one malthouse to every nine domestic buildings. Moreover, 120 of the houses were said to serve as alehouses, for Derby was a thoroughfare town as well as the county capital and a great market centre. Houghton noted that malt was exported down the Trent as well as across the Pennines: 'Formerly a great deal of Malt was carried to the Ferry by Land, which is five Miles; which cost as much as from the Ferry to Hull by Water, which is 60 Miles'. The other towns in the region had fewer maltsters, but Sheffield had a few substantial men in the trade, like Richard Bradford (1696), who had 100 quarters of dry malt, twenty quarters of green malt and twenty quarters of barley, worth in all £138, or John Almond of Bridgehouses (1718), whose malt was valued at £110. Samuel Thompson, who was described as a yeoman upon his death in 1717, was an innkeeper who did his own brewing with malt from the fertile barley lands further east; his inventory records a debt of £6.5s. for five quarters of malt to Mr Richard Spencer of Tickhill. [25]

Cheese and Butter

In the early seventeenth century demand for cheese and butter sometimes exceeded that which the markets could supply. A 1608 petition claimed that Sheffield consisted of:

> *hamdicraftes men, in great numbers who have no meanes to make their provision but only to the markett, and that the cuntrie there aboutes affoardeth not sufficient store of white meates, chiefly butter, and cheese, to serve the towne.*

Gilbert, the seventh Earl of Shrewsbury, who as lord of the manor owned the tolls of Sheffield market, was therefore persuaded to allow Elizabeth Heywood, a local widow, to buy butter and cheese at Ashbourne and other market centres and to re-sell these products in Sheffield. Later that century cheese-making became the great speciality of Cheshire and north Shropshire and of the region centred upon the Dove valley in south Derbyshire and east Staffordshire. Rich pastures and meadows, wrote Robert Plot in 1686:

> *supply Uttoxater Mercat with such vast quantities of good butter and cheese, that the Cheesemongers of London have thought it worth their while to set up a Factorage here, for these Commodities, which are brought in from this, and the neighbouring County of Derby, in so great plenty, that the Factors many Mercat days (in the season) lay out no less than five hundred pounds a day, in these two commodities only.*

The spectacular growth of this trade had nothing to do with the introduction of new grasses, nor with irrigation schemes; the natural grasses of the region were perfectly adequate and the greatly increased production can be accounted for only as a response to growth in national demand.

Much Cheshire cheese went via Liverpool and the sea to London and the naval ports or overland to the capital and provincial market towns, but some factors favoured the arduous journey across the Pennines to Doncaster and so by river to Hull and by sea to London. In 1703 the London cheesemongers who supported a petition to make the Don navigable claimed that this was 'the easiest and readiest way' and a letter written twenty years later at the time of renewed attempts to improve the navigation observed that cheese from the west was brought to the markets at Barnsley, Sheffield and Wakefield and that 'The commodities to serve London and the Fleet ... come allways through Barnesley, being the more passable way than the moor towards Sheffield'. Malt, other grains and flax served as back carriage. [26]

4 Badgers and swailers

A statute of 1563 ordered that 'no Drover of Cattell Badger [i.e. corndealer etc., see over] Lader Kidder Carrier Buyer or Transporter of Corne or Grayne Butter or Cheese' should be allowed to trade without an annual licence granted by the justices of the peace at the quarter sessions. The government was worried about vagrancy and about rising prices, and packmen who wandered about the countryside and who frequently avoided established markets were a natural cause of suspicion. Each dealer had to pay a shilling for an annual licence and eightpence to have it registered with the clerk of the peace. To obtain a licence he had to be a married householder over the age of thirty years, he had to provide a £20 bond and find someone willing to stand surety of £10 (later, £20) for his good behaviour, and he had to have dwelt in his place of residence for at least three years. The inhabitants of the northern counties of Cumberland, Westmorland, Lancashire, Cheshire and Yorkshire were exempted from the terms of this Act and were allowed to 'do as they have heretofore Lawfully done'. [27] The difficulty of obtaining meal and malt in regions where corn production did not meet demand probably explains this exemption, but if so the inhabitants of the Derbyshire Peak District surely had equally as strong a case.

We do not know how widely this licensing system was evaded, but a great number of regular dealers certainly took the precaution of observing the law. During the three years beginning July 1746 the Derbyshire J.P.s issued 319 licences, including eighteen to women. Amy Lancaster of Duffield and Gertrude Hoole, alias Mason, of Dronfield were widows and so perhaps were the other women. They probably continued to run their businesses without doing the travelling. In the previous century the Somerset J.P.s had licensed 'Edith Doddington of Hilbishopps, widow, to be a badger of butter and cheese and to carry the same into the counties of Wilts, Hampshire, Dorset and Devon, and to return again laden with corn, and to sell it again in any fair or market within this county'. We have already mentioned the similar activities of Elizabeth Heywood, a widow who brought corn from Ashbourne to Sheffield. In 1630 Edith Doddington had three horses with which to carry on her business and in the same year Anthony Banbury of Pitney was granted a licence for two horses. [28] The number of horses are not specified in the Derbyshire licences, but the limited evidence for the region suggests similar small-scale trading. Many badgers may have had only a single horse.

Anthony Banbury was licensed 'to buy barley and oats, and the same to convert into malt, and to sell again in any fair' in Somerset, while Elizabeth Doddington was allowed to trade in butter, cheese and corn. Another description of a badger's activities is contained in Richard Gough's *History of Myddle*, an account of a north Shropshire parish written in the opening years of the eighteenth century: Gough's neighbour, Ralph Guest, 'was a sober peaceable man; his imployment was buying corne in one markett towne, and selling it in another which is called Badgeing'. But the badgers did not restrict their trading to the market place; they sold their meal and malt in the villages and hamlets and in return bought butter, cheese, eggs and spare poultry from the farmers to sell in the market towns. In time they became general dealers or middlemen, so that by the end of the nineteenth century the term had acquired many meanings. In 1898 Joseph Wright defined badger as corn-dealer, miller or miller's man, huckster, itinerant dealer who buys up farm produce and carries it elsewhere to sell, small shopkeeper (groceries and provisions) and even wholesale grocer. [29]

The word badger is incorporated in several minor place-names, some of which, however, may be derived from the surname (which arose from the occupation). Local badger place-names do not come from the animal, which was normally called by the Celtic word brock (hence the many Brockholes place-names). Robert le Bagger owned land in North Anston about 1290 and a place called le Bagourhouses was recorded near Hemsworth in 1309. The Badger Lanes at Ashover, Langsett and Stainborough have doubtful origins, but further north Badger Gate farm stands alongside an old highway which crossed the moors from Marsden. And though 'to badger someone', meaning to pester, is often thought to derive from the old sport of badger-baiting, the phrase can be more properly ascribed to the sales talk of a hawker. *The English Dialect Dictionary* gives the sense as 'to beat down in price, to haggle over a bargain'. [30]

'The badgers come farre, many of them', wrote Henry Best of Elmswell in 1641, 'wherefore theire desire is to buy soone, that they may be goinge betimes, for feare of beinge nighted'. Local authorities were concerned to see that badgers bought their corn within the market place and that they and other dealers did not try to forestall normal transactions. In 1609, for example, the 'Sembly Quest' of the manor of Sheffield appointed William Allin and John Creswick 'to see that whitemeate as butter and egges be broughte into the markett and none to be sould in the feildes' and Francis Staniforth and George Clayton 'to see and search that corne be brought into the markett and none to be sould until the markett bell rynge'. [31] In times of dearth the poor were served first and normal trading began only when the market bell was rung a second time. George Towgoode was charged with sharp practice in this connection when it was claimed at the Derbyshire quarter sessions held on 6 June 1631 that 'hee being a badger (or dealer) was in the markett of Ashbourne on the last markett daye before the seconde belle was runge by the clarke'. Another fraudulent practice is illustrated by the records of the West Riding quarter sessions held at Rotherham in 1638, when Christopher Fisher, badger, John Walker, badger, and Margaret Browne, widow, all of Sheffield, were convicted and fined 'for on Tuesday, the 3rd of July, 1638, and divers other times, both before and after, at Sheffield, selling to divers of the King's subjects in open market a shilling of oats fraudulently mixed with dust and chaff'. [32]

James Hall, a Doncaster badger, was elected one of the twenty-four common councilmen of Doncaster corporation in 1560 and 1561, [33] but nothing has been found elsewhere to suggest that other badgers were such substantial figures. At the Bakewell sessions in July 1748 the list of licensed badgers was headed by Mr Buxton of Chelmorton, but elsewhere he was plain John Buxton and all the other 318 badgers were known by their Christian names. The probate inventory of John Green, a Sheffield badger, who died in 1726, indicates the standard of living of one such trader. He had also been described as badger ten years previously when his son had been baptised at Sheffield parish church. [34] His inventory comprised the following items:

Purse & Apparell, £10, Range & furniture, £1.5s.0d, pewter & Longsettle, £1.5s.0d, 4 Tables 3 Buffetts, £1.10s.0d, 5 Chairs warming pan & Candlesticks, 14s.0d, 2 Spits racks & other materialls, 7s.0d, 1 iron pot 2 brass pans, 10s.0d, 1 frying pan 1 driping pan, 2s.0d, 1 Chest of meal, £1.10s.0d, 1 Tub & Oates, 5s.0d, 2 Tin pans & 1 Lantern, 2s.6d; Brewhouse: 1 Lead 1 Trough & Tubs, £2, One horse Saddles & paniers, £3, Hay & Coles, £1.10s.0d; Sellar: ten barrells 1 Tub, £2, Ale 3 kitts & Tunells, £2.2s.6d, Gantryes, 5s.0d; At the stairs head: 1 bed, 15s.0d; Little Chamber: 2 beds & beding, £4, 1 box & Linnen, £4, 4 Chairs a Chest & a box, 12s.0d, One Table, 1s.0d; Great chamber: 1 range, 3s.0d, 6 Chairs, 8s.0d, 2 Tables a form & a Buffett, 10s.0d, One Bed & Beding, £4; In the malt Chamber: the miln, £1, Malt, £10, Sacks & other Materialls, £1; Debts inward, £8.8s.0d.

Green was evidently supplying malt, but the only other indications of his trade are his horse, with its saddles and panniers, and possibly the small debts that were due to him.

Badgers provided an essential service in rural districts that were unsuitable for growing corn and during the eighteenth century they found additional employment in manufacturing areas. From 1 October 1698 to 30 September 1703 the Sheffield baptism and burial registers recorded the occupations of 1,149 men, but of these only Francis Scholey was a badger. [35] No doubt badging was still a part-time occupation for some men who were described otherwise in the registers. Five badgers and a swailer were named in the registers between 1739 and 1741. [36] The growth of an industrial population naturally increased the demand for the services of badgers and other itinerant traders. Further north, the number of badgers in Bradford and surrounding villages had risen considerably by the early nineteenth century, judging by the number of dealers who were fined at the quarter sessions for having defective weights. The surviving records do not deal specifically with Sheffield, but it is clear that growing numbers of badgers, hawkers and pedlars served the heavily populated and urbanised parts of the country during the next few decades. As D. Alexander has written, 'Country people were accustomed to buying from market traders and pedlars, and when they moved into more urban environments they searched for known, or at least familiar, distribution services'. The term badger was still used in some parts of Derbyshire in the closing years of the nineteenth century. [37]

The Yorkshire badgers were exempt from the terms of the 1563 statute, [38] but their Derbyshire counterparts had to obtain a licence each year at a meeting of the quarter sessions,

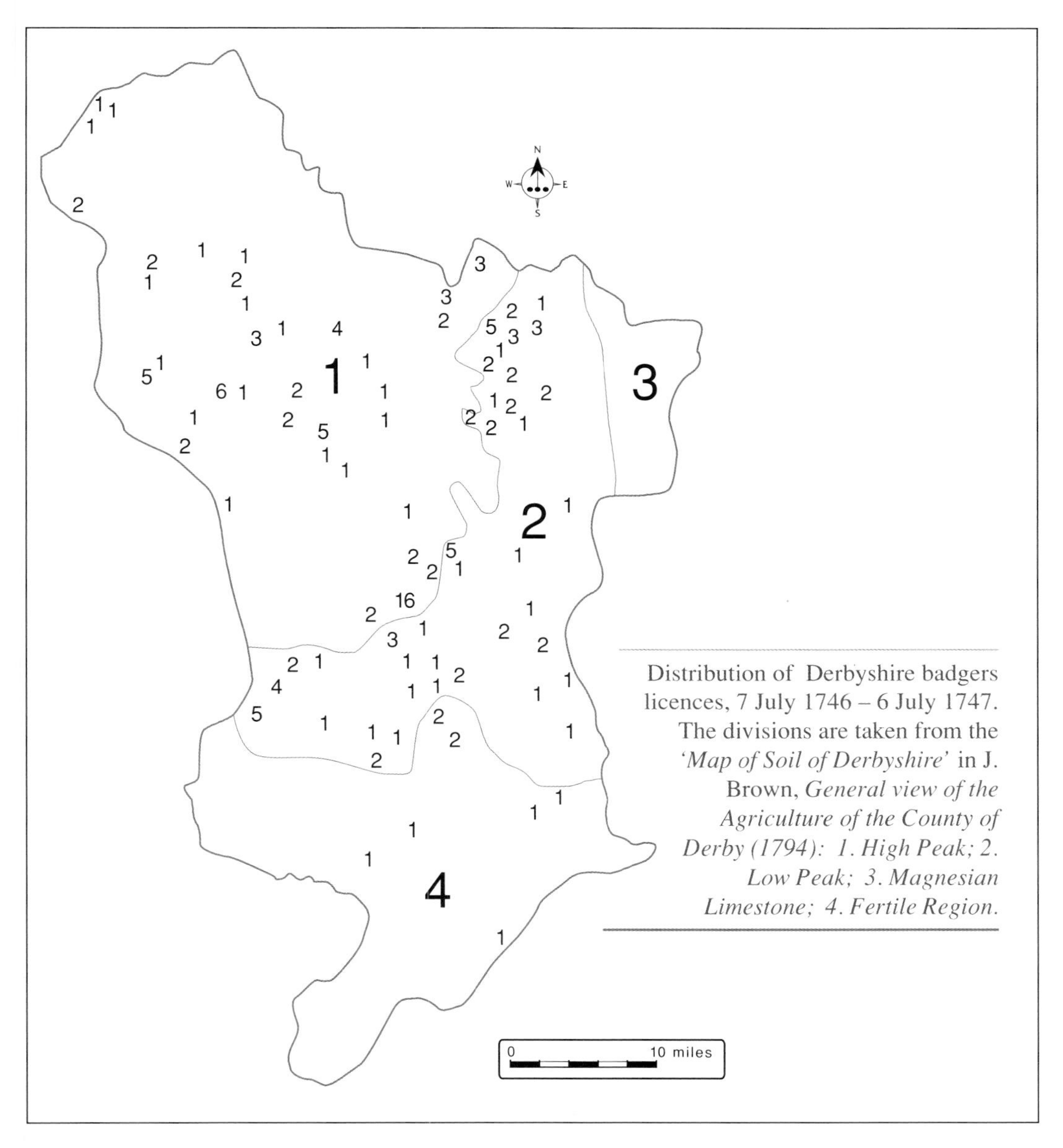

Distribution of Derbyshire badgers licences, 7 July 1746 – 6 July 1747. The divisions are taken from the *'Map of Soil of Derbyshire'* in J. Brown, *General view of the Agriculture of the County of Derby (1794): 1. High Peak; 2. Low Peak; 3. Magnesian Limestone; 4. Fertile Region.*

either at Derby (twice) or Chesterfield or Bakewell. Early records for Derbyshire do not survive, but at the Easter sessions in 1713 the J.P.s decided to enforce the law strictly. At the following Michaelmas sessions eighty-six dealers were presented for trading without a licence and at the Epiphany sessions early the following year a further 128 people were presented for a similar offence. [39] A few more were charged with 'badging without lycence', some with 'useing the business of a drover without lycence', and one or two with 'useing the Trade of a Swailer without Lycence', but in the great majority of cases the particular trade was not specified.

The word swailer has been used on two occasions above and it is now time to examine what was meant by the term. J. C. Cox suggested that swailers were dealers in one or more articles that were named on their licences, like those of the Wirksworth swailers who in 1693 dealt separately in cloth, in tobacco and in salt. [40] However, such specialities are not mentioned in

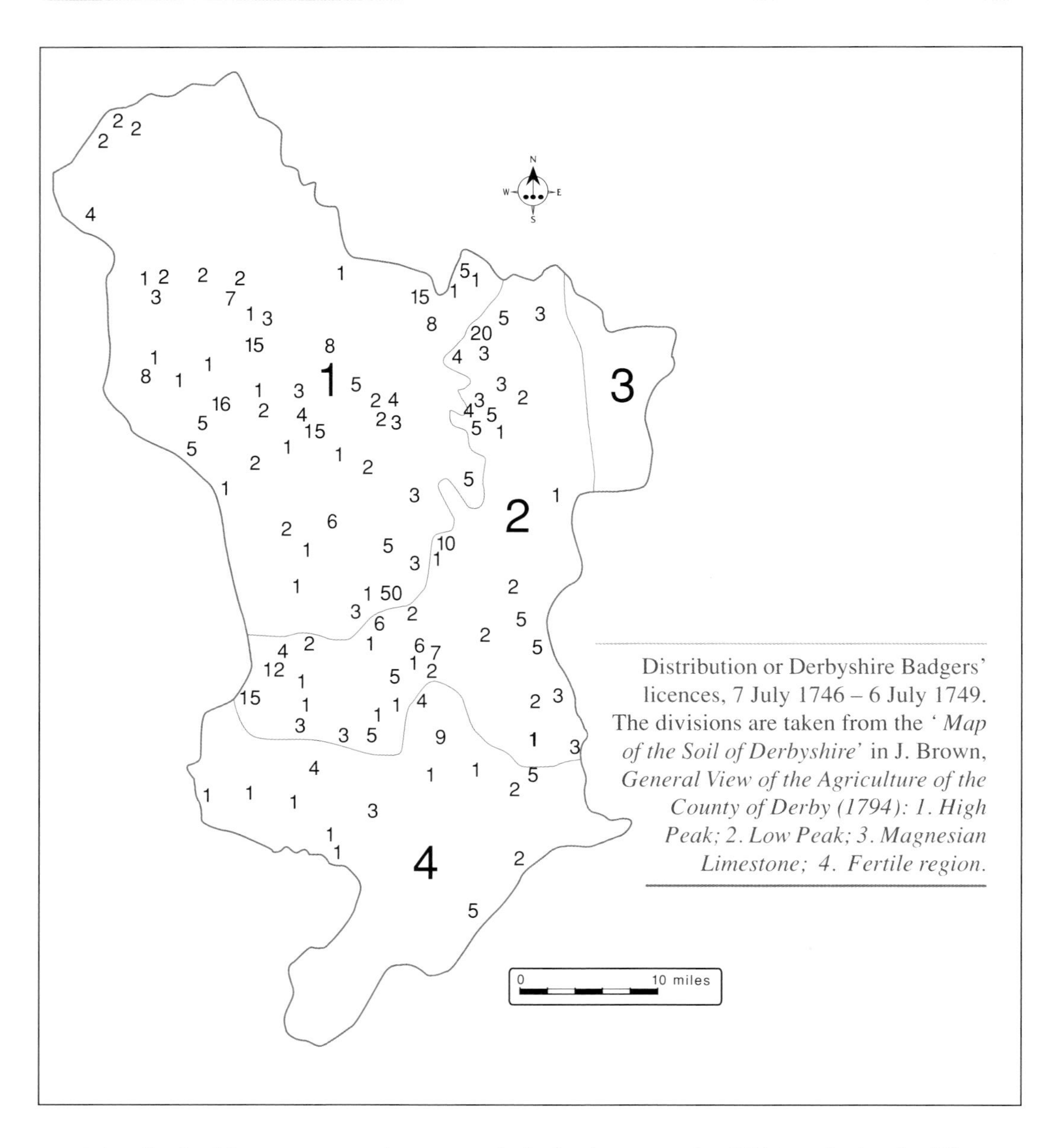

Distribution or Derbyshire Badgers' licences, 7 July 1746 – 6 July 1749. The divisions are taken from the '*Map of the Soil of Derbyshire*' in J. Brown, *General View of the Agriculture of the County of Derby (1794): 1. High Peak; 2. Low Peak; 3. Magnesian Limestone; 4. Fertile region.*

surviving Derbyshire quarter sessions records; indeed an entry for 1746 reads simply, 'Thomas Fernihough of Dore in the County is Lycensed to be a Common Swailer for one year'. *The English Dialect Dictionary* of 1898-1905 gives the meaning of swailer as 'a wholesale corn or provision dealer; one who buys corn and converts it into meal before he sells it again'; in other words, swailer was synonymous with badger in north midlands dialect. Much earlier than this, in 1829 Glover had written, 'The people who deal in oatmeal are called swalers or mealmen' and in 1796 Samuel Pegge observed that the badger 'is called also a swailer, I suppose from melting or swealing the oats; for the badger or swailer is one who sells oatmeal'.

The terminology used in the records of the Derbyshire quarter sessions confirms that by the middle of the eighteenth century the terms were interchangeable. In the early 1750s all the licensed dealers (other than drovers) were listed as swailers, but from January 1757 all were listed as badgers. Occasionally, as for example at the sessions held at Bakewell in July 1760, the clerks reverted to the use of swailer, but normally badger was preferred. William Roe, swailer, had a child baptised at Norton parish church in 1733, Samuel Cartledge, swailer, was buried at Sheffield in 1740, and Joseph Hoole, alias Mason, of Summerwood Top, Dronfield, swailer, died in 1741, but the term is not commonly found outside the records of the quarter sessions. Even so, J. C. Cox claimed that swailer was still used in parts of Derbyshire in 1890. [41]

At the meetings of the Derbyshire quarter sessions during the year beginning 7 July 1746 no less than 174 licences were issued to 'drovers, badgers, swailers or hucksters', the great majority to badgers and swailers bringing meal and malt from the southern and eastern arable districts and returning to the market towns with butter, cheese and eggs. Wirksworth, which was ideally situated where the limestone hills came down to the fertile Midland Plain, had sixteen licensed dealers, far more than any other place. Next came the White Peak village of Taddington with six, Bakewell and Buxton each with five, and Tideswell with three. Most places, including Chesterfield, had only one itinerant dealer and Derby had none at all. The 174 licensed traders came from eighty-seven different places within the county.

Many of these traders renewed their licences in subsequent years, but for many others badging was obviously only a temporary occupation.

Table 1 Licensed Traders at Derbyshire Quarter Sessions, 1746-49 [42]

year	total number of licences	renewals	new names	number of places
1746-47	174	—	—	87
1747-48	149	79	70	76
1748-49	179	104	75	84

The number of new names that appears each year is very striking. Occasionally, someone else in the family took over the business, but more often than not the newcomers had surnames that were different from those in previous years. The number of places with badgers and swailers remained about the same and their geographical distribution over the three-year period was similar to the pattern for any one year. Most places relied upon the services of only one or two badgers, but Wirksworth was exceptional in having twenty-one dealers licensed in 1748-49.

The spatial pattern was similar in later years. In 1770-71, for instance, the 206 licensed badgers came from ninety-seven different places within the county. Ten years previously, the 186 licenses were arranged according to the hundred or wapentake in which the badger resided. Wirksworth hundred had unusually few badgers that year but otherwise the figures give a good general indication of the places which needed the badgers' services. They read: 'Scarsdale 45, High Peak 94, Appletree 26, Morleston & Litchurch 9, Wirksworth 12'. Most of the badgers are mere names to us, but they played a crucial role in the rural economy, at times even a vital one.

8 THE RETAIL TRADE

1 Haddon Hall accounts

Although we cannot be certain how ordinary people purchased consumer goods during the age of the Tudors, we can see how Sir George Vernon of Haddon Hall obtained provisions for his family and household. His steward's accounts for the years 1549-51 and 1564-65 shed a great deal of light on the available services and the range of groceries that could be obtained even in the heart of Derbyshire. [1] The several different sources of supply included local markets and fairs, urban shops, local families, and hawkers. Surprisingly few goods were bought just down the road at Bakewell; the steward sent there for some shoes, a few drinking mugs, 'a hundred of nails and twelve wain clouts', but little else. The exotic groceries which appear so often in his accounts were not obtained from Bakewell market. When the steward needed hops, spices, wines, sugar or prunes he or his underlings went instead to Chesterfield, ten difficult miles beyond the East Moor, or they journeyed fifteen miles in the opposite direction to Ashbourne.

Haddon Hall and bridge of 1663.

During the sixteenth, seventeenth and eighteenth centuries hops for flavouring beer were a favourite item of back carriage for carriers taking materials and manufactured goods to London or to the ports or the great provincial fairs. Defoe spoke of vast quantities of hops being taken into Yorkshire, Derbyshire and Lancashire as back carriage from Stourbridge Fair in Cambridgeshire. We do not know whether the hops that reached Tudor Chesterfield came by land or water (or by both), but in 1549 the steward of Haddon Hall paid Richard Baslow a shilling for his costs in going to Chesterfield to buy hops and candlewicks. Perhaps the hops were bought at a shop rather than in the open market, for later that year the accounts refer to £1.6s.10d. paid to Robert Wilson of Chesterfield for ninety-two pounds of hops. The probate inventory of Thomas Hethcote, a Chesterfield butcher, who died in 1559, shows that hops were also purchased by more humble men. [2]

On his visits to Chesterfield the Haddon steward also bought rye, veal, mustard, malt, a kiln hair to dry malt, drinking cups, and more unexpectedly 'all kinds of seafish', prunes, raisins, and a a gallon of claret wine. Whether these goods came overland from London or via the coast and rivers to Bawtry we cannot say. Wine could certainly be brought safely over many miles of rough country, for in October 1549 Sir George received a rundlet of claret wine from Manchester and in 1568 Robert Stringer paid for three hogsheads of wine to be delivered from Chester to his home in Derby. On Christmas Eve 1564 the Haddon steward paid 13s.4d. to his tenants in Baslow for carrying a tun of wine. Probate inventories make it clear that wine was another commodity that was available to people further down the social scale. At the very end of the sixteenth century Henry Norman of Chesterfield had wine valued at £3 in his cellar and wine casks worth sixteen shillings. [3]

Chesterfield had direct links with the inland port of Bawtry, a possible source of supply for wines and groceries, but few places in the country were more landlocked than Ashbourne. Yet here the Haddon steward was able to purchase wines, vinegar, spices, raisins, prunes, pepper, sugar, cloves, mace, and beef for Christmas pies. Such groceries must have been sold to anyone who could afford them, otherwise they would have been delivered directly to the great houses. Ashbourne lay on the main highway from London and Derby to Manchester and presumably received its groceries this way. If James Backhouse, a Kirkby Lonsdale shopkeeper, could stock such items in Westmorland in 1578, it should not surprise us that market towns on the edge of the Peak could provide similar facilities. No doubt people who lived several miles away from the towns were amongst the grocer's customers. We do not have local evidence from the sixteenth century, but on 21 December 1647 Adam Eyre of Hazlehead Hall bought pepper and aloes at Sheffield, fifteen miles from his home. [4] The Haddon steward also purchased 'all kinds of spices' at Lenton fair, Nottingham, and on occasion bought on the doorstep from 'Hanson's wife', probably a local hawker. On 8 October 1549, for instance, she sold him three pounds of sugar, a pound of pepper, two pounds of prunes, two pounds of great raisins, and small quantities of ginger, nutmegs, cloves and mace. The steward rarely thought it worth his while to buy in bulk, even when he or one of his men went further afield: to Derby for rye, to Chapel en le Frith for beasts, to Staffordshire for hops, or to Lichfield for fish.

Oysters, mussels, eels, pike, white herring and other fish were consumed at Haddon Hall in the middle years of the sixteenth century. Local people occasionally came with 'a dysshe of fresshe fyssche' for sale at modest prices, but Sir George Vernon was prepared to pay much more for the taste of sea fish, not only during Lent but at other times of the year. On 7 July 1550, for example, the steward paid 3s.4d. 'at Chesterfylde of all Kynds of Seyfysshe for my Master'. Once again, it is clear that such commodities were available to other people, for in 1585 Thomas Heathcot of Chesterfield was earning his living as a fishmonger. On 13 February 1550 the Haddon steward sent someone 'to by fyssche at lychefylde fayer', on 23 March he paid 3s.4d. 'unto peter Elliotte for j houndrethe of whyette hearinge', on 18 June he gave Henry Savage eightpence 'For the Caryege of sault Fysshe to my Mr to harleston', and most unexpectedly of all, on 1 February 1551 he paid four shillings 'for see fysshe wyche wyllm aylestre sente forthe of lankyeshyer'. Nearly two hundred years later, Defoe saw fish carried alive in 'great buts fill'd with water in waggons' all the way from the Lincolnshire fens to London. [5]

Eggs and dairy produce were presumably obtained from the home farm, but at Christmas time extra supplies were bought at the doorstep. On 27 December 1549 fourpence was paid 'unto the Egwhoman for Eggs' and on the following day fourpence was given to a man 'for the brengynge of a dysshe of Eggs unto my Master'. At the same time eggs were delivered from Monyash, five miles away, by a woman called Margaret. Edward Bylson, who brought a horseload of quinces and pears in 1564, sounds like a hawker, but other payments that feature in the accounts may have been to local people who were prepared to do some occasional carrying but who were otherwise occupied on neighbouring farms. The services provided by hawkers were certainly appreciated, for on 14 January 1565 'John Basford and Crosse and other hawkers' were given a tip or seasonal present of ten shillings. T. S. Willan has drawn attention to the surprisingly large tips given by great landowners to those who carried their goods. He writes: 'In the early seventeenth century the Howards of Naworth Castle ... regularly rewarded the bringers of presents with sums that were two to four times as large as the daily wage they were paying to their labourers. It was a curious practice, deeply embedded in a paternalistic view of social and economic relationships'. [6]

In the 1550's, exotic spices and other groceries were sold at Ashbourne Market. *C.L.M. Porter.*

2 Shops

The market and the shop were complementary, both in a physical sense (for shops tended to congregate around or near to the market place) and in the range of goods which they offered for sale. A shopkeeper such as William Stout of Lancaster was always at his busiest on a market day. Celia Fiennes was impressed by the range of provisions on sale in Chesterfield market, but seventeenth-century probate records show that the town also had its shopkeepers, including grocers, chandlers, mercers, drapers, ironmongers and even a confectioner. The craftsman's workshop formed another outlet for the retail trade. In Tudor Chesterfield shoes, saddles, gloves, metalware and various other products were sold by craftsmen directly to the customer. An outstanding example was the bellfounder, Ralph Hethcote, who described himself in his will as brazier. Upon his death in 1577 he had pots, pans, kettles, chafing dishes, mortars, ladles, candlesticks, pewter, lead and other things for sale; much of his capital was invested in his farm, and in his warehouse he had bell moulds valued at £10 and a bell that had been newly made. [7]

Seventeenth-century shopkeepers kept a fairly mixed stock in trade and were prepared to make money wherever they could. Celia Fiennes thought Derby was a dear place for strangers and one where 'they had only shops of all sorts of things'. The probate inventory of John Lee of Sheffield (1696) provides a good, contemporary illustration of the type of shop she must have seen. A few years before his death, he was known to the Attercliffe group of ironmasters as Mr Lee, the Hartshead ironmonger, but the contents of his shop included groceries, haberdashery, pigments, medicines, stationery and other items of hardware. That part of his inventory which lists his stock in trade is worth quoting in full to show the varied nature of the goods that he was offering for sale: [8]

> *Goods in the Kitchen Chamber: One Duz. & 6 Barrells Lamb Black, 6s.0d, Six Bundles of Course Paper, 14s.4d, 2 Hundred Weight of Blistred Steell, £2.4s.0d, 3 Hundred Weight of iron Potts & Pans, £3, Half a Hundred of Shoomak, 11s.0d, 28 pound of iron Wier, 19s.0d, Five old Frying Pans, 5s.0d, 28 pound Block Tin, 16s.6d, A Small parcell Raisins, 2s.4d.*
>
> *Goods in the cellar: 15 Hundred of Organs iron, £12.15s.0d, Half a Hundred of Allam, 10s.0d, A Small parcell of Copperas, 1s.6d, A Parcell of Pitch, 15s.0d, A parcell of Sweet Oyle, 3s.4d, 3 Hundred & a half Tobbacco, £20.8s.4d, 3 Quarters of a Hundred Treakle, £1.4s.9d, A Small parcell of Old Currans, 5s.6d, 18 Gallons Civen Oyle, £3.6s.0d, 2 leaden Cesterns, £2.*
>
> *Goods in the Warehouse: A Small parcell of Nutmegs, 2s.0d, 14 Loaves of Sugar, £2.9s.0d, One Hundred & a half Browne Sugar, £3.15s.0d, A Parcell of Browne Candy, £1.*

Goods in the Shopp: On Hundred Browne Sugar, £3, One Hundred White Lead, £1.8s.0d, One Hundred Starch, £1.4s.0d, 16 Reame of White Paper, £2.8s.0d, 5 pound of Turpentine, 2s.6d, 2 Duz. Hour Glasses, 14s.0d, 33 pound of Black and Browne Thred, £3.11s.6d, One Gr[oss] and a Half laces, 4s.6d., Psalters Testam[en]ts & Catechismes, 13s.6d, Fine Thred 1 pound, 4s.9d, 13 pieces Holland tape, 9s.6d, 3 pieces fillitting, 3s.6d, Laces, 5s.0d, Fine Thred, 9s.11d, Skein Thred, 3s.0d, Tape and Caddis 1 duz. 1/2, 5s.3d, Brass Curtain Rings, 2s.8d, Bone Rings, 6d, Powder Hornes and Inkhornes, 5s.9d, Horne Combs, 4s.7d, Bees Wax, 1s.10d, Umber, 1s.6d, 5 duz. Cardes, 9s.6d, 1 duz. 1/2 Primmers, 3s.0d, Horse Spice and Turmerick, 3s.9d, Flower of Sulpher, 9d, Litharge, 2s.0d, Half a pound Gum Draggon, 6d, 17 pound of Seeds, 5s.11d, 3 pound White Pepper, 5s.3d, 6 pound Black pepper, 8s.0d, 5 pound of Gum, 2s.6d, 3 pound of Pack thred, 2s.0d, 6 pound of Horse Spice, 2 pound Fenecrick, 5s.0d, 1 duz. Ropp., 2s.4d, 3 pound of Assidew, 5s.0d, 5 gr[oss] of Tobacco pipes, 8s.4d, 5 pound Swines grease, 1s.0d, 4 Reames of White paper, 12s.0d, 2 pound Frankinsence, 1 pound of Wax, 1s.4d, 14 pound of Bole, 1s.0d, One pair Large Scales 17 Stone Lead Weights, £2, 5 pair Brass Scales 4 pound in Brass weights, 8s.0d, The Shop Window Grate, 7s.0d, 2 Shop Counters, 3 Nest Drawers with the Shelves and all the Emty Boxes, £2.10s.0d, 1 old pepper Mill, 1s.6d.

Shortly after John Lee's death, the Sheffield baptism and burial registers give the occupations of the men they record. Between October 1698 and September 1703 they name six ironmongers, six mercers, four drapers, four chandlers, three grocers, three bakers, two hatters, a salter, a watchmaker, a clock maker, a pewterer, and a stationer or bookseller, as well as four glovers, four saddlers, twenty-four shoemakers and twenty-five butchers, who may or may not have been shopkeepers but who can probably be described as retailers. Probate inventories survive for such tradesmen, particularly the grocers, whose shops were packed with goods imported from all over the world. Henry Hancock, a Sheffield grocer who died in 1689, kept the following goods for sale in his shop, cellar and warehouse: [9]

Loafe Sugar 2 c.ls. 1 lb, £6.15s.7d, Six hundred of Sugar, £11.8s.0d, powder Sugar, £3, One hundred pound weight of peper, £7, Sixty pound of Fine pouder Sugar, £1.15s.0d, A box of browne Sugar Candy Sixty pound, £1.17s.6d, Fifty Five Realmes of paper, £7, Foure dozin of Thrid, £4, Twelve dozin of Soape, 12s.0, Two dozin and A halfe of Twine, 15s.0d, Eight Rheames of ordinary paper, 10s.0d, Three hundred weight of starch, £2.10s.0d, One box of Flower of Sulpher, 7s.0d, Borax seaven pound, £1, Forty pound of Red Lead, 6s.8d, Thirty two pound of Brimstone, 5s.6d, Forty pound of Annyseeds, 17s.6d, Six pound of Coriander seeds, 2s.6d, graines and Longe peper, 2s.6d, Three pound of Turmerick, 4s.6d, Liquorish powder foure pound, 2s.8d, Cinoman One pound, 12s.0d, wormseeds three pound, 13s.0d, Cena 3 qrs, 3s.0d, verdegrease, 4s.0d, Twenty Foure pound of Rice, 6s.0d, white Sugar Candy one pound and A halfe, 2s.0d, Allois one pound and A halfe, 6s.0d, Diapente one pound, 1s.0d, A parcell of Nailes, 10s.0d, Seaven grose of pipes, 4s.8d, Fennell seeds, 4s.0d, nyne Gramers, 6s.0d, six Psalters, 4s.0d, Two dozin of Primers, 4s.0d, nyne dozin of Cards, 10s.0d, Six pound of Nutmeggs, £1.16s.0d, Six pound of Gum Arabick, 6s.0d, Two pound and A quarter of Cloves, 18s.0d, Eighteene pound of Sugar, 10s.6d, Six pound of Carroway seeds, 2s.0d, Counters drawers and severall weights and scales & boxes in the Shopp, £8, Thirteene pound of blew, 12s.0d, Iron grate and frying pan, 13s.0d, Three hundred and A halfe of Currans, £6.10s.0d, One hundred weight of Raisons, £1.4s.0d, Coarse treackle foure hundred weight, £4, Forty Five Gallons of Brandy, £9, three qrs of [a hundredweight] of Allom, 15s.0d, Soape, 16s.0d, pruans, 9s.0d, Indian Red and Rosell, 3s.0d, white vinager, 6s.8d, Eight Barrells of Tobacco, £90, Callis sand, 5s.0d, A bagg of Hopps, £4, Six hundred weight of Suggar, £1§1.8s.0d, One hundred ounces of plate, £25.

Groceries formed the bulk of Hancock's stock in trade, but he also acted as a stationer and tobacconist. The wide range of foreign imports that were available in Sheffield at modest prices is even more apparent from the inventory of Benjamin Paramore, taken early in 1689. The 250 separate items that were valued together at about £200 included Jamaican pepper, Jordan almonds, Spanish juice, Macedonian parsley seed, French barley, and 'London Treackle'. Several contemporary Sheffield inventories list similar goods.

Unfortunately, most south Yorkshire inventories made before 1689 have been destroyed, and though a few shopkeepers are named in other records we learn nothing of their trade. Four mercers were recorded in Sheffield between 1585 and 1631, a grocer and two woollen drapers were each married at Sheffield in the 1650s and three Sheffield grocers, two mercers and a haberdasher were indicted at the West Riding quarter sessions between 1663 and 1708. [10] The probate inventories of Thomas Heaton (1718) and William Swaine (1728) are the first records to describe Sheffield men as shopkeepers. Robert Swyft, a mercer who died in 1561, is commemorated by a brass tablet in Rotherham parish church and two Rotherham pewterers, a woollen draper and a grocer appear in the quarter sessions records of 1651-85. [11] And in Wirksworth in 1693 a list of tradesmen included six grocers, four ironmongers, three applemongers, two softmongers, two chandlers and two bakers. [12] Six grocers and four ironmongers sounds a lot for a moderately-sized market town, but demand for the sort of goods listed above must have been considerable.

In 1688 Gregory King estimated that the nation's shopkeepers numbered 4,000. Most of them were based in towns, but a contemporary tract claimed that shops were to be found 'in every country village'. T. S. Willan's analysis of G. C. Williamson's three-volume catalogue of tokens issued by tradesmen and shopkeepers between 1649 and 1672 has shown that 7,787 tokens survive for no less than 1,534 places up and down the country (excluding London and Southwark). At least 2,151 of these tokens belonged to shopkeepers in 822 different settlements. These figures are obviously minimal, for only a proportion of the original tokens survive and no doubt some shopkeepers never issued any, but they provide clear evidence that many rural villages had at least one shop during the third quarter of the seventeenth century. About 330 of the 822 places had no market rights. In south Yorkshire rural tokens survive for grocers only in Attercliffe and Hatfield, but Derbyshire has many more extant tokens, with 106 issuers from thirty-three different places, including ten grocers and eight mercers. Twenty-two of the 106 issuers came from a total of seventeen villages that had never had market rights or where such rights had lapsed. The occupations of most rural issuers are not recorded, but Bonsall had two butchers and a grocer, Eckington and Melbourne each had a mercer, Youlgreave had a grocer, Brailsford a chandler, and Brassington an ironmonger. [13]

Local parish registers occasionally name other rural shopkeepers. William Lee of Silkstone, mercer (1656) and Francis Stafford of Hope, linen draper (1660) were each married at Sheffield, Thomas Gaythorne, mercer (1661) and William Parkin, a retailer (1723) are recorded at Worsbrough, and in 1748 the Wath upon Dearne register describes John Shirtcliffe as shopkeeper. An Elizabethan mercer from Dronfield is known to have apprenticed his son to a member of the London Carpenters' Company and other rural shopkeepers are known from wills and probate inventories. Thomas Mapplewell, a Campsall draper (1695), had a large farm and goods in his shop to the value of £345, but regrettably they were not listed. Samuel Staniforth (1692) lived in Attercliffe when it was still a separate village to the east of Sheffield.

The appraisers of his inventory described him as a pinner, presumably because he sold pins and haberdashery, but his shop offered stationery, medicines, groceries and ironmongery for sale. On the shelves raisins, sugar, candy, soap, nuts and cloves were arranged alongside items labelled 'dragon's blood', 'diascordium and methridale' and suchlike, or the customer could reach for the testaments, psalters, horn books, primers and grammars, which were separated from the usual items of haberdashery and from the six stithies and fourteen hammers waiting to be bought by local cutlers. Stored at the back shop, or in the warehouse and chamber, could be found Jamaica peppers, sugar, currants, treacle, rice, hops, starch and dyes, brandy, wine, tobacco and various iron ware. [14] The range of goods, especially imported groceries, available in seventeenth-century shops is very impressive.

3 Hawkers and pedlars

Hawkers, hucksters, tinkers and pedlars are elusive figures who can rarely be found in local records, so the task of describing their activities is a difficult one. Joan Thirsk has written, 'Chapmen, trowmen, higglers and others distributed [their] wares more silently and stealthily than the smuggler by moonlight'. England was virtually a free-trade area and though this was a great benefit to the nation it means that the historian of internal trade has no recognised set of records to work upon. Even those towns which had the right to charge tolls have rarely preserved the relevant documents and most traders managed to avoid duties altogether. Itinerant traders were regarded with suspicion by successive Tudor and Stuart governments and as early as 1552 an Act declared that, 'tynkers, pedlers and suche like vagrant persons are more hurtfull then necessarie to the commen wealth of this realme'. Shakespeare's character, the thieving pedlar, Autolycus, was a easily-recognised type. [15] But all attempts to enforce a licensing system or to forbid such activities were doomed to failure. The glassmen, for example, were classified as rogues by an Act of 1604, but that did not prevent their travelling throughout the realm in search of customers for glasses; John Ward, glassman, had his daughter baptised at Sheffield parish church in 1716 and had his occupation recorded quite openly. [16]

A few tinkers are known from parish registers. Thomas Brown and Thomas Snowden of Rotherham were each described as tinker upon their marriages in the early 1720s; James Heeley, a Barnsley tinker, appears in the 1732 register of Worsbrough chapelry; the Sheffield burial register of 1741 notes the death of Edward Hodgkinson, tinker; and in 1750 the Wath upon Dearne register records the burial of Thomas Hopkinson, a tinker from nearby Swinton. [17] In the West Riding quarter sessions records, John Hopkinson of Sheffield was described as a tinker in 1640 and in the previous year George Jackson, a Chesterfield tinker, was cleared of a charge that he had practised the pewterer's trade in Rotherham without having served a proper apprenticeship. [18] Most of the tinkers named above were urban dwellers and perhaps the charge against George Jackson arose from confusion over the nature of the goods that he was selling. Tinkers are generally regarded as men who travelled through the countryside in search of work mending pots and pans and later the name became used pejoratively to mean a rogue and a clumsy botcher of his work, but in the sixteenth and seventeenth centuries some tinkers were retailers of cheap metalware.

Ralph Hethcote, a Chesterfield brazier and bellfounder, who died in 1577, had in his warehouse 'in flawnders ware pannes and kettles eight score powndes' valued at £6.13s.4d, 'in Tynckers ware and suche lyke tenne score and 2 powndes' worth £7.11s.6d, and '2 tinker Candlesticks' priced at one shilling. On the other hand, rural tinkers occasionally hawked different goods if the opportunity arose, as on 25 October 1550 when the steward of Haddon Hall paid fourpence 'unto the Tynker of Rousley for a dysshe of freshe fysshe'. [19] Distinctions between different occupations were not hard and fast.

A well-known term for a dealer in small articles was huckster, which was originally the feminine form of hawker. [20] A glimpse of their activities in the sixteenth century is afforded by a Doncaster corporation regulation of 1560, which was designed to protect the town's famous Saturday market. It was ordered that: 'No huckster that buyeth salt to sell again shall buy now from Thursday at night to Saturday at three of the clock. No huckster that buyeth

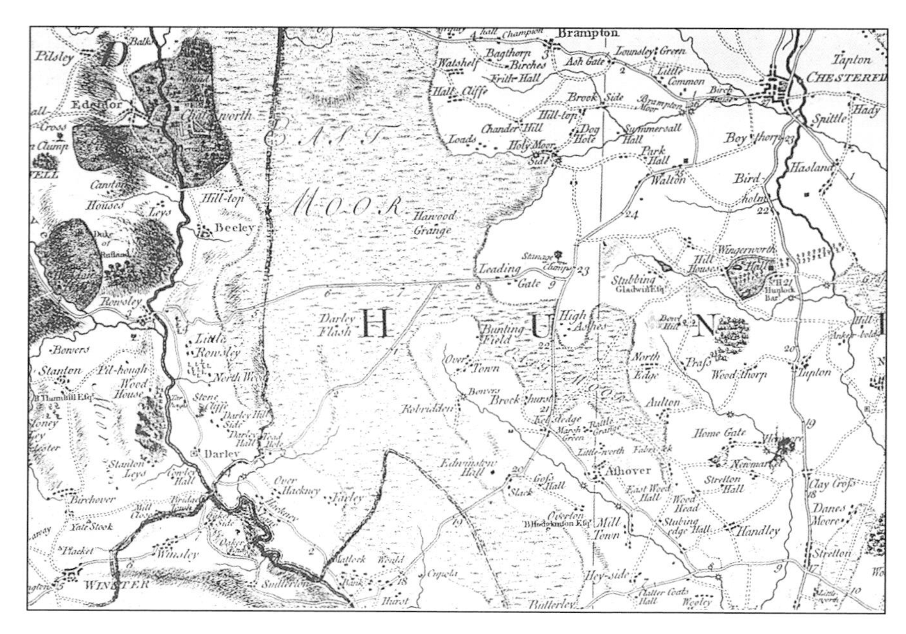

Chesterfield and the East Moor, shown on Peter Burdett's map of Derbyshire in the 1760's. A network of roads converge on the market town.

butter and eggs to sell again shall buy now afore eleven o'clock. No man or woman shall meet no victuals to buy, but shall suffer it to come to the market-cross to be sold'. In *The English Dialect Dictionary* of 1898-1905 Joseph Wright gave the meaning of huckster as petty tradesman or small shopkeeper; in Cumberland and East Yorkshire the term was then used to mean a middleman who dealt in farm produce. In 1778 Henry Thickett was described in the Tickhill parish register as huckster, but the word rarely appears in local records. The three Killamarsh hucksters who were licensed at the meeting of the Derbyshire quarter sessions held at Chesterfield on 7 October 1766 were exceptional. But J. C. Cox tells us that the word was still well-known in Derbyshire in 1890, and in his first novel, published in 1911, the young D. H. Lawrence wrote:

> *Far off on the highway could be heard the sharp trot of ponies hastening with Christmas goods. There the carts of the hucksters dashed by to the expectant villagers, triumphant with great bunches of light foreign mistletoe, gay with oranges peeping through the boxes, and scarlet intrusion of apples, and wild confusion of cold, dead poultry. The hucksters waved their whips triumphantly, the little ponies rattled bravely under the sycamores, towards Christmas.* [21]

The activities of pedlars have left few traces, but the traditional picture of their going round the villages, farms, inns and big houses is probably accurate. Pedlars supplied rural customers with miscellaneous consumer goods purchased from craftsmen, shopkeepers and stallholders in market towns or at seasonal fairs. They were concerned not with local subsistence needs but with those little extras that added spice to life. With only a pack strapped to his back, or perhaps with a single horse, the pedlar was a distinctive figure in rural society. A. E and E. M. Dodd have described how pedlars from Flash, high in the Peak District, traded in silk, mohair, and twist buttons from Macclesfield:

> *The Flash pedlars were known locally as 'fudge-mounters'; they travelled the country with their packs 'kippering and twanning' as they went, that is, sleeping in barns and begging their food. They got a bad name, but not all of them merited Samuel Smiles' description 'wild and*

barbarous'; the pedlar John Lomas (1747-1823), for example, built the Methodist chapel at Hollinsclough and his initials can be seen on a tablet above the entrance.

A few earlier pedlars are known by name from parish register and quarter sessions records. Nicholas Medley and John Stewart appear in the Worsbrough chapelry register of 1716-19, Thomas Liversiege of Haugh in the Rotherham marriage register in 1720, and Robert Chreighton in the Sheffield burial register in 1740; in October 1639 Thomas Beale, a Masborough pedlar, was fined five shillings for abusing two J.P.s with foul language, and in 1665 Richard French, a Tickhill pedlar, was brought before the justices after being involved in a bad-tempered quarrel. [22]

Seventeenth-century commentators and local officers tended to describe pedlars as Scotsmen, possibly because the first pedlars had sold cheap Scottish linen. The Congleton borough court referred to them in 1642 as 'all Scotchmen and other persons carrying packs'. [23] Some connection with this type of activity must explain why the pub opposite Hathersage church acquired the name of the *Scotsman's Pack*. A Sheffield inn, the *King's Head*, had a room known in 1716 as the 'Scotchman Chamber', which was no doubt set aside for trading activities. [24] A rare and vivid picture of the way of life of these pedlars (in this case an undoubted Scotsman) is provided by a seventeenth-century deposition before a Derbyshire Justice: [25]

Archibald MacLeod of Glasgoe in the kingdome of Scotland saith upon his oath before Charles Agard Esqr of Foston, that upon Friday the last day of March, 1665, about tenn of the clocke in the forenoone passinge as a Traveller with severall sortes of linnen Clothe brought out of Scotland to sell here in England and callinge at the house of John Wetton in Sudbury, Innkeeper, to enquire for customers to buy his cloth, was demanded by Jane, the wife of the afore-named John Wetton, the price, which being disliked by the said Jane as too great, shee gave this informant many ill words as Scotche Dogge and traitor, and afterwards stroke him with her fist upon the face, where upon this Informant endeavoured to defend himselfe. A certain man to him unknowne but was informed hee was a Chesherman and a Carrier in the house aforesayd then beinge with a certaine paire of tonges stroke this informant upon the head three or four tymes and gave three dangerous wounds to this informant upon the left side of his head in soe much that this informant bled exceedingly.

We do not know Jane Wetton's and the carrier's version of the story.

After the civil war, as the range of light-weight consumer goods increased, a 'prodigious number' of pedlars plied their trade throughout the kingdom. A 1691 tract claimed that pedlars and hawkers had multiplied daily and within the last few years had trebled in number. Their relationship with shopkeepers was an uneasy one. Henry Best of Elmswell tells us that Holland cloth was 'brought over by our merchants, and sold to our linen drapers, at whose shops our country pedlars furnish themselves', but as well as buying from shopkeepers pedlars bought at the markets and fairs an directly from the producer, and it was this competition that the shopkeepers feared. Town corporations and guilds tried to defend the interests of shopkeepers by insisting that everyone kept to his particular trade. In 1622, for example, the Doncaster shoemakers ordered that 'noe tradesman of that occupation shall at any time either on the markett dayes or any other weeke dayes goe upp and down this towne hawkeing any ... wares to sell', and in 1686 the corporation were told that William Crowther had several times illegally hawked and sold kersey cloths within the town on days other than market days. However, when the House of Commons debated the matter in 1691, the convenience and cheapness of having goods brought to the door won the day and the motion to suppress hawkers and pedlars was lost. [26]

At a meeting of the quarter sessions held at Leeds in July 1683 the West Riding J.P.s ordered that:

the respective cheefe Constables within this Ryding doe Imediately upon sight hereof issue forth their warrants to the petty Constables within their respective divisions to make diligent search ... for all Rogues Vagrants petty Chapmen of what sort soever, especially for those of the kingdome of Scotland, and such as are the Harborers or Receivers of them. And if they fynd any such That then they convey them before the next Justice of peace, to the end they may be examined and committed as the said Justice shall fynd them to bee Dangerous.

Earlier that year at the January meeting held at Doncaster the J.P.s had ordered that two 'Scotchmen beeing Pedlers or Petty Chapmen ... who are by law declared to be Rogues' should be whipped and returned to their legal place of settlement 'in the kingdom of Scotland'.[27] Some of the 'Scotchmen' or 'Scotch pedlars' who appear in local records have surnames that could have come either from northern England or lowland Scotland. The Sheffield baptism register for 1717-19, for example, names Walter Miller and Andrew Hutton as Scotchmen and when James Hallywell was married in Rotherham church in 1719 and William Cass was buried there four years later they were described in the register as 'Scotch pedlar, sojourner'.[28]

The 'Scotchmen' recorded in the Sheffield parish register between 1698 and 1703 were mostly new to the area, except that John Maxfield had been born in Sheffield in 1665. Robert Blackstocke first appeared in the register upon his marriage to a local girl in 1697; he was described as a Scotchman when he baptised his daughter early in 1702, but when his son was baptised three years later Robert's occupation was given as innkeeper. George Crabbe wrote about another pedlar who rose in status, in his poem *The Parish Register*, published in 1807:

Dawkins, a dealer once, on burthen'd back
Bore his whole substance in a pedlar's pack;
To dames discreet, the duties yet unpaid,
His store of lace and hyson he convey'd:
When thus enrich'd, he chose at home to stop,
And fleece his neighbours in a new-built shop.

The West Riding order of July 1683 was directed at 'petty Chapmen of what sort soever' and at their meeting in the previous January the J.P.s had delt with 'Scotchmen beeing Pedlers or

The Scotsman's Pack, Hathersage. *H. Smith.*

Petty Chapmen'. The term 'chapman' was applied loosely to traders ranging from substantial wholesalers like the Sheffield ironmongers and prosperous middlemen such as the nailchapmen and the cutlery factors, down to petty traders and hawkers. The Sheffield parish register of 1698-1703 names Hosea Emott of Bridgehouses, Joseph Riglesworth of Heeley, Ezra Simon of Bridgehouses and Joshua Pell, Joseph Ridley, Joseph Ward and William Ward of the town of Sheffield as chapmen, but it is not at all clear to which grade they belonged. Samuel Shore appeared as chapman, hardwareman and ironmonger. James Robinson, a Chesterfield chapman who died in 1587, had meagre personal possessions but left £96 'in moneye' and made bequests to the poor and towards the foundation of a free school. The image of a travelling chapman is conjured up by the two dozen knives and three dozen sheaths recorded in his inventory and by his 'purse and girdle, dagger and money in his purse'.

In 1647 Abel Tilly, another Chesterfield chapman, had £20 in ready money and was owed £11.16s,6d. His wares 'in his pack and abroad' and in boxes in his house and parlour were valued at £12.8s.10d, his seeds and bags made of harden cloth were valued at £1.4s., two pairs of brass scales and weights were worth five shillings, and his hay and horse gears were valued at £1. The furniture in his simple two-roomed house was worth a further £15.13s. [29] Peter Firth, an Orgreave chapman who was married in Rotherham parish church in 1731, was possibly an itinerant trader rather than a substantial middleman, but William Steer, a prominent cutlery factor from Darnall, was content with the description 'chapman' when he made his will in 1726. R. E. Leader, writing in 1901, believed that the eighteenth-century distributors of Sheffield cutlery wares were called 'chaps' or chapmen:

Their chief resort was The Bird-in-Hand, Church Lane ... When a 'chap' arrived, the ostler went round to inform the manufacturers of the fact, and received one penny from each one for his trouble. Sometimes, there were two, three or four 'chaps' in the house at one time, and each had a separate room for business ... The 'chaps' usually brought with them mules, or packhorses, for the removal of such wares as they might purchase ... A busy street at dawn would often see a train of no fewer than fifty animals making ready to start. And accompanying them would be travellers and friends, and merchants who, either in charge of their wares or on some other business, were journeying to provincial towns or to the capital. [30]

Leader was writing long after these events took place, but his knowledge of local topography and oral traditions was unrivalled.

Petty chapmen provided a link between manufacturer and customer. They were described in 1639 as people who 'buy up commodities of those that sell by wholesale and sell them off dear by retaile, and parcel them out'. When Matthew Bedell surveyed Rothwell, near Leeds, in 1628 he commented, 'In this town the inhabitants make great store of bone lace, whereby their poor are employed and themselves much enriched. They make a quick return of this commodity for it is fetched and carried away from their doors by chapmen continually resorting thither'. Such activities were not usually recorded, but a deposition made before a Derbyshire J.P. affords a rare glimpse of the way of life of a petty chapman or hawker in the middle of the seventeenth century. On 25 March 1652 John Holt, a Chesterfield chapman, claimed that:

on Thursday at night last himselfe Edward Holt and his wife and Godfry Hodgkinson and his wife lodged in a Barne of George Hodgkins in Worsop, and that when [he] and the rest afore mentioned were preparing to goe to bed Henry Firth came in amongst them, and laid himselfe downe upon a hawkinge bagge of Edward Holts wherin were a bible 3 pairs of cordevant gloves one paire of sheeps leather gloves two tobacco boxes two silver seales and a dozen and eleaven pairs of bondstringes and that after a little time the said Firth pretending to goe home to Troway where he lives left ... and before any one else come into or went out of the said Barne, the said hawkinge bagge and commoditcase in it before mentioned was gone, for which reason [he] positively accuseth the said Firth for conveyinge away and stealinge the said bagge and said commodityes in it. [31]

Was the Bible in Edward Holt's hawking bag for sale or was it his personal possession? Pedlars and other wayfarers were often said to be dissenters and the authorities tried to keep a watchful eye upon them. At a meeting of the quarter sessions held at Derby in 1682 the J.P.s ordered

that the further Observacon of the Order of last Sessions by which the receavinge of the Sacrament within Twelve Moneths and constant resortinge to Church and not frequentinge Conventicles and Certificates thereof was required from those whoe desired to bee Licensed Alehouskeepers Badgers or Drovers bee suspended untill further Order.

The quarter sessions order books prior to 1682 do not survive, so the background to the original order is not known. Nor is it clear why the original measure was abandoned, unless it was deemed impractical to enforce. No further orders along these lines were issued by the J.P.s, either in Derbyshire or in the West Riding of Yorkshire. Samuel Shore and Field Sylvester, two of Sheffield's most prominent chapmen, were leading members of Upper Chapel, and the names of other tradesmen appear frequently in the records of local nonconformity, but the religious activities of the petty chapmen are as elusive as their business affairs. [32] Hosea Emott and Ezra Simon, the Bridgehouses chapmen, attract our attention, but of course they were not responsible for their own names. They christened their own children with common names.

Further government measures to licence chapmen proved ineffective. When a national register of chapmen was attempted in 1697-98, about 2,500 names were recorded, but. only nineteen were from Derbyshire and fourteen from south Yorkshire. [33] In the summer of 1805 when Gill Greenwood, pedlar, agreed to serve as a substitute in the Chesterfield militia, he gave his abode as Dewsbury or Sheffield, places that are some twenty-five miles apart, with some thirty-seven miles separating Dewsbury from Chesterfield. [34] Such wayfarers are not easily tracked down in earlier records. Some were obviously prepared to travel long distances, but most probably confined themselves to a recognised territory or even a regular circuit based on one or two market towns. We have seen them trading in inns, buying at shops, and providing a service between producer and customer. Another source of supply was the seasonal fair, which sometimes catered specifically for the pedlar's needs. In 1770 William Owen's *Book of Fairs* noted that Doncaster had four annual fairs each year for horses, cattle, sheep and pedlary, that Thorne had two fairs each year for horned cattle, horses, and pedlary, and that Chesterfield had several fairs for livestock and pedlary, including a special one on 25 September which was devoted to the sale of cheese, onions, and pedlars' wares. Rivalry between pedlars and shopkeepers was as strong in the late eighteenth century as it had been under the Stuarts. In 1772 Doncaster corporation lobbied M.P.s on behalf of 'the settled trader' against hawkers and pedlars and as a result of shopkeepers' pressure an Act was passed in 1785 forbidding pedlars to sell goods in towns where they were not resident, except on market days. The J.P.s subsequently punished persistent offenders such as Joseph Leuty of Gowdall, a hawker and pedlar who in 1804 traded illegally in Selby, seven miles from his home, but generally their task was an impossible one. The 1851 census recorded 25,747 hawkers, pedlars and hucksters in England and Wales, and according to Henry Mayhew this figure was a gross understatement, indicating only the permanent core of full-time hawkers and pedlars. [35]

9 CARRIERS

1 Part-time carriers

During the early-modern period families within our region, and indeed throughout much of the realm, frequently combined farming with a craft or a trade. Metalworkers, leadminers, colliers and others followed this traditional way of life until the national population grew to such an extent that insufficient land was available for men to have a smallholding as well as another source of revenue. The packmen and carriers were no exception. They, too, had a little land with which to supplement their earnings and much short-distance carrying was undertaken by husbandmen in the slack spells before and after the hay harvest when the roads were normally dry and firm. Dual occupations probably account for the fact that very few people were described in local records as carriers. If carrying was normally a by-employment in which men took goods no further than the market towns or the inland ports, then the carrier would probably have been known instead by the name of his principal occupation. In the West Midlands it was already being said by 1700 that the growing army of carriers, waggoners and 'horse followers' were mainly local farmers who depended heavily on this contribution to their income. 'Several persons have offered to fetch limestone for your lordship', the Earl of Strafford was told in June 1722, 'but the roads have been so bad by the wetness of the weather that they have been unable to do so'. [1]

Jaggers Lane at Hathersage reminds us of the former packhorse men. *H. Smith.*

When Samuel Silcock's children were baptised at Sheffield parish church in 1698 and 1701 he was described in the register as husbandman, but when he died in 1715 the grant of letters of administration to his estate referred to him as a carrier. Perhaps he had changed to carrying in later life (for his inventory mentions neither farm animals nor crops), or perhaps his carrying was a part-time business; we cannot be sure, for carrying was something that a man could turn to when other things had failed. In 1701 Richard Gough, of the Shropshire parish of Myddle, wrote that his neighbour, Richard Maddocks, was 'a carpenter by trade, and an ingeniouse workman, but hee was very slow, or as some said idle, soe that few men imployed him, and therefore hee left his trade and turned carryer; but the death of an old horse broke him', and he became the keeper of an alehouse. Samuel Silcock had only two horses and meagre personal possessions when he died. His inventory reads: [2]

Purse and Apparell, £2, Two horses and Materialls, £4.10s.0d; Gods in the house: a range and furniture, 5s.0d, An Iron pot and other Iron things, 4s.0d, Pewter, 10s.0d, Two Tables, 10s.0d, Chairs, 10s.0d, Other things in the house, 2s.6d; Goods in the Shop: Cheese and other things, £2.5s.0d; Goods in the Chamber: A bed and its furniture, £2.5s.0d, A chest of Drawers and a looking glass, 15s.0d, half a dozen Markett Chairs, 6s.0d, A box and Table, 5s.0d, Linnens, 5s.0d, Other odd things, 2s.0d; Another Chamber Goods: Three beds and furniture, £3, A Table Chairs and other things, 5s.0d, Wood, 10s.0d: [total] £18.9s.6d.

The market chairs and the cheese in the shop suggest that he was also a retailer, but only in a small way.

Packmen and carriers were known by a bewildering variety of names, many of them having a strong regional flavour. Their occupation is commemorated by Packman's Bridge near Ulley and Treeton on the great highway from Rotherham to Mansfield, Nottingham and London, and in Packman Lane, the modern successor to the ancient Ricknield Street which separates the parishes of Harthill and Thorpe Salvin near the southern border of south Yorkshire. The Packman Gate that was mentioned in the 1625 register of the parish of Wath upon Dearne is doubtless the same thoroughfare as the present Packmen Road at Brampton, and the Packman Lane recorded at Mortomley in John Harrison's survey of the manor of Sheffield in 1637 can be identified with the modern Packhorse Lane which leads the traveller away from the busy main road to the Packhorse Inn. Inns of the same name still provide refreshment at Little Longstone and Chapel en le Frith; others formerly catered for travellers arriving at Barnsley, Rotherham or Sheffield; and the Packhorse Inn at Silkstone, which was demolished in the 1970s, was described in 1791 as a 'spacious and well-accustomed inn', with barns, stables and twenty acres of land. [3]

2 Inns and alehouses

It has been said that the golden age of the English inn lasted from the reign of Queen Elizabeth to that of Queen Victoria, from the start of an era of marked growth in the country's internal trade to the coming of the railways. In 1577, when this golden age was about to dawn, the government took a census of the nation's alehouses and inns and found about 20,000 distributed around the country. The great majority of these, of course, were humble alehouses. Derbyshire was credited with 726 alehouses and eighteen inns and Nottinghamshire had over 1,000 alehouses but apparently only five inns. These figures have to be used with caution but they indicate the general pattern. Not surprisingly, given its size and the importance of its county town as a regional capital, Yorkshire headed the list with 239 inns and nearly 3,700 alehouses. [5]

The number of licensed alehouses scattered throughout Elizabeth's realm is truly remarkable. Derby alone had sixty-one in 1577 and by the 1690s as many as 120 of the 694 houses in the borough were licensed to sell ale. In 1631 the corporation of Doncaster (another great thoroughfare town with approximately 3,000 inhabitants) issued the equally staggering number of 135 alehouse licences. Justices of the Peace continually struggled to control such premises, for the alehouse was mistrusted as a centre of social unrest where all sorts of troublesome and undesirable characters gathered together. The constables of Wirksworth wapentake reported in 1631 that they had 'put down a full third part of all the alehouses', but they agreed reluctantly that 'there are so great a multitude of poor miners within this wapentake that we are enforced to leave more alehousekeepers than otherwise we would'. Most alehouses were purely local concerns, but those situated alongside great highways catered for all sorts of traffic and were watched particularly carefully by the J.P.s. In July 1638, for example, the West Riding justices, fearing the spread of plague, restrained those who sold ale and beer 'in the open street to passengers and travellers travelling on the high road between Doncaster and Wentbrigg ... because they entertain and discourse with all manner of passengers and travellers, wanderers and idle beggars'. [6]

In 1577 seven of Derbyshire's eighteen innkeepers lived in the county town. The rest were to be found in places situated on or near to the principal highways, especially one or the other branches of the great road from Derby to Manchester, at Brailsford, Mercaston, Mugginton, Ashbourne or Buxton (where the traveller had the choice between two inns). Another couple

Packhorse Inn, Little Longstone. *H. Smith.*

of inns at Sudbury catered for the traffic on the Derby and Nottingham to Uttoxeter road, and in the hundred of Scarsdale a hostelry at Clowne served travellers on the Richmond to London highway, and inns at Chesterfield and (probably) Morton lay on or near the Sheffield to Derby road. [7] Eighteen inns for the whole of the county is not a large number but they must have seemed adequate for the small amount of through traffic that required such facilities. During the following century accommodation was improved to meet a significant rise in demand. We have already noted the tremendous growth in the provision of guest beds and stables, as demonstrated by the War Office returns of 1686. Much of the accommodation that was made available in rural settlements, and probably quite a lot of that in towns, was undoubtedly in private houses, but late seventeenth-century probate inventories show that inns had been established not only in towns but in such rural villages as Silkstone, Wentworth and Woolley. [8]

The improvement in quantity was not always matched by a rise in quality. Edward and Thomas Browne were far from satisfied with the accommodation provided at Bakewell after their hazardous journey across the East Moor from Chesterfield in the autumn of 1662. They found neither litter nor oats for their horses, which were therefore 'forc'd to pack out and lay abroad this wet night, poor jades, in a cold rotten meadow ... but alas horses and all here were forc'd to shift themselves'. In the great thoroughfare towns the standard of innkeeping was naturally much higher. When Daniel Defoe arrived in Doncaster on his journeys in the early eighteenth century, he noted that as the town 'stands upon the great northern post-road, it is very full of great inns'; the landlord of the post-house was not only mayor of the town but fit company for any gentlemen in the neighbourhood. [9]

Alan Everitt has shown that inns gradually acquired new functions so that by the eighteenth century they provided a whole range of services. In particular, as the number of travelling chapmen grew and the practice of dealing by sample was adopted, many inns became trading centres. In 1603 the York mercers expressed alarm at the way that some of their members had gone 'to the common inns where the chapmen, buyers of flax, and other merchandise have lodged, and there have often solicited them to their own shops, warehouses, or cellars, for the venting of their own flax, iron, and other merchandise'. When the 'good accustomed inn in Barnsley, known by the name of the Packhorse Inn' was advertised for sale in 1786, its rooms included 'nine corn chambers rented by corn dealers'. [10]

We have seen how other chapmen and hawkers used the services provided by local inns. An unusual insight into a different kind of trading is obtained from Thomas Baskerville's notes on his journeys during the reign of Charles II. He observed that at Doncaster 'they make excellent stockings for horsemen of very fine yarn and variety of colours, and the women of the town are so importunate for they go with bundles of the stockings on their arms from inn to inn where travellers are, that you can hardly evade laying out money with them, for they will follow you up into your chamber and will not be denied without a great deal of trouble'. He was not displeased by these hard selling methods, but felt rather that 'they are to be commended for it, for this being the great road between London and York, and Scotland, they do by this means vend a great deal of goods'. [11]

One of the most important functions of inns was to provide accommodation and business premises for carriers. The commercial directories of the late eighteenth century make it clear that although some carriers started their journeys from a warehouse, most of them were based at an inn, where parcels and letters could be delivered or collected, bills paid and fresh bookings made. Often the innkeeper would set a room aside for such transactions; Edmund Hague, a Rotherham innkeeper (1725), had a room that the appraisers of his inventory called the 'Carriars Parlour'. [12] Carriers also made regular overnight stops at inns along their way and used other inns as their destination points. The network of inns along the major highways of the kingdom was vital to the efficient running of long-distance carrying services.

The Mermaid Inn on Morridge, North Staffordshire. Formerly Blakemere House, a drovers road and saltway passed by the left hand side and troughs existed in the foreground. *C.L.M. Porter.*

3 London carriers

By the reign of Queen Elizabeth parts of Derbyshire and the West Riding were connected with the capital by regular carrying services. The evidence is scanty, but something can be gleaned from letters of great lords or their servants and occasionally from other records. A letter to the fifth Earl of Shrewsbury dated sometime between 1547 and 1551 mentions several pieces of cloth that had been sent to London by the Derby carrier and in 1584 a servant of the earl wrote from the capital to a Mr Stringer of Whiston to say that he was sending two stag skins by Hobson the carrier and that he hoped to hear of their safe arrival by the return carrier. The service between the West Riding and the capital was so regular by 1617 that the highway from Rotherham to Mansfield and Nottingham via Mile Oaks and Whiston was described as 'the Auncient Rode way or London way for carryers'. When a flitch of bacon was sent from Worksop to London in 1604 it was taken by the carrier of Harthill, a village that lay six miles or so to the west of Worksop. Likewise, in 1584, Sir Ralph Sadler wrote from the Dove valley to advise that various household things required by Mary, Queen of Scots, at Tutbury 'maye be brought downe on horsback by the caryers of Derby and of this town for less than 1d. a *lib*. And so may the plate be also brought in a trunk, well malid in canvas, much better chepe than by cart'. [13] Elizabethan carriers obviously transported quite a variety of goods; no doubt they were also prepared to take passengers whenever they could.

A pattern of weekly services connecting the capital with both near and distant parts of the country can be reconstructed from *The Carriers' Cosmographie* of 1637, in which John Taylor gave details of the usual lodgings of provincial carriers in London, together with their times of arrival and departure.

The Carriers from Sheffield, in Yorkshire', he wrote, 'doth lodge at the Castle in Woodstreet, they are to bee found on Thursdaies and Fridayes ... The Carriers of Doncaster in Yorkshire, and many other parts in that country, doe lodge at the Bell, or Bell Savage, without Ludgate, they do come on Fridaies, and goe away on Saturdaies or Mundaies ... The Carriers of Derby, and other parts of Derbyshire, doe lodge at the Axe in St. Mary Axe, neere Aldermanbury, they are to be heard of there on Fridaies.

Derby carriers were also to be found at the Castle in Wood Street every Thursday or Friday and the carriers of Halifax, Leeds and Wakefield also had their favourite inns and their accustomed times of departure. This remarkable account of a well-established carrying service in the reign of Charles I shows that the largest towns within our region had weekly contacts with the capital. A generation later, when the plague was active in London, local J.P.s were concerned that carriers should not spread the infection. An order of the West Riding quarter sessions issued at Wakefield on 11 January 1666 reads:

> *This Courte takeing into consideration the dangerous consequences that may follow by permitting Carriers to travell to the Citye of London and bring goods from there into the severall parts of the west side of the County aforesaid the Contagion there beeing not yet ceased, It is therefore ordered that noe Carriers do passe from any parts of the west syde of the Countye aforesaid to the said Citye neither be permitted to bring any goods from there until it shall please god to Cease his heavie Judgement there that free Commerce may be without danger.* [14]

Although John Taylor informs us that Sheffield carriers visited London regularly by 1637, few local people could have been involved in this trade, for no carriers are named amongst those whose occupations were recorded in the Sheffield marriage register of 1653-60 and none is to be found amongst the 1,149 men whose occupations were recorded in the baptism and burial registers of 1698-1703. In 1591 when Lawrence Hobson of Millhouses in the parish of Sheffield leased 'the scythe wheeles or cutlers wheels called Moscarr Wheels' to a Norton scythesmith, he described himself as a carrier, but we do not know whether he took goods all the way to London. Nor do we know anything about the activities of John Browne, a Sheffield carrier, who in 1584 leased a messuage in Water Lane. John Armitage of Chesterfield is the first 'London Carrier' to be found in local records. This was the way he described himself in his will in 1661. Perhaps he was living in retirement at the time of his death, for he had only two rooms and his probate inventory mentions neither horses nor any other aspect of his business. His personal estate was valued at a little over £50, of which £35 was due to him 'by speciality'. Another Chesterfield carrier, John Greaves, had personal estate valued at £76.15s.8d. (including bonds worth £30) upon his death in 1692. His home consisted of a living room or 'house', two parlours, a kitchen, buttery, chambers, and a barn. He had a stock of oats and hay and he kept a cow as well as the horse which presumably did his carrying. [15] Such men probably typified the majority of local carriers.

The few London carriers must obviously have been involved full-time. The most important carrier in late seventeenth-century Doncaster was moderately prosperous and of some standing in his community. When the mayor went to London to see King James II about renewing the town's charters, it was Abraham Pilling who escorted him. A tradesman's token that has survived is marked 'Abraham Pilling, 1665, A.E.P.' on one side and 'Carrier of Donkester. His Halfe Penny' on the reverse, and when he was buried in 1695 his occupation was entered in the parish register as London carrier. In 1672 he was taxed on four hearths in his house in Frenchgate, the main thoroughfare in the town, and when he died he bequeathed both this property and a barn in Far St Sepulchregate to his wife, Frances. Amongst his bequests was one to his son, William, who had been absent so long that the family did not know whether or not he was still alive. The probate inventory attached to his will shows that he had neither a cart nor a waggon and that his carrying was done by a team of sixteen packhorses and mares. His personal possessions also included a warehouse and a large amount of fodder for his horses. The inventory concludes with 'Booke debts whereof some may be desperate, £15'. [16]

J. A. Chartres has used *The Carriers' Cosmographie* and later accounts to show that carrying services from London to the provinces grew at an appreciable rate between 1637 and 1681 and then multiplied in response to a general growth in domestic trade between 1681 and 1715. Locally, we read that in April 1708 Jonathan Clark of Whaley, near Bolsover, 'did begin to be a carrier with a waggon to London', no doubt on the old Rotherham-Mansfield road. 'Great gangs of London carriers as well as drifts of malt-horses and other carriers and passengers' were said to cross the Lathkill at Alport when a petition for a new bridge was presented to the Derbyshire quarter sessions in 1718. This 'ancient waye' was one of the routes linking Manchester and Stockport with Derby and London. The *Derby Mercury* of 27 December 1733 advertised the fact that:

Alport bridge, near Youlgreave. A county bridge of 1718 over the River Lathkill.

> *George Paschall, now the old Derby carrier to London, sends a Wagon from his House adjoining to the Red-Lyon Inn in Derby every Monday and is at the Bull and Mouth Inn near Aldersgate, London every Saturday: Also sets out again every Monday from thence and is at his house every Friday or Saturday following. Note, That those are the days of setting out and coming in, for the Winter season and all Persons that are disposed to Travel by the said Waggon shall have Handsome Usage; also those that have Goods or Parcels of any kind to send or have brought shall be kindly received and well us'd: He also returns money to and from London but if any be put into Parcels unknown to him or without Notice given to his Bookeepers thereof, he will not be accountable for any such money lost.*

A rival service was advertised by Thomas and Henry Patridge in May 1734, taking five days to get to the capital and deposit goods and passengers at Loughborough, Leicester, Market Harborough and places adjacent on the way. [17]

In July 1741 the *Derby Mercury* reported that:

> *the Derbyshire Waggon which inns at the Bell in Woodstreet, was robbed by two footpads on Finchley Common. They took from the Waggoner about 7 [shillings[who making a stout Resistance they stabbed him in three places in the back, each about two inches deep and cut the Sinews of his neck so that his Head lay on his Shoulder: after which the Villains made off: Some Higglers soon after passing that Way took up the Waggoner and carried him to Finchley but his Life is Despaired of.*

Such barbaric deeds were mercifully rare, judging by the columns of the weekly newspapers. Footpads and highwaymen posed a threat that few travellers did not care to worry about, but much of their supposed activity lies in the realm of romantic fiction rather than historical fact. On her travels throughout the country Celia Fiennes only once 'had reason to suspect' highwaymen. The Derby to London coach was stopped many miles south of our region on five occasions in the 1770s, but the only coach to be held up locally in the eighteenth century was the mail coach stopped by Spence Broughton and an accomplice as it passed over Attercliffe Common in February 1791. After his arrest and execution the following year, his body was hung in chains at the scene of the crime (now called Broughton Lane) until the gibbet was finally dismantled in 1827. Petty pilfering from waggons was far more common than forcing vehicles to halt so that passengers could be robbed. An advertisement placed in the *Derby Mercury* of 11 November 1757 by a Sheffield woman who had been robbed indicates the type of goods commonly carried by stage-waggon. It reads:

> *Stolen out of a Waggon standing at the door of the White Lion Inn at Derby on the night of the 9th instant a large round Portmanteau Trunk covered with the Skin and the Hair on it and marked with a M in nails. In the said Trunk there was 5 Guineas in Gold, six tea Spoons, a Pair of tea Tongs and a large Table Spoon all Silver, marked with an M and no other letter. One Blue Damask gown and a brown Tabby Gown, the Cuffs lined with Red and one cross Barr'd Poplin Gown with French pocket holes. Two quilted Petticoats, one of them Green, also two hats one is paper covered with Tinsel and bound with a Red Ribbon.*

A two guineas reward was offered for a safe recovery. [18]

Until the last quarter of the eighteenth century carriers remain shadowy figures, mere names in the local records. John Walker, senior and junior, of Rotherham (1717), William Pool of Worsbrough (1723), Matthew Osborne of Masbrough (1738) and Joseph Eyre of Sheffield (1744) are named in parish registers. The Sheffield register of 1740-41 also names Joseph and Thomas Wright as London carriers. Thomas had long been engaged in the carrying business, for a schedule of the goods belonging to John Holdsworth of Clayton, near Bradford, taken in the winter of 1725-26, mentions a sum of money owed to him for carrying packs. [19]

The handful of London carriers stand apart; the destinations of other local carriers are difficult to determine. One firm piece of evidence is that in 1707 the vicar of Sheffield wrote to Ralph Thoresby of Leeds to say that as the enclosed papers were too bulky for the post, he had sent them by the Bradford carrier. In 1700 the executors of Mr John Bigge, curate and lecturer of Worsbrough, paid 'Wharton the Carrier for bring in his books and things from York, 18s.0d.' This implies a door-to-door service over a distance of about forty-five miles without having to leave a major highway. The Whartons were old-established carriers of yeoman status from Osbaldwick, just east of York. When Christopher Wharton, carrier, died there in 1687, his possessions included two waggons, nine horses and eight oxen. The value of a service such as Wharton's was that it was adaptable to customers' requirements.

Anything from correspondence and money to bulky items of merchandise could be carried, and if goods were not always delivered directly they could be collected at the inns where the carriers made their regular stops. Adam Eyre of Hazlehead Hall noted in his diary on 26 April 1647, 'Wm. Wainwright brought mee home from Wakefield a box which came from London, which cost 8s. ... and for his wadges and his horse 2s.'. Hazlehead was rather remote, on the edge of the Pennines, fifteen miles or so from Wakefield, yet by the middle of the seventeenth century goods took only about a week to arrive there from the capital. Nor were such services restricted to the summer months; James Clegg of Chapel en le Frith expressed no surprise when he received legal papers brought by a London carrier at the end of January 1733. There can be no doubt about the importance of land carriage to the inhabitants of our region. A spate of petitions drawn up in 1729 against an Act of Parliament passed ten years earlier includes one from the Cutlers' Company and 'the Freeholders, Dealers, Traders, and Artificers' of Sheffield, 'complaining of Inconveniences, and the great Increase of the Price of Land Carriage of Goods, arising from the Act ... which restrains the Number of Horses, drawing Carts travelling for Hire'. [20]

The evidence from Clegg's diary that London carriers were operating even in the winter is confirmed by quarter sessions records. Following a complaint in 1691 that 'waggoners and other carriers, by combination among themselves, [had] raised the prices of carriage of goods in many places to excessive rates, to the great injury of trade', an Act of Parliament authorised J.P.s to fix standard rates of carriage at their annual Easter sessions. Rates were to be posted in public places for all to see and offenders faced a fine of £5. Many years passed before the Derbyshire justices used these powers, but the West Riding J.P.s acted immediately. It seems, however, that the J.P.s could do no more than lay down guidelines. After studying the rates fixed by some other counties, T. S. Willan came to the conclusion that theJustices did not make an effective assessment but simply complied with the law in a formal manner; he doubted whether the county rates were observed, except perhaps in the first few years. [21]

4 Sheffield carriers in 1787

The commercial directories that appeared during the second half of the eighteenth century do not cover the whole of our region, but that published by Gales and Martin in 1787 gives details of the carrying services available to and from Sheffield along roads which had already been turnpiked. [22] It shows that in addition to the stage-coach facilities offered by the proprietors of the *Angel* and the *Tontine*, three carriers provided between them eight weekly services to London by waggon. Every Tuesday Royle's waggon left the *Travellers* at West Bar and proceeded via Chesterfield, Mansfield, Newark and Grantham; his Friday waggon went by way of Nottingham, Loughborough, Leicester, Market Harborough and Northampton. Clarke's waggons left the *Mitre* in Fargate every Monday, Tuesday, Thursday and Friday along the Mansfield-Nottingham route and on Wednesdays and Fridays Heaton and Jackson's waggons left the *Hotel* for Doncaster and then turned south down the Great North Road to the capital. Between them they offered a daily service to London, taking six to eight days to complete the journey. Those in a hurry could reach the capital in twenty-six hours by the flying coach.

Provincial directories make it clear that although the London carriers were the more conspicuous figures they were greatly outnumbered by carriers who provided regular services to other centres. Co-operation between carriers ensured end-on connections between market towns in most parts of England. [23] How long such services had operated before the publication of directories is difficult to judge. In 1773 the *Derby Mercury* advertised the fact that Bromwell Powell's waggon came weekly from Bewdley on the Severn, through the Black Country to Lichfield, Burton and Derby, where it met John Anderton's Sheffield waggon, which in turn connected with northern carriers going as far as Kendal.

In August of the same year the *Mercury* published an advertisement of 'S. Smith, the Three Crowns, High Street, Sheffield [who] sets out on Wednesday morning and arrives at the Dog and Partridge, Derby on Thursday evening and delivers goods to Joseph Saxon who keeps a regular weekly stage to Birmingham and forwards goods to the West of England'. Likewise, in 1772 two Sheffield carriers made a formal arrangement whereby Thomas Lidgard, who operated a service from Lincoln to Sheffield, promised to deliver all Manchester-bound goods to Richard Gardiner, who in return accepted goods at his Manchester warehouse that were bound for places on Lidgard's route. [24]

In 1787 Sheffield people could take advantage of forty-two services linking Sheffield directly or through connections to most parts of the country. Obviously, such a system had not grown up overnight but its origins are obscure. Anderton's waggons (which we have seen in operation fourteen years earlier) offered four services a week from a warehouse in China Square. At noon on Mondays a waggon left for Kendal via Barnsley, Wakefield, Leeds, Bradford, Skipton and Settle, arriving a week later and beginning the return journey the same day. Goods could be forwarded from Kendal to Keswick, Cockermouth, Whitehaven, Penrith, Carlisle, Dumfries, Glasgow, and (it was claimed) all parts of Scotland. A shorter journey in this direction was taken from Sheffield every Friday afternoon to Barnsley and Wakefield, arriving at Leeds on Monday morning. Goods taken to Leeds could be sent on to Knaresborough, Boroughbridge, Northallerton, Darlington, Newcastle and elsewhere in the north. Anderton also provided services to the West Midlands. Every Monday evening his waggon left for Bewdley, calling at Chesterfield, Derby, Walsall, Wolverhampton, Stourbridge and Kidderminster, arriving the following Saturday and returning the same day. From Bewdley other carriers took goods to all parts of Worcestershire, Gloucestershire, Herefordshire, Bristol, Exeter, Bridgwater and different parts of the West Country. Another of Anderton's waggons left China Square every Tuesday and headed for Derby, Lichfield and Birmingham, arriving on Saturday and returning the following Monday. From Birmingham goods could be dispatched to Coventry, Oxford, Worcester, Gloucester, Hereford, Bristol, Bath, Exeter and other places in the west.

Birmingham could also be reached from Sheffield twice a week by Sim's cart, via Ashford, Leek and Newcastle under Lyme. Another major destination was Manchester, which was reached by six services. Hibberson's waggons left his warehouse in Arundel Street on Tuesday and Friday evenings by way of Chapel en le Frith and Stockport, arriving on Thursdays and Mondays, and Goddard's waggon left the *Bird in Hand*, Church Lane, every Thursday evening along the same route, arriving on Monday morning. Oliver's Friday waggon chose the same highway, but his Tuesday and Saturday waggons went instead via the Woodhead road, calling at Wortley and Ashton under Lyne. From Manchester goods could be sent on to Chester, Liverpool and Macclesfield; alternatively, Macclesfield could be reached directly by Farnsworth's waggon, which crossed the moors three times a week by way of Hathersage, Hope and Chapel en le Frith. Each journey took a week. Other parts of Derbyshire were reached by Gregory's waggon, which used the new turnpike road down Froggatt Edge to Stoney Middleton, Hassop and Bakewell, or by three cart services; Jackson's cart linked Sheffield with Winster, Wirksworth and Ashbourne, and both Swinden's and Robinson's carts went by way of Stoney Middleton to Tideswell.

Anderton was not the only carrier to provide regular services to northern towns. Pashley's waggon went to Wortley, Penistone, Huddersfield and Halifax and Leadman's waggons followed the same route or went to Leeds. Longer journeys were undertaken twice a week by Sim's carts to Doncaster, Tadcaster and York, and each Monday and Friday Nicholson's waggons left the *King's Head* in Change Alley for Doncaster, Ferrybridge and Tadcaster, arriving at York on Saturdays and Tuesdays. They connected with carriers heading for Pontefract or Scarborough or Hull. Other parts of eastern England were reached by Gleddall's carts from the *Royal Oak* in King Street, which went twice a week to Tickhill, Retford and Gainsborough, or by Wasteney's two carts which started at the *Bay Horse* in High Street and headed for Worksop and Retford, thus linking with carriers to Gainsborough, Horncastle and Louth. Every Tuesday and Saturday Rodger's waggons left the *Black Swan* in Snig Hill for Dronfield, Chesterfield and Mansfield, and Oliver's waggon made a weekly journey to Cambridge, calling at Worksop, Newark, Grantham, Stamford and Huntingdon. By 1787 Sheffield carriers provided services in all directions and connecting services meant that no part of the kingdom was out of reach. The directory claimed that not only London but Birmingham, Wakefield, Doncaster, Hull, Leeds, Manchester, and even Carlisle and Edinburgh could be reached by stage-coach.

Few of these carrying businesses seem to have lasted more than one generation. Hibberson's waggons were still providing a regular service over the Pennines in 1822 and his business had expanded in other directions, but the firm that catches the eye in Baines's directory published that year is that of T. and M. Pickford & Co., who offered to convey or forward goods to all parts of the kingdom. This famous firm of national carriers was in business in the mid eighteenth century when an advertisement in the *Manchester Mercury* of 17 August 1756 described James Pickford as 'the London and Manchester waggoner'. By 1776 Pickfords had introduced 'fly waggons' which did this journey in 4½ days, averaging forty-two miles a day. By 1803 this service was provided six days a week and the firm had 400 horses to haul their waggons. [25] Pickfords successfully adapted to the rapid changes during the three or four decades following the publication of Gales and Martin's directory. An advertisement in the Sheffield newspaper, *The Iris*, dated 2 April 1816 shows how another firm had moved with the times:

> *Deacon, Harrison & Co., Carriers to and from Sheffield and London, By Waggons and Canal, Daily from Johnson and Sons' Warehouse, Gibraltar Street, Sheffield, by way of Chesterfield, Codnor Park Wharf, Nottingham, Loughboro', Leicester, Northampton, etc, to No. 90 London Wall, London, and No 6 Wharf, Paddington. D. H. & Co., return thanks to the Merchants and Manufacturers of Sheffield, and its Vicinity, for the very flattering encouragement they have experienced since they commenced the Carrying Business on the Grand Union and Junction Canals ... every morning for London, and every afternoon for Wakefield, Huddersfield, Leeds and York, whence goods are conveyed to all parts of the North and East, by the most respectable Carriers. N.B. A wagon every Day as usual from Wakefield to London, and Cambridge by way of Doncaster, etc.*

Deacon, Harrison & Co. took pains to thank the merchants and manufacturers, for although carriers were prepared to take virtually anything their main source of employment was the local tradesman. It is more than likely that this had always been the case.

Saltersbrook. The ancient saltway from Cheshire to South Yorkshire was made a turnpike road in 1732-41. It now forms part of the Trans-Pennine footpath. *Sheila Edwards.*

10 CONCLUSION

The recovery of the national economy from the reign of Queen Elizabeth onwards was matched by a steady growth in the size of the population. Whereas in the 1520s England contained some $2^1/_4$ million people, by the end of the seventeenth century numbers had risen to about $5^1/_2$ millions. For a century or so after 1640 the rate of growth slowed appreciably and at times the total number of inhabitants was only just maintained. However, even during this period of general stagnation the economy of certain regions continued to expand and the population of towns including Sheffield, Birmingham, Bristol, Liverpool, Manchester, Norwich and Nottingham grew at a rate which was astonishing to contemporaries. In order both to feed and to employ all those extra people the national economy underwent fundamental changes and the two centuries that followed the accession of Elizabeth saw substantial increases in production and trade. These improvements cannot be measured precisely, for statistics for this period are mere approximations, if they are available at all; nor was progress smooth and uninterrupted, for all trades had frequent periods of recession. Nevertheless, the country was clearly successful not only in coping with its greatly increased population but in raising the general standard of living. The role of the transport sector of the economy was obviously vital to this success.

During the early-modern period agricultural regions became more clearly defined and at the same time more efficiently integrated as farmers responded to market forces by specialising to a degree unknown before. The farmers of the Dove valley and of the Cheshire Plain found that they could pay for their imported malt and bread corn by selling cheese to the industrial workers of nearby towns or by sending their produce all the way to London. In the opposite direction the south Nottinghamshire farmers sent malt 'by land-carriage to Derby, through all the Peak as far as Manchester, and to other towns in Lancashire, Cheshire, and even into Yorkshire itself; to which end all the lower lands of this county, and especially on the banks of the Trent, yield prodigious crops of barley'. The hill-farmers of the Peak District were able to abandon most of their arable 'town fields' and to pay for imported corn and malt through the profits of their cattle and sheep and their industrial occupations.

Upon his visit to Halifax Daniel Defoe noted that hardly any corn was sown and little beef or mutton was reared, for the sale of cloth paid for imported food. 'Their corn', he observed, 'comes up in great quantities out of Lincoln, Nottingham, and the East Riding, their black cattle and horses from the North Riding, their sheep and mutton from the adjacent counties every way, their butter from the North and East Riding, their cheese out of Cheshire and Warwickshire, more black cattle also from Lancashire'. At the time that he was writing enormous quantities of food were being moved along the nation's highways, strapped in packs, stacked in carts and waggons, or simply taken on the hoof. Much of it was moved relatively short distances to local markets and fairs, but on certain routes traffic was as heavy as that on the great highway from Ipswich to London, a road described by Defoe as 'most worn with waggons, carts and carriages; and with infinite droves of black cattle, hogs, and sheep', and amazing numbers of geese and turkeys. [1]

This progress towards commercial agriculture was paralleled by unprecedented developments in industry. Joan Thirsk has shown how a deliberate government policy initiated in the 1540s fostered new industries so as to reduce the country's dependence upon foreign imports and to provide employment for the growing population. [2] Great numbers of women and children as well as men found work in the many new, labour-intensive crafts that spread to the far corners of the land during the sixteenth and seventeenth centuries. One of the most successful of these crafts was framework knitting; 'One would scarce think it possible', wrote Defoe, 'so small an article of trade could employ such multitudes of people as it does'. for the whole of the people of Leicestershire and much of those in Nottinghamshire and Derbyshire seemed to find employment in it. [3] The hand-knitting of stockings in the Doncaster district was another trade that had been introduced deliberately. Long before the Industrial Revolution England had a consumer society catered for by an astonishing variety of industries. In our region old-established crafts underwent qualitative changes and spread into rural hamlets well away from the original centres. The cutlers of Sheffield produced quality goods, certain rural parishes concentrated upon particular products, such as scythes, sickles or forks, and other rural workers turned out cheap, common wares. Hallamshire products were sold in distant markets, from Herefordshire to Scotland and from Kendal to King's Lynn, but the expansion of the metal trades was brought about not only by increased demands from other parts of the country but by the spectacular growth of the American market from the late seventeenth century onwards. In 1721 the Cutlers' Company claimed that more than half their products were sold abroad. The beneficial effects of overseas trade on certain sectors of the economy must be stressed even though historians now recognise that the nation as a whole was far more dependent upon internal trade, which handled perhaps a quarter or even a third of Gross National Product in the sixteenth and seventeenth centuries. [4]

Based originally on local deposits of iron ore, the metalworking trades became increasingly dependent upon Continental imports for the manufacture of high-class products. The Hallamshire cutlers spent much energy and money on improving the Don navigation, which served both as their supply route for Continental iron and their major outlet towards their markets. But they appear to have had no difficulty in selling their wares in towns and villages that were accessible only by packhorse routes over the hills and they did not turn their attention to turnpike roads until the mid 1750s, when the Don navigation was complete. The lead merchants and quarry owners had to wait until the succeeding canal age before they could improve their waterway, but as they too were in a sellers' market this did not prove much of a hindrance. Even though the Peak District was one of the most landlocked places in the country and the Peakland roads amongst the most difficult, these trades flourished mightily. The coalfield, however, could not be properly exploited until canals and railways were built, for the coalmasters of north-east England had the inestimable advantage of immediate access to the sea.

The region was also fortunate in that its farming was geared towards the rearing of cattle rather than the growing of corn. Throughout the seventeenth century good prices could be obtained for beef and dairy produce, but farmers whose land was more suited to cereals and sheep found that the prices they were offered were continually depressed. Whereas in the arable areas of the country smallholders could no longer earn a living, in the pastoral district small farmers not only survived but flourished. [5] In our region smallholdings were supplemented by generous common rights and farmers had the opportunity of additional employment in rural industry. The origins of the Industrial Revolution are to be sought not in those areas where the peasant structure of society was destroyed but precisely in those regions which long retained the characteristic features of the peasant way of life. The industrial crafts that were nourished in the early-modern period eventually provided the capital, the labour force, the technical knowledge and the entrepreneurs that were necessary to launch and sustain the Industrial Revolution. The new industrial era was forged in the countryside as well as in the towns.

The growth of a consumer society during the two centuries that elapsed between the accession of Queen Elizabeth and the start of the reign of George III meant that the number of middlemen increased significantly. Defoe observed that

> *the shopkeepers in Bristol who in general are all wholesale men, have so great an inland trade among all the western counties, that they maintain carriers just as the London tradesmen do, to all the principal counties and towns from Southampton in the south, even to the banks of the Trent north; and tho' they have no navigable river that way, yet they drive a very great trade through all these counties.* [6]

The middlemen of the early-modern period ranged from lowly pedlars, badgers and part-time carriers to substantial factors and merchants. The wealthiest dealers did not reside in our region, for agricultural conditions did not favour the emergence of rich graziers or corn factors, and the prosperous men in the lead trade were mineral owners and smelters, not middlemen.

Even in Hallamshire few cutlery chapmen or ironmongers were known as merchants and hardly any of them rose to the prominence achieved by the merchant-manufacurers in the textile trades. But middlemen of less exalted status were essential in the development of the local economy and numerous families supplemented their earnings by part-time carrying, especially in the summer season. Throughout the country middlemen operated in a favourable climate, for English internal trade was largely free of taxes and in the later seventeenth century attempts to enforce the old restrictive statutes were largely abandoned. Though the market place and the fair ground remained the most important venues for trade, much private buying and selling was done at the inn or the farmhouse. By 1726 Daniel Defoe could describe the internal trade of the nation as 'the wonder of all the world of trade'.[7]

In retrospect, the extent of the foreign trade of our region is equally astonishing. This cannot be measured with firm statistics or even with approximate figures, but time and time again unexpected insights are received from snippets of information. We are taken by surprise when we read that in the middle of the seventeenth century Norton scythesmiths made a special type of scythe for Scottish farmers and later were producing goods for America; that in the 1730s south Yorkshire nailers were exporting their wares to Newfoundland, Jamaica and the Leeward Isles; that in the middle sixteenth century exotic spices could be purchased in Ashbourne market; and that in 1587 the appraisers of the probate inventory of Thomas Fletcher, a yeoman-clothier of the parish of Chesterfield, had no difficulty in giving an English value to the six Spanish coins that they found in his purse. [8]

Bills, bonds and other debts recorded in thousands of inventories from all over the country show how widespread was the use of credit. Even before 1700 borrowing and lending were normal features of English life amongst all classes and in all parts of the country. [9] The use of credit for commercial purposes formed only part of a well-developed system. Short-term liquidity problems could usually be dealt with from local sources and longer-term commercial credit formed the very basis of the nation's trade. As J. A. Chartres has written, the growth of credit mechanisms and the diffusion of credit downwards to lesser producers and traders added significantly to the absolute volume of inland trade. [10] Derbyshire and Yorkshire probate inventories make it abundantly clear that credit was readily available for trade and other purposes throughout our region.

The growth of trade in the early-modern period meant that the range of carrying services had to be expanded. Although most goods were carried over relatively short distances by part-timers, long-distance carriage required the services of professionals. Yorkshire and Derbyshire had well-established weekly carrying services to London by 1637, for the capital was not only a major centre of consumption but the distribution centre for much of the home market and, later, for the trade with America. By the early eighteenth century, if not before, Derbyshire lay just near enough for goods to be taken all the way by waggon, whereas Yorkshire carriers such as Abraham Pilling of Doncaster relied upon packhorses. Although wheeled traffic was used for short-distance work within the region during the early-modern period, Yorkshire waggoners did not travel to the capital regularly until the roads were turnpiked. The same appears to be true of Lancashire, for near the close of the eighteenth century John Aikin reflected on the changes that had occurred during the lifetime of old people in the Manchester area:

> *For the first thirty years of the present century, the old established houses confined their trades to the wholesale dealers in London, Bristol, Norwich, Newcastle, and those who frequented Chester fair. The profits were thus distributed between the manufacturer, the wholesale, and the retail, dealer ... When the Manchester trade began to expand, the chapmen used to keep gangs of pack-horses, and accompany them to the provincial towns with goods in packs, which they opened and sold to shop-keepers, lodging what was unsold at small stores at the inns. The pack-horse brought back sheep's wool, which was bought on the journey, and sold to the makers of worsted yarn at Manchester, or to the clothiers of Rochdale, Saddleworth, and the West Riding of Yorkshire. On the improvement of turnpike roads waggons were set up, and the packhorses discontinued; and the chapmen only rode out for orders, carrying with them patterns in their bags. It was during the forty years from 1730 to 1770 that trade was greatly pushed by the practice of sending these riders all over the kingdom, to those towns which before had been supplied from the wholesale dealers in the capital places before mentioned.* [11]

The general drift of his remarks also applies to the Sheffield cutlers, though they were tardier than the Manchester men in establishing turnpike roads and in discarding packhorses for waggons.

John Leland, who toured the country late in the reign of Henry VIII, rarely complained about the condition of the nation's highways, but during the next generation or two the ancient roads of the kingdom had to take the strain of an unprecedented volume of traffic. [12] Lengthy trains of packhorses, great droves of animals, and heavy waggons and carts became increasingly familiar sights on routes leading to the capital and to the provincial markets and fairs or to the river and sea ports. Purely local traffic such as grindstones for the cutlers, rod iron for nailers, charcoal for the furnaces, coal for domestic and industrial consumption, building stone, leather goods, meat and dairy produce, lime for the fields, and a large assortment of other goods that were moved relatively short distances far exceeded in quantity anything that had gone before. Successive Tudor and Stuart governments responded to the problem of how to maintain roads used by so much traffic by creating and extending a new system of administration based on the parish.

Numerous individual bequests supplemented the work of the official system as people became conscious of the need for better highways. Though road surfaces were often muddy and rutted and unusable in winter, this did not prevent the movement of heavy goods in dry seasons. Sensational accounts of eighteenth-century travellers must not blind us to the fact that horse-drawn waggons and carts could negotiate poor roads, albeit slowly, and that packhorses needed only a track. As T. S. Willan has observed, given the size of the sixteenth- and seventeenth-century population and the nature of the economy, it would have been a waste of resources to have improved roads to later standards. Nor would such improvement have necessarily reduced transport costs, for transport agencies were small and labour intensive and could practice no economy of scale. [13]

Justices of the Peace responded to the increasing volume of traffic in the late seventeenth and early eighteenth centuries by providing guide stoops, causeys, and stone bridges. Whereas in the Middle Ages only the most important bridges were built of stone, by the 1720s Defoe could find no timber bridges in the north. [14] Even the parish authorities now built their packhorse bridges of stone. The century after the Restoration saw substantial improvements in the means of carriage, particularly in the provision of wheeled vehicles. By 1715, for instance, London was connected to all parts of the provinces by over 900 weekly coach services and the number was soon to grow again. [15] At that time south Yorkshire could be reached from the capital in three days, despite the difficulties of crossing the heavy midland clays, which Defoe thought were 'perfectly frightful to travellers'. On the road from London to Northampton, Leicester and Nottingham or Derby 'these terrible clays' were found all the way from Dunstable to the Trent, so that 'it has been the wonder of foreigners, how, considering the great number of carriages which are continually passing with heavy loads, those ways have been made practicable'. [16]

The inability of the parish repair system to cope with the increasing amount of traffic on the most important thoroughfares led to the formation of turnpike trusts empowered to levy tolls for the upkeep and improvement of particular stretches of road. Petitions presented to the House of Commons frequently claimed that certain highways could not be maintained by the ordinary laws of the realm unless tolls were levied to supplement statutory labour. The first turnpike trust was established in 1663 to deal with a particular difficult section of the Great North Road in Hertfordshire and Cambridgeshire, but the experiment was not repeated elsewhere until 1696. The idea spread slowly at first but after 1750 gathered momentum quickly. [17] The first turnpike road in our region (the fiftieth in England) was that from Manchester to Buxton and Chapel en le Frith, part of the great highway to London which was wholly turnpiked by the middle of the eighteenth century.

A petition presented to the House of Commons on 16 December 1724 claimed that the Manchester to Buxton or Chapel road was 'the most direct Way from the Town of Manchester to the City of London; and is very deep and bad, and in some Parts so bad, that Coaches and Waggons cannot pass through the same with safety'. Less than five years later, William Wright claimed that before these roads were turnpiked in 1725 they 'were so bad in many Places, that they were almost impassable', but now they were fit for wheeled vehicles as well as packhorses. The turnpike trustees appear to have been taken by surprise by the speed with which wheeled vehicles replaced many of the packhorse services. An amending Act of 1731 stated that, 'Whereas the manner of carriage over the said roads was usually by packhorses ... by the great amendment and widening of the said roads [it] is of late changed into wheeled traffic, whereby the said tolls have been greatly diminished'. William Wright explained that 'the greatest part of the Toll has been raised by Horses, carrying Malt from Derby, and the parts adjacent into Cheshire; but Malt has, since the Road was in part repaired, been chiefly carried by Carts, drawn with Two Horses; which has very much lessened the Profit of the Toll'. [18]

Early attempts at improvement elsewhere in the region were concentrated upon cross-country routes heading for the inland ports. A scheme of 1739 improved the roads from Chesterfield to Mansfield and Worksop (and so on to Bawtry), but failed in its ambition to provide a turnpike road across the moors from Bakewell to Chesterfield. Two years later, the great Pennine highway from Manchester and Stockport via Saltersbrook was turnpiked as far as the Don navigation at Rotherham and Doncaster. The river had been made navigable to Rotherham by 1740 and the bulk of the exports of south-west Yorkshire went this way. Water transport was still so much cheaper than land carriage.

The local thoroughfares and by-ways that were mapped by Burdett and Jeffreys in the 1760s had existed from time immemorial. Some went back to prehistoric times, many others to before the Norman Conquest, and most of them had been firmly established by the end of the Middle Ages. In the half-century or so following the publication of these maps the ancient pattern was altered radically for the first time when enclosure commissioners laid out their distinctive straight lanes across the former commons and wastes and new turnpike trusts scorned the cautious approach of their predecessors by constructing roads along the valleys instead of merely improving the old hill routes. The turnpiking of the most important highways led to a rapid decline in the status of other through routes. Some continued to cater for local traffic and were straightened and widened by enclosure commissioners, but as we have seen others are now abandoned and overgrown, hardly recognisable as ancient tracks.

Derelict highways on the Coal Measure sandstones tend to survive only in short stretches, but on the Pennine moorlands the whole pattern is preserved, for the blanket of peat that covers the moors has been deeply cut by hooves and wheels. The Big Moor, in particular, retains a great deal of evidence on the ground in the form of an extensive network of sunken tracks, short lengths of laid causeys, several guide stoops and one or two slab bridges. Vast quantities of lead and great numbers of millstones came this way and malt, coal and other goods went in the opposite direction. The amount of traffic in the summer time must have been considerable. The fully-fledged turnpike system helped the much greater industrial expansion that took place later, but the initial growth of trade occurred before the old highways were improved substantially. Heavy and bulky goods were transported regularly over some of the most difficult terrain in the land. As Daniel Defoe said upon visiting the High Peak: 'This, perhaps, is the most desolate, wild, and abandoned country in all England'. [19]

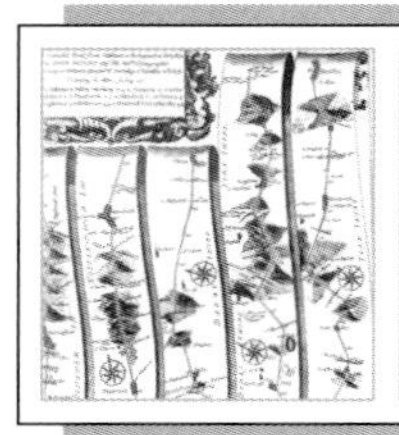

ABBREVIATIONS

AHR:	*Agricultural History Review*
Bestall and Fowkes:	J. M. Bestall and D. V. Fowkes (eds), *Chesterfield Wills and Inventories, 1521-1603 (1977)*
Borthwick:	Borthwick Institute of Historical Research, York
Cameron:	K. Cameron, *The Place-Names of Derbyshire*, 3 vols (1959)
Cox:	J. C. Cox, *Three Centuries of Derbyshire Annals*, II (1890)
DAJ:	*Derbyshire Archaeological Journal*
Defoe:	D. Defoe, *Tour through the Whole Island of Great Britain*, Everyman edition, 2 vols (1962)
Dodd:	A.E. and E. M. Dodd, *Peakland Roads and Trackways*, 3rd ed. 2000
EcHR:	*Economic History Review*
Hobson:	'The Journal of Mr. John Hobson, late of Dodworth Green', *Surtees Society*, LXV (1875)
JHC:	*Journal of the House of Commons*
Morris:	C. Morris (ed.), *The Journeys of Celia Fiennes* (1947)
RO:	Record Office
Ronksley:	J. Ronksley (ed.), *John Harrison: An exact and perfect survey and review of the manor of Sheffield, 1637* (1908)
SA:	Sheffield Archives
Smith:	A. H. Smith, *The Place-Names of the West Riding of Yorkshire*, I (1961)
THAS:	*Transactions of the Hunter Archaeological Society*
VCH:	*Victoria County History*
YAS:	*Yorkshire Archaeological Society*

44 *Ibid.*, 7; W. T. Jackman, *The Development of Transportation in Modern Britain* (1916), 34; SA, *Calendar of the Talbot Correspondence*, 2/155.
45 A. Browning (ed.), *The Memoirs of Sir John Reresby* (1936), 34, 169, 196-7, 341, 388, 429. A Hackney carriage was a four-wheeled and cumbersome vehicle that seated six people. The name comes from an Old French word for an ambling horse, which by the fourteenth century was anglicised to mean 'let for hire'.
46 Hobson, 193, 252.
47 Advertisement in the *Sheffield Public Advertiser*, 4 November 1760; M. Walton, *Sheffield: Its story and achievement* (1969), 130; H. S. Twells, 'Derby's flying machines and earliest coaches', *DAJ*, LXIV (1943), 64-82.
48 *Calendar to the Records of the Borough of Doncaster*, IV (1902), 10-11, 13; Hobson, 248, note.
49 Defoe, II, 181.
50 Buckley and Ward, *op. cit.*, 13-16, quoting *State Papers Domestic, Charles II* (SP 29), I, 88, no. 100.
51 3 George II, c.4.
52 Hobson, 307.
53 Brotherton library, Wilson, CLIX, fos. 59, 71, 64.

Chapter 5 Water transport

1 T. S. Willan, *The Inland Trade* (1976), 1; E. Pawson, *Transport and Economy: The turnpike roads of eighteenth century Britain* (1977), 22-5; D. Hussey, *Coastal and River Trade in Pre-Industrial England: Bristol and its Region, 1680-1730* (2000); M. D. G. Wanklyn, 'The impact of water transport facilities on English river ports, c.1660- c.1760', *EcHR*, XLIX (1996), 1-19.
2 *JHC*, XXIII (1737-41), 575.
3 T. S. Willan, *River Navigation in England, 1660-1750* (1936), 96-7.
4 Borthwick, wills and inventories.
5 British Library, Lansdowne, 897; Public RO, WO/30/48.
6 D. Hey, *The Making of South Yorkshire* (1979), 58-60; D. Holland, *Bawtry and the Idle River Trade* (1976), 1. Excavations in 1990-91 have proved the existence of a late Anglo-Saxon settlement near the wharf; R. E. Sydes and J. Dunkley, 'Excavations in Bawtry', *Archaeology in South Yorkshire, 1990-1991* (1991), 32-39.
7 L. T. Smith, *Leland's Itinerary in England and Wales*, I (1964), 34.
8 SA, MD 192; Bestall and Fowkes, xxv, 17.
9 T. W. Hall, *A Descriptive Catalogue of Sheffield Manorial Records*, II (1928), 217; Public RO, E134/15 and 16 Charles I/Hil.10.
10 L. Stone, *The Crisis of the Aristocracy, 1558-1641* (1965), 341-4 (in 1579 Earl George tried unsuccessfully to obtain from the queen a lease of the customs of lead throughout the country); R. Davis, *The Trade and Shipping of Hull, 1500-1700* (1964), 13.
11 SA, Crewe, 1,679.
12 Public RO, E134/17 James I/Mich.7.
13 Public RO, E134/18 James I/East.21/no.78 York.
14 *Cf.* Thomas Bartholomew, 'mariner, at the common stay' in 1567 (Hall, *Sheffield Manorial Records*, II, *op. cit.*, 217); Stephen Bartholomew of Bawtry, 'boatman' in 1597 (SA, Crewe, 1,740); Peter Bartholomew, 'waterman' in 1611 (SA, Crewe, 1,611).
15 SA, Crewe, 1,792.
16 SA, Crewe, 1,680 and 1,696; Public RO, E134/15 and 16 Charles I/Hil.10.
17 D. Hey (ed.), *The Hearth Tax Returns for South Yorkshire, Ladyday 1672* (1991), 17; SA, Crewe, 1,902; in 1779 Misses Elizabeth and Judith Lister sold Bawtry hall and manor to Pemberton Milnes of Wakefield, esquire, whose descendant became (in 1895) the Earl of Crewe.

18 Holland, *op. cit.*, 3; J. Hunter, *South Yorkshire: The history and topography of the deanery of Doncaster*, I (1828), 234.
19 SA, Crewe, 1,698.
20 L. A. Clarkson, 'The leather crafts in Tudor and Stuart England', *AHR*, XIV (1966), 25-39; D. F. E. Sykes, *History of Huddersfield and the Valleys of the Colne, the Holme and the Dearne* (n.d.), 169-70.
21 Public RO, WO/30/48.
22 SA, Crewe, 1,704 and 1,705; SA, Staveley iron records, 12 and 13 mention exports of ironware through Bawtry in the early 1690s.
23 Defoe, II, 181.
24 Holland, *op. cit.*, 4-9.
25 SA, Tibbits, 515 and 516.
26 SA, *Calendar of the Talbot Correspondence*, 2/74; G. G. Hopkinson, 'The business transac tions of Richard Dalton, raff merchant, 1739-49', *THAS*, VIII, I (1958), 16-18.
27 T. S. Willan, *The History of the Don Navigation* (1965), 1; *cf.* 147: cheese was brought from Cheshire through Barnsley, 'being the more passable way than the moors towards Sheffield'.
28 *Calendar to the Records of the Borough of Doncaster*, I (1899), 92; SA, Staveley iron records, 17.
29 A. Everitt in J. Thirsk (ed.), *The Agrarian History of England and Wales*, IV, *1500-1640* (1967), 499, 503; Public RO, WO/30/48; Defoe, II, 181.
30 The following account is based on Willan, *Don Navigation, op. cit.*
31 Hopkinson, *op. cit.*, 17.
32 A canal from Tinsley to Sheffield was opened in 1819.
33 West Yorks RO, quarter sessions order books (Pontefract, 11 April 1738).
34 E. Baines, *History, Directory and Gazetteer of the County of York*, I (1822), 140; D. Holland (ed.), *New Light on Old Bawtry* (1978), 1-8.

Chapter 6 The carriage of minerals and manufactured goods

1 *JHC*, XIX (1718-21), 230; W. G. D. Fletcher (ed.), 'Philip Kinder's Ms "Historie of Darbyshire"', *The Reliquary*, old series, XXIII (1882-3), 9.
2 D. Kiernan, *The Derbyshire Lead Industry in the Sixteenth Century* (1989); D. Crossley and D. Kiernan, 'The Lead-Smelting Mills of Derbyshire', *DAJ*, CXII (1992), 6-48; N. Kirkham, *Derbyshire Lead Mining through the Centuries* (1968), 98; *VCH Derbyshire*, II (1907), 324; P. Dover, *The Early Medieval History of Boston, 1086-1400* (1972), 9; O. Coleman (ed.), *The Brokage Book of Southampton, 1443-4*, II (1961), 258, 280.
3 Cameron, I, 88-9; J. H. Brooksbank, 'The Forest of the Peak'. *THAS*, I, 4, 337-55; Smith, 174; Crump, 4; T. Wright, *Dictionary of Obsolete and Provincial English* (1857), 599; Bestall and Fowkes, 196, 287; J. Wright, *The English Dialect Dictionary* (1898-1905), 343-4.
4 A. Wood, *The Politics of Social Conflict: The Peak Country, 1520-1770* (1999), 53-66.
5 Kirkham, *op. cit.*, 25, 85, 92; T. D. Ford and J. H. Rieuwerts (eds), *Lead Mining in the Peak District* (2000), 26-29, Landmark.
6 SA, Beauchief, 80; SA, Bagshawe Eyre, 1,366 A and 358; S. C. Newton, 'The gentry of Derbyshire in the seventeenth century', *DAJ*, LXXXVI (1966), 1-30.
7 A. Raistrick and B. Jennings, *A History of Lead Mining in the Pennines* (1965), 268-9.
8 W. A. Carrington, 'Selections from the steward's accounts preserved at Haddon Hall, for the years 1549 and 1564', *DAJ*, XVI (1894), 61-85; J. Radley and S. R. Penny, 'The turnpike roads of the Peak District', *DAJ*, XCII (1972), 93-109 (note 2); H. Harris, *Industrial Archaeology of the Peak District* (1971), 162; *Sheffield Clarion Ramblers' Handbook for 1953-4*, 79; Notts. RO, DDP 42/10.
9 Raistrick and Jennings, *op. cit.*, 270.
10 I. S. W. Blanchard, 'Economic change in Derbyshire in the late Middle Ages, 1272-1540' (unpublished PhD thesis, University of London, 1967), 417; *VCH Derbyshire*, II (1907), 346.

11 J. P. Polak in V. S. Doe (ed.), *Essays in the History of Holmesfield, 1550-1714* (1975), 22; Notts.RO, Foljambe, 617; Cox, 227; T. S. Willan, *The Inland Trade* (1976), 74.
12 J. Houghton, *A Collection for Improvement of Husbandry and Trade* (1692), II, no. 38.
13 SA, *Calendar of the Talbot Correspondence*, 2/75; SA, BR 51; Polak, *op. cit.*, 72.
14 Carrington, *op. cit.*, 70; D. Kiernan, (ed.), 'Lawrence Oxley's Accounts, 1672-81' in *A Seventeenth-Century Scarsdale Miscellany* (Derbyshire Record Society, XX, 1993), 121-83; *JHC*, XIX (1718-21), 222.
15 Lichfield Joint RO, probate inventories, quoted in A. Hopkinson, 'Study of a Village: Killamarsh, 1535-1750', dissertation for the Certificate in Local History, University of Sheffield (1984), on which this paragraph is based.
16 YAS, Duke of Leeds collection, DD5/5/155.
17 Notts. RO, DDP 65/47.
18 L. T. Smith, *Leland's Itinerary in England and Wales* (1964), IV, 13-14.
19 J. T. Cliffe, *The Yorkshire Gentry from the Reformation to the Civil war* (1969), 61; SA, Beauchief, 80. See also J. V. Beckett and J. P. Polak (eds), 'The Scarsdale Surveys of 1652-62' in *A Seventeenth-Century Scarsdale Miscellany* (Derbyshire Record Society, XX, 1993), 69.
20 L. Stone, 'An Elizabethan coal mine', *EcHR*, III, 1 (1950), 97-106; G. G. Hopkinson, 'The development of the south Yorkshire and north Derbyshire coalfield, 1550-1775', *THAS*, VII, 6 (1957), 295-319.
21 Hopkinson, *op. cit.*, quoting *Magna Britannia et Hibernia*, VI (1730), 448; SA, MD 1,769; Defoe, II, 183.
22 SA, Bagshawe Eyre, 1,213; Cliffe, *op. cit.*, 59. Sea-coal was so-called because it was taken to the capital by sea.
23 C. Kerry (ed.), 'Ashover memoranda by Titus Wheatcroft, AD 1722', *DAJ*, XIX (1897), 24-52; W. Bray, *Sketch of a Tour into Derbyshire and Yorkshire* (1783), 174-5.
24 F. Thompson, *A History of Chatsworth* (1949), 91.
25 I am indebted to John Heath for this reference.
26 *VCH Derbyshire*, II, 350.
27 Houghton, *op. cit.*, II, no. 38.
28 Cox, 227; Cameron, I, 75. See A. F. Roberts and J. R. Leach, *The Coal Mines of Buxton* (1985), 13-24 for a discussion of the holloways leading from pits on Axe Edge and in the Goyt valley and the markets for this coal.
29 B. Elliott, 'John Foster of Woolley: an early eighteenth century coal master', in D. Holland (ed.), *The South Yorkshire Historian*, no. 3 (1976), 18-21.
30 SA, WWM D 1,727; G. L. Gomme (ed.), *Topographical History of Worcestershire and Yorkshire: A classified collection of the chief contents of the Gentleman's Magazine from 1731 to 1868* (1902), 227-30.
31 Smith, 184 (and 212 re Pitsmoor); *cf.* a thirteenth-century reference to 'les Orepittes of Brimington' in T. W. Hall and A. H. Thomas, *A Descriptive Catalogue of the Jackson Collection* (1914), 108; T. W. Hall, *A Descriptive Catalogue of Sheffield Manorial Records*, II (1928), 224-5; Derbys. RO, 1005 Z/EI; D. Crossley and D. Ashurst, 'Excavations at Rockley Smithies, a water-powered bloomery of the sixteenth and seventeenth centuries', *Post-Medieval Archaeology*, II (1968), 10-54.
32 SA, Beauchief, 80; A. Raistrick, 'The South Yorkshire iron industry, 1698-1756', *Trans. Newcomen Soc.*, XIX (1938-9), 51-86; A. Raistrick and E. Allen, 'The South Yorkshire ironmasters, 1690-1750', *EcHR*, old series, IX (1939), 168-85; P. Riden (ed.), *George Sitwell's Letterbook, 1662-66* (1985).
33 D. Hey, 'The ironworks at Chapeltown', *THAS*, X, 4 (1977), 252-9.
34 A. Raistrick, *Industrial Archaeology* (1972), 210, 231; M. Jones, *Trees, Woods and People: Habitat, History and Heritage* (2000); SA, Staveley iron records, 12-16; G. G. Hopkinson, 'The charcoal iron industry in the Sheffield region', *THAS*, VIII, 3 (1961), 122-51; SA, *Calendar of the Talbot Correspondence*, 2/162.

35 Raistrick, *Industrial Archaeology, op. cit.*, 231; SA, *Calendar of the Talbot Correspondence*, 2/132; SA, Sp.St. 60493-1.
36 P. Riden, *George Sitwell's Letterbook, 1662-66* (1985), xxii-xxiii; C. R. Andrews, *The Story of Wortley Ironworks* (1956), 69-70; SA, Sp.St. 60,471, 60,464; K. Barraclough, *Sheffield Steel* (1976), 11: the transport charges of pig iron from Bank furnace to Wortley forge in 1696 were higher in the winter.
37 SA, Staveley iron records, 12-15.
38 This account is based on D. Hey, *The Rural Metalworkers of the Sheffield Region* (1972).
39 L. T. Smith, *op. cit.*, IV, 14; D. Hey, *The Fiery Blades of Hallamshire: Sheffield and its Neighbourhood, 1660-1740* (1991); C. Binfield and D. Hey (eds), *Mesters to Masters: A History of the Company of Cutlers in Hallamshire* (1997).
40 Hey, *Rural Metalworkers, op. cit.*, 8-9; T. W. Hall, *Sheffield, 1297 to 1554* (1913), 100; SA, MP 1,479 M; Lichfield Joint RO, probate Inventories.
41 *Cf.* J. Roper, *Early North Worcestershire Scythesmiths* (1967); W. Cobbett, *Rural Rides*, II (1930), 609; J. Pilkington, *A View of the Present State of Derbyshire* (1789), II, 380; SA, BM 54 (the accounts of Jonathan Hopkinson, scythesmith of Hutcliffe Wheel in the late 1780s refer to customers in Lincoln, Nottingham, Peterborough, Stamford, Grantham and Newark).
42 D. M. Woodward, *The Trade of Elizabethan Chester* (1970), 18; A. D. Dyer, *The City of Worcester in the Sixteenth Century* (1973), 91-2.
43 M. B. Rowlands, *Masters and Men in the West Midland Metalware Trades Before the Industrial Revolution* (1975), 32; SA, Wheat, 1,961 and Tibbits, 1,053a; W. Davies, *Agriculture of North Wales* (1810), 386.
44 P. Riden (ed.), *George Sitwell's Letterbook, 1662-66* (1985), 172; Defoe, II, 183; T. S. Willan, *The History of the Don Navigation* (1965), 6; *JHC*, XXIII (1737-41), 302 and XX (1722-7), 16.
45 Borthwick, inventories: 'olivante' is a phonetic spelling of elephant, implying ivory; R. E. Leader, *A History of the Company of Cutlers in Hallamshire*, I (1905), 151.
46 Barraclough, *op. cit.*, 10-11; Bestall and Fowkes, XXV, 17; SA, MD 192; R. E. Leader, *op. cit.*, I, 151; J. D. Leader, *The Records of the Burgery of Sheffield* (1897), 149, 178; Borthwick, inventories.
47 SA, Leader, 70-78; D. Hey, *Fiery Blades, op. cit.*, 183-96; R. E. Leader, *op. cit.*, I, 153; G. Jackson, *Hull in the Eighteenth Century: A study in economic and social history* (1972), 31, 40.
48 SA, MD 3,483; J. D. Marshall (ed.), *The Autobiography of William Stout of Lancaster, 1665-1752* (1967), 160; SA, Tibbits, 1,043.
49 Marshall, *op. cit.*, 90, 96, 106, 109, 113-14, 160, 256 (and note 11).
50 J. Aikin, *A Description of the Country from Thirty to Forty Miles around Manchester* (1795), 548; SA, *Calendar of the Talbot Correspondence*, 2/133; Borthwick, inventories; *cf.* SA, Leader, 70-8 (16 March 1726 letter from Sheffield to London saying that razors, knives, forks and scissors are being sent in James Smith's bags).
51 D. Hey, *Fiery Blades*, *op. cit.*, 156-62.
52 Rowlands, *op. cit.*, 66, 99.
53 Borthwick, wills; SA, Jackson, 1,693; Thomas Parkin of Sheffield, ironmonger, appears in the West Riding quarter sessions records for 1702.
54 SA, Sp.St. 60,471 and Staveley iron records, 14 and 15.
55 R. G. Wilson, *Gentlemen Merchants: The merchant community in Leeds, 1700-1830* (1971).
56 Borthwick, wills and inventories: John Holland (1698) 'Stock in Lead, £150, A part of a Ship, £17, Mortgage, £400, 2 bonds, £280', etc: Field Sylvester, gent. (1717). Samuel Shore appears as merchant in the Sheffield parish register in 1716.
57 L. H. Butcher, 'Archaeological remains on the Wharncliffe-Greno upland, South York shire', *THAS*, VII, 1 (1957), 38; Smith, 246, 199-300.
58 J. Radley, 'Peak Millstones and Hallamshire grindstones', *Trans. Newcomen Soc.*, XXXV (1963-4), 168; D. G. Tucker, 'Millstones, Quarries and millstone-makers', *Post-Medieval Archaeology*, XI (1977), 1-21; E. Curtis, 'Sheffield in the fourteenth century: two Furnival

inquisitions', *THAS*, I, 1 (1914), 41; Blanchard, 'Economic change', *op. cit.*, 371; R. Meredith, 'Millstone Making at Yarncliff in the reign of Edward IV', *DAJ*, CI (1981), 102-6; Dodd, 65.

59 J. P. Polak, 'The Production and Distribution of Peak Millstones from the Sixteenth to the Eighteenth Centuries', *DAJ*, CVII (1987), 55-72; Dover, *op. cit.*, 24; G. C. Dunning, 'The stone mortar in Little Baddow Church', *Medieval Archaeology*, XIX (1975), 161-3.

60 SA, Crewe, 1,679; Cameron, I, 112; S. Wilkin (ed.), *Sir Thomas Browne's Works* (1836), 29; R. Blome, *Britannia* (1673), 257, 75; J. Hunter (ed.), *The Diary of Ralph Thoresby*, I (1830), 164.

61 Radley, *op. cit.*, 168, quoting SA, BR 185 (c) 263. The probate inventory of Thomas Sutton of Oakerthorpe (1618) refers to 'one paire of Milnstones standinge at Handley', valued at £8, and to two pairs of millstones worth £22.10s. Sutton was a yeoman farmer who appears to have been carting millstones (Lichfield Joint RO, inventories).

62 Houghton, *op. cit.*, II, no. 44.

63 Brotherton library, Wilson, CLIX f. 79.

64 Fletcher, *op. cit.*, XXII (1881-2), 184; A. H. Thomas, 'Some Hallamshire Rolls of the fifteenth century', *THAS*, II, 1 (1920), 65-79; Ronksley; G. I. H. Lloyd, *The Cutlery Trades* (1913), 153-4.

65 M. Plant, 'A scythestone industry on Beeley Moor', *DAJ*, LXXXVIII 1968), 98-100; Kerry, *op. cit.*

66 E. Miller, *The History and Antiquities of Doncaster and its Vicinity* (1804), 317; E. Rhodes, *Yorkshire Scenery* (1826), pt I, 69.

67 Hobson, 315, 323.

68 L. F. Salzman, *Buildings in England Down to 1540; A documentary history* (1952), 131-2; L. T. Smith, *op. cit.*, I, 35.

69 Public RO, E 317 Yorks. 15; Morris, 95; Ronksley.

70 B. Stallybras, 'Bess of Hardwick's buildings and building accounts', *Archaeologia*, LXIV (1912-13), 386, and *cf.* 366 (19 July 1589: 'To Parker the slater for XX hundred slate of Whittington More'). See also D. N. Durant and P. Riden (eds), *The Building of Hardwick Hall*, I (1980) and II (1984).

71 Morris, 54, 170, 238; H. Martineau, *Guide to the Lakes* (1855), illustration of Honister Crag from the quarry road to Yew Crag. An eighteenth-century painting of 'Bristol Docks and Quay' in Bristol City Art Gallery shows goods being transported on horse-drawn sleds.

72 *Sheffield Clarion Ramblers' Handbook for 1927*, 104. This map has not been located.

73 SA, Bagshawe, 313, printed in R. Meredith, 'Hathersage Affairs', *THAS*, XI (1981), 14-27.

74 Brotherton library, Wilson, CLIX f. 94-5.

75 Stallybras, *op. cit.*, 386; British Library, Lansdowne, 897.

76 Corporation of London RO, rental 6.16, f. 18; SA, Bright papers, JE 97, JE 99.

77 SA, Elmhirst, M 1,005 and 1,006.

78 Public RO, E 317 Derbys. 12 and 20; Kerry, *op. cit.*, 25; Derbys. RO, D803/ME3.

79 Bray, *op. cit.*, 174-5' Pilkington, *op. cit.*, II, 312; Harris, *op. cit.*, 163.

80 D. Hey, *The Making of South Yorkshire* (1979), 103, 124.

81 J. Thirsk (ed.), *The Agrarian History of England and Wales*, IV, *1500-1640* (1967), 12.

82 D. Hey, 'Introduction' to Bestall and Fowkes, xi-xxxiv.

83 Lichfield Joint RO, probate inventory of S. Bamford (I am indebted to D. Kiernan for this reference); H. Heaton, *The Yorkshire Woollen and Worsted Industries* (1965), 79-80; Defoe, I, 182.

84 W. B. Crump and G. Ghorbal, *History of the Huddersfield Woollen Industry* (1967), 39; Crump, 112; F. Atkinson, *Some Aspects of the Eighteenth Century Woollen and Worsted Trade in Halifax* (1956), 53.

85 Defoe, I, 82 and II, 206-7; Dodd, 92.

86 J. Tait, *The Domesday Survey of Cheshire* (1916), 217-25; Salt Museum, Northwich, leaflets

on 'Salt Making in Domesday Cheshire' and 'The Cheshire Salt Industry in Tudor & Stuart Times (1485-1714)'; West Yorks. RO, quarter sessions order book, October 1696, duties on salt: 'for every peck of Salt containing fourteen pound weight, Eight pence; for every Bushel of Salt containing fifty six pound Weight, 2s.8d.' Rock salt mining at Northwich began in 1671.

87 *VCH Staffordshire*, II (1967), 278-9.
88 W. B. Crump, 'Saltways from the Cheshire wiches', (1940; reprinted from *Trans. Lanca shire and Cheshire Antiquarian Soc.*, LIV). Some different interpretations are suggested here.
89 The earliest spellings read Saltern, so the evidence is not clear cut.
90 Hall and Thomas, *op. cit.*, 34.
91 E. Heaf, *Tideswell Tracks* (Tideswell Local History Club, 1999).
92 Cameron, I, 174; SA, Bagshawe Eyre, 2,051 and 2,055.
93 SA, Fairbank, FB 35; Belvoir castle, perambulation of the manor of Baslow, 1614.
94 The grid reference to Salter Wood is SK 335739. Salterswelsick is recorded in Notts, RO, Portland, DDP/84/5.
95 H. J. Morehouse, *The History and Topography of the Parish of Kirkburton and the Graveship of Holme* (1861), 141; Notts RO, DD SR/1/17/65; Barnsley Archives, Thurlstone enclosure award.
96 J. Addy (ed.), *A Further History of Penistone* (1965), 24.
97 SA, Fairbank, MB 160 and Ecc 13L.
98 SA, Fairbank, MB 521 and Wath 32L; Rot 65L and E(289)8L.
99 Grid reference SK 252972; D. Hey, 'Fresh light on the South Yorkshire saltways',*THAS*, IX, 3 (1967), 151-7 suggests a possible route.
100 SA, Fairbank, Ecc 2L and MB 160.
101 Smith, 277.
102 T. W. Hall, *A Descriptive Catalogue of the Edmunds Collection, and Court Roll and Parliamentary Survey of the Manor of Eckington* (1924), 207.
103 Raistrick, *Industrial Archaeology, op. cit.*, 199.
104 A. K. Clayton, *Hoyland Nether* (1974), 17.
105 Carrington, *op. cit.*, 82-3. A crannock was a dry measure that varied greatly; it was two or four bushels for corn, but much larger for salt (*Oxford English Dictionary*).
106 SA, Tibbits, 413/9.

Chapter 7 The transport of livestock and farm produce

1 D. Hey, *The Making of South Yorkshire* (1979), 57-8; D. M. Palliser in A. Everitt (ed.), *Perspectives in English Urban History* (1973), 53; W. Owen, *Book of Fairs* (1770).
2 B. E. Coates, 'The origin and distribution of markets and fairs in medieval Derbyshire', *DAJ*, LXXXV (1965), 92-111; Hey, *op. cit.*
3 H. C. Heathcote, 'Winster market house', *DAJ*, XXVIII (1906), 169-73; SA, Bagshawe, 303; R. Millward and A. Robinson, *The Peak District* (1975), 235-6; Brotherton library, Wilson, CLIX f. 3 and CCVI f. 21.
4 Brotherton library, Wilson, VII fos. 78-116; D. Hey, 'Penistone Market and Cloth Hall' in B. Elliott (ed.), *Aspects of Barnsley, 5* (1998), 173-88.
5 Public RO, WO/30/48. J. A. Chartres kindly provided the figures for Derbyshire.
6 British Library, Lansdowne, 897. Pryme uses 'town' in the old sense of township, a unit of local government.
7 Morris, 96.
8 Derby had fifteen per cent of the county's stables, compared with 34.8 per cent of the guest beds.
9 Ronksley; *Calendar to the Records of the Borough of Doncaster*, IV (1902), 71, 75.
10 *Ibid.*, iii. On droving see K. J. Bonser, *The Drovers* (1970); A. R. B. Haldane, *The Drove Roads of Scotland* (1952), R. Colyer, *The Welsh Cattle Drovers* (2001), 2nd ed. Landmark.
11 J. Clare, *The Shepherd's Calendar* (1817), the original version of 'July'.

12 SA, PR47/2; Borthwick, wills and inventories; Derbys. RO, quarter sessions records. In the south Derbyshire hundred of Appletree only four drovers were recorded in 1729. The quarter sessions indictment book for Michaelmas 1713 occasionally mentions those 'useing the business of drover without Lycence', but these cannot be quantified, nor can drovers be isolated in later records.
13 SA, WWM/BR164, WWM/A224, Sp.St.60656/1; Borthwick, probate inventory of Robert Blackburn of Bate Green (1727).
14 31 George II, c.63.
15 A. Everitt in J. Thirsk (ed.), *The Agrarian History of England and Wales*, IV, *1500-1640* (1967), 499, 539-40, 551.
16 SA, MD 192; 'Rural economy in Yorkshire in 1641, being the farming and account books of Henry Best of Elmswell, in the East Riding of the county of York', *Surtees Soc.*, XXXIII (1857), 112-14; Nottingham University library, Galway, G12,362.
17 W. Marshall, *The Rural Economy of the Midland Counties*, I (1796), 229-30; E. Baines, *History, Directory and Gazetteer of the County of York*, I (1822), 257; *cf.* J. Blackman, 'The food supply of an industrial town: a study of Sheffield's public markets, 1780-1900', *Business History*, V (1962-3), 83-97.
18 Borthwick, inventories; Sheffield City library, Local pamphlets, 115, no. 2, Acts of Parliament relating to Sheffield (1739-1894), no. 3.
19 Mrs Barbara Bestall kindly supplied this list.
20 D. Hey, 'Introduction' to Bestall and Fowkes; Hobson, 308, 314.
21 Defoe, II, 143; J. T. Cliffe, *The Yorkshire Gentry from the Reformation to the Civil War* (1969), 2; J. Thirsk and J. P. Cooper (eds), *Seventeenth-Century Economic Documents* (1972), 35-6; J. Brown, *General View of the Agriculture of the County of Derby* (1794), 15.
22 John Rylands library, Manchester, Bagshawe, 5/4/1; E. J. T. Collins, 'Dietary change and cereal consumption in Britain in the nineteenth century', *AHR*, XXIII, 2 (1975), 97-115.
23 SA, Beauchief, 80; J. Hunter, *The history and topography of the deanery of Doncaster*, I (1828), 208-9; Brotherton library, Wilson, VII f. 79; Hobson, 275.
24 T. S. Willan, *The History of the Don Navigation* (1965), 74; *JHC*, XIV (1702-4), 59-60; John Rylands library, Manchester, Bagshawe Eyre, 2,591 B; W. G. D. Fletcher, 'Philip Kinder's MS "Historie of Darbyshire"', *The Reliquary*, old series, XXII (1881-2), 23, 181; Cox, 223.
25 Derby library, f. 3,343a; J. Houghton, *A Collection for Improvement of Husbandry and Trade* (1692), II, nos 39 and 41; Borthwick, wills and inventories.
26 SA, Jackson, 1,321; R. Plot, *The Natural History of Staffordshire* (1686), 108; D. Hey, 'The north-west midlands' in J. Thirsk (ed.), *The Agrarian History of England and Wales*, V:I, *1640-1750*, 129-158; Willan, *op. cit.*, 5, 154, 147, 148; *cf.* Derbys. RO, D231M/4549: 'There will be 200 of cheese by Berisford the Hognaston carrier at Blossoms in Cheap-side on Friday and Saturday morning. Price of cheese £2.12s.0d; cost of carriage 16s.' .
27 5 Elizabeth c.12; R. H. Tawney and E. Power, *Tudor Economic Documents*, II (1914), 152-5. An earlier attempt to licence badgers, etc. was made in 1552.
28 Derbys. RO, quarter sessions records; A. E. Bland, P. A. Brown and R. H. Tawney, *English Economic History: Select Documents* (1914), 385.
29 D. Hey (ed.), *Richard Gough: the History of Myddle* (1981), 183; J. Wright, *The English Dialect Dictionary* (1898-1905), 125; T. Wright, *Dictionary of Obsolete and Provincial English* (1877), 149; J. C. Atkinson, *Forty Years in a Moorland Parish* (1891), 10.
30 SA, former South Yorks RO archives, 36/2/1/1; Smith, 226; Crump, 101.
31 J. D. Leader, *Records of the Burgery of Sheffield* (1897), 318. The 'Sembly Quest', or assembly inquest, made annual regulations.
32 Cox, 191; J. Lister (ed.), 'West Riding sessions Records, II', *YAS record series*, LIV (1915), 75.
33 *Calendar to the Records of Doncaster, op. cit.*, II (1900), 174, 181.
34 Borthwick, inventories; Sheffield baptism register, 20 May 1716.
35 Sheffield burial register, 11 June 1703.

36 Namely, Thomas Markham, John Ibberson, Henry Marriott, John Owen, Roger Goodwin and Samuel Cartledge.

37 West Yorks RO, quarter sessions records, unclassified summary convictions; D. Alexander, *Retailing in England during the Industrial Revolution* (1970), 60-6; Cox, 246.

38 However, *cf. Calendar to the Records of Doncaster, op. cit.*, IV (1902), 108, Cuthbert Gybson presented by the corporation for buying and selling corn and grain without licence.

39 Derbys. RO, quarter sessions indictment book (1711-28).

40 Cox, 199-200. Wirksworth had two other swailers without a special product.

41 J. Wright, *op. cit.*, 862, which records the use of the word in Lancashire, Cheshire, Staffordshire, Derbyshire and Leicestershire; S. Glover, *History of Derbyshire*, I (1829), 148; *Oxford English Dictionary*; Cox, 246; Lichfield Joint RO, inventories.

42 The 'renewals' figure for 1748-9 includes all those who renewed licences issued in either of the two previous years. The residences of two traders who obtained licences in 1748-9 were not given.

Chapter 8 The retail trade

1 W. A. Carrington, 'Selections from the steward's accounts preserved at Haddon Hall, for the years 159 and 1564', *DAJ*, XVI (1894), 61-85.

2 Defoe, I, 83; Bestall and Fowkes, 91-3.

3 D. M. Woodward, *The Trade of Elizabethan Chester* (1970), 117; Bestall and Fowkes, 268.

4 Woodward, *op. cit.*, 37-8 (vinegar, peeper, oranges, sugar, cinnamon, raisins and figs were amongst the groceries imported from Spain and France into Elizabethan Chester); T. S. Willan, *The Inland Trade* (1976), 60-1; 'A Dyurnall, or Catalogue of all my Accions and Expences from the 1st of January 1646[7] - Adam Eyre', *Surtees Soc.*, LXV (1875), 81.

5 Bestall and Fowkes, 181; Defoe, II, 100-1.

6 Willan, *op. cit.*, 71.

7 *Ibid.*, 53, 60-83; J. D. Marshall, (ed.), *The Autobiography of William Stout of Lancaster, 1665-1752* (1967), 96; Morris, 96; Bestall and Fowkes, 137-42.

8 Morris, 170; Borthwick, inventories; SA, Staveley iron records, I2, 13. Hartshead in central Sheffield takes its name from an inn.

9 C. Drury and T. W. Hall, *The Parish Register of Sheffield* (1917-27), IV and V; Borthwick, inventories.

10 SA, Sheffield Church Burgess Trust, 107 (Robert Bower, mercer, 1585), 1,215 (William Skargell, mercer, 1621), 1,211 and 1.216 (Robert Rollinson, mercer, 1609 and 1631); Drury and Hall, *op. cit*, III: Lionel Revell, grocer, William Cooke and Joseph Butler, woollen drapers; West Yorks. RO, quarter sessions indictment books: Henry Hancock (1663) and Jeremy Butler (1708), mercers, William Savage, Samuel Savage and Lionel Revell, grocers (1664), Thomas White (1684), haberdasher.

11 Borthwick, inventories (SA, Church Burgess Trust, 625 describes Thomas Heaton as an ironmonger in 1725); West Yorks. RO, quarter sessions order and indictment books: Matthew Oxley (1651) and Nathaniel Nelson (1659), pewterers, William Mandevyle (1670), woollen draper, John Martison (1685), grocer.

12 Cox, 197-200, which also records a shopkeeper in Tideswell in 1693.

13 Thirsk and Cooper, (eds), *Seventeenth-Century Economic Documents* (1972), 393; Willan, *op. cit.*, 83-9 (if doubtful cases are included, 2,683 tokens were issued from 949 places, about 400 of which did not possess market rights); G. C. Williamson, *Trade Tokens Issued in the Seventeenth Century* (1967), 3 vols.

14 Drury and Hall, *op. cit.*, III; SA, PR3, Worsbrough registers; *YAS parish registers*, XIV: Wath (1902); Willan, *op. cit.*, 60; Borthwick, inventories.

15 J. Thirsk, *Economic Policy and Projects* (1978), 3; 5/6 Edward VI c.21; *cf.* the ballad of

Anthony Painter, the Blaspheming Caryar, printed in 1613 for John Trundle, Christ Church Gate, London.

16 I James I c.7; Drury and Hall, *op. cit.*, V.
17 C. S. James (ed.), *Rotherham Marriage Registers*, I (1914), 146, 148; SA, PR3; *YAS*, typescript of Sheffield parish registers; *YAS*, Wath registers, *op. cit.*
18 J. Lister (ed.), 'West Riding Sessions Records, II', *YAS record series*, LIV, 140, 195.
19 Bestall and Fowkes, 137-42; Carrington, *op. cit.*
20 *Cf.* baker/baxter. I wish to thank John Widdowson for this explanation.
21 *Calendar to the Records of the Borough of Doncaster*, II (1900), 170; J. Wright, *The English Dialect Dictionary* (1898-1905), 265; SA, PR7/3, Tickhill registers; Cox, 246; D. H. Lawrence, *The White Peacock* (1950), 120.
22 Dodd, 77; SA, PR3; James, *op. cit.*, 141; *YAS*, typescript of Sheffield parish registers; *YAS record series*, LIV, 159; West Yorks. RO, quarter sessions indictment books.
23 Thirsk, *op. cit.*, 122-4.
24 Borthwick, inventory of Samuel Tompson of Sheffield (1716).
25 Cox, 80.
26 Thirsk and Cooper, *op. cit.*, 417-20; C. B. Robinson (ed.), 'Rural economy in Yorkshire in 1641', *Surtees Soc.*, XXXIII (1857), 105-6; *Calendar to the Records of Doncaster, op. cit.*, IV (1902), 89, 110.
27 West Yorks. RO, quarter sessions order books.
28 Drury and Hall, *op. cit.*, IV and V; James, *op. cit.*, 139.
29 Drury and Hall, *op. cit.*, IV and V; Bestall and Fowkes, 191-3; Lichfield Joint RO, inventories. (I am grateful to Mrs B. Bestall for the A. Tilly reference.)
30 James, *op. cit.*, 159; Borthwick, wills; R. E. Leader, *Sheffield in the Eighteenth Century* (1905), 92-4.
31 R. B. Westerfield, *Middlemen in English Business: Particularly between 1660 and 1760* (1915), 314; Thirsk, *op. cit.*, 157; Cox, 79; *cf.* Thirsk and Cooper, *op. cit.*, 341 for another petty chapman's losses in Dorset.
32 Derbys. RO, quarter sessions order books; *cf.* Thirsk and Cooper, *op. cit.*, 412 (carriers and pedlars suspected of distributing seditious literature, 1684); D. Hey, 'The pattern of nonconformity in South Yorkshire, 1660-1851', *Northern History, VIII (1973), 86-118.*
33 Public RO, AO 3/370; M. Spufford, *Small Books and Pleasant Histories: Popular Fiction and its Readership in Seventeenth-Century England* (1981).
34 Derbys. RO, militia records.
35 *Calendar to the Records of Doncaster, op. cit.*, IV (1902), 243; West Yorks. RO, quarter sessions, unclassified papers; D. Alexander, *Retailing in England during the Industrial revolution* (1970), 64.

Chapter 9 Carriers

1 M. Rowlands, 'Society and industry in the West Midlands at the end of the seventeenth century', *Midland History*, IV, 1 (1977), 48-60; *JHC*, XIV (1702-4), 59-60; SA, Vernon Wentworth, 308/2.
2 Borthwick, wills and inventories; C. Drury and T. W. Hall, *The Parish Register of Sheffield*, IV (1927); D. Hey, *Richard Gough: The History of Myddle* (1981), 151.
3 *YAS*, Wath registers; Ronksley; *Sheffield Register*, 17 June 1791; SA, MD 1,055, p. 249 (sketch of Old Pack Horse Yard, Snig Hill, Sheffield); the *Packhorse Inn* at Barnsley stood in Shambles Street and that in Rotherham at the corner of Wellgate and Doncaster Gate.
4 Cameron, I, 88-9; J. H. Brooksbank, 'The Forest of the Peak', *THAS*, I, 4, 337-55; Smith, 174; Crump, 4; T. Wright, *Dictionary of Obsolete and Provincial English* (1857), 599; Bestall and Fowkes, 196, 287; J. Wright, *The English Dialect Dictionary* (1898-1905), 343-4.

5 A. Everitt, 'The English urban inn, 1560-1760' in A. Everitt (ed.), *Perspectives in English Urban History* (1957), 91-137; W. H. Hart, 'A list of the "Alehouses, Innes and Tavernes" in Derbyshire in the year 1577', *DAJ*, I (1889), 68-80.

6 J. Houghton, *A Collection for Improvement of Husbandry and Trade* (1692), II, no. 39; Doncaster RO, AB/MR/1/4 (I wish to thank Tim Alexander-Macquiban for this reference); A. E. Bland, P. A. Brown, R. H. Tawney (eds), *English Economic History Select Documents* (1914), 389; J. Lister (ed.), 'West Riding Sessions Records, II', *YAS record series*, LIV, xli.

7 The entry is under Morton, Pilsley and Brampton. Scarsdale hundred had three inns and 123 alehouses, High Peak hundred had two inns and 110 alehouses, and Wirksworth hundred had one inn and 110 alehouses.

8 Borthwick, inventories of Edward Houlden of Woolley (1695) and Hugh Walker of Silkstone (1698); SA, NBC, inventory of Robert Stanistreete of Wentworth (1689).

9 S. Wilkin (ed.), *Sir Thomas Browne's Works* (1836), 30; Defoe, II, 181.

10 J. Thirsk and J. P. Cooper (eds), *Seventeenth-Century Economic Documents* (1972), 328; Barnsley library, Burland's Annals of Barnsley, I (1880), 172.

11 *Royal Commission on Historical Manuscripts, Portland,* II: *Thomas Baskerville's Journeys in England, temp. Car. II*, 310.

12 Borthwick, inventories.

13 SA, *Calendar of the Talbot Correspondence*, 2/259, 2/65, 2/176; J. Guest, *Historic Notices of Rotherham* (1879), 380; J. Crofts, *Packhorse, Waggon and Post: Land carriage and communications under the Tudors and Stuarts* (1967), 4.

14 J. Taylor, *The Carriers' Cosmographie* (1637); West Yorks. RO, quarter sessions records. *The Merchant and Tradesman's Daily Companion and Traveller's and Countryman's True Instructor* (London Bridge, 1729) confirmed the *Castle* and the *Bell*, both in Wood Street, as the venue for the carriers of our region (I wish to thank Mrs Margaret Furey for this reference).

15 SA, Oakes 770; SA, Church Burgess Trust, 105; Lichfield Joint RO, wills and inventories (I wish to thank Mrs B. Bestall for these references).

16 J. Tomlinson, *Doncaster from the Roman Occupation to the Present Time* (1887), 329; D. Hey, 'Doncaster People of Ten Generations Ago' in B. Elliott (ed.), *Aspects of Doncaster*, I (1997), 119-52 (which prints A. Pilling's inventory).

17 J. A. Chartres, 'Road carrying in England in the seventeenth century: myth and reality', *EcHR*, XXX (1977), 73-94; D. Gerhold, 'The growth of the London carrying trade, 1681-1838', *EcHR*, XLI (1988), 392-410; *cf.* C. W. Chalklin, *Seventeenth-Century Kent* (1965), 165; P. Yeatman, 'The diary of Benjamin Granger of Bolsover, 1688-1708', *DAJ*, IX (1887), 55-69; Cox, 223; H. S. Twells, 'Mr. Drewry and the Derby wagons', *DAJ*, LXIII (1942), 61-78. 'John Peat a London waggoner' appears in the Bradfield chapelry register on the baptism of his son in 1747.

18 Morris, 225; Twells, *op. cit.*; *cf.* Crump, 110; R. E. Leader, *Sheffield in the Eighteenth Century* (1905), 54-7; SA, Bright, JT 59 (1674: rumours of a highwayman at Doncaster but they arrived safely).

19 SA, Worsbrough registers; *YAS*, Sheffield registers; C. S. James, *Rotherham Marriage Registers*, I (1914), 166; M. J. Dickenson, 'The West Riding woollen and worsted industries, 1689-1770: an analysis of probate inventories and insurance policies' (unpublished PhD thesis, University of Nottingham, 1974), 187-8.

20 W. T. Lancaster (ed.), *Letters addressed to Ralph Thoresby*, Thoresby Soc., XXI (1912), 164; Borthwick, wills and inventories; *Surtees Soc.*, LXV (1875), 29; V. S. Doe (Ed.), *The Diary of James Clegg of Chapel en le Frith, 1708-55* (1979), I, 162; *JHC*, XXI (1729), 472; W. B. Bunting and L. L. Simpson, *Derbyshire Parish Registers*, XII (1914), 37, 39, 40, 45 names the following carriers who were married at Chapel en le Frith: Henry Howard (1757), James Ford of the parish of Hope (1757), Joseph Lowe (1760), Samuel Kirk (1760, coal carrier) and Peter Hallam of the parish of Glossop (1772); a field in Chapel en le Frith still bears the name of Carriers' Meadow (Dodd, 80).

21 T. S. Willan, 'The Justices of the Peace and the rates of land carriage, 1692-1827', *Journal of Transport History*, old series, V, 4 (1962), 197-204.
22 S. O. Addy (ed.), *A Directory of Sheffield published by Gales and Martin in 1787* (1889).
23 G. L. Turnbull, 'Provincial road carrying in England in the eighteenth century', *Journal of Transport History*, IV, 1 (1977), 17-39.
24 Twells, *op. cit.*; SA, Parker, 1,088. A service between the West Midlands and Sheffield is also recorded in Sketchley's *Birmingham, Wolverhampton and Walsall Directory* (1767), 100.
25 E. Baines, *History, Directory and Gazetteer of the County of York*, I (1822), 358; G. L. Turnbull, *Traffic and Transport: An economic history of Pickford's* (1979), 27.

Chapter 10 Conclusion

1 Defoe, I, 45, 59 and II, 121, 146, 199.
2 J. Thirsk, *Economic Policy and Projects* (1978).
3 Defoe, II, 88-9.
4 J. A. Chartres, *Internal Trade in England* (1977), 10.
5 J. Thirsk, 'Seventeenth-century agriculture and social change' in J. Thirsk (ed.), *Land, Church and People: Essays presented to Professor H. P. R. Finberg* (1970), 148-77.
6 Defoe, II, 36.
7 D. Defoe, *The Complete English Tradesman* (1726), 389.
8 Bestall and Fowkes, 188-91.
9 B. A. Holderness, 'Credit in English rural society before the nineteenth century, with special reference to the period 1650-1720', *AHR*, XXIV, 2 (1976), 97-109.
10 Chartres, *op. cit.*, 53.
11 J. Aikin, *A Description of the Country from Thirty to Forty Miles around Manchester* (1795), 308-9.
12 B. P. Hindle, 'Seasonal variations in travel in medieval England', *Journal of Transport History*, IV, 3 (1978), 170-8.
13 T. S. Willan, *The Inland Trade* (1976), 4.
14 Defoe, II, 211. Celia Fiennes often commented on the stone bridges of the North: Morris, 219, note 9.
15 Chartres, *op. cit.*, 55.
16 Defoe, II, 118.
17 W. I. Albert, *The turnpike road system in England, 1663-1840* (1972); E. Pawson, *Transport and Economy: The turnpike roads of eighteenth century Britain* (1977); B. P. Hindle, *Roads, Tracks and their Interpretation* (1993).
18 3 George II c.4; *JHC*, XX (1722-7), 363 and XXI (1727-32), 435.
19 Defoe, II, 179.

BIBLIOGRAPHY AND ACKNOWLEDGEMENTS

1 Documentary sources

I am grateful to the copyright holders for permission to quote from the following documents:

SHEFFIELD ARCHIVES: *Fairbank*, FB 13, 31, 35, 111, MB 160, 521, E(289) 8L, Ecc 2L, 3L, Kirk 1L, Pen 4S, 31S, Rot 65L, Wath 32L, Whis 26L, 40S; *Crewe*, 662, 1,611, 1,679, 1,680, 1,696, 1,698, 1,704, 1,705, 1,740, 1,792, 1,902; *Tibbits*, 407/27, 408/27, 409/71. 413/3, 413/9, 515, 516, 1,043, 1,053a; *Spencer-Stanhope*. 60, 217, 60, 464, 60, 471, 60,656/1; *Ronksley*, 161, 162, 952, 1,141, 1,552, 7,523, 9,291, 9,295, 9,299; *Miscellaneous,* MD 192, 1,055, 1,769, 3,339, 3,483, 5,786, MP 1,479M; *Wentworth Woodhouse*, WWM A 224, A 1,273, C 138, D 1,727, MP 95, BR 51, 164, 185 (c), 263, Bright papers, JE 97, 99, JT 59; *Bagshawe*, 303, 313; *Bagshawe Eyre*, 358, 1,213, 1,366A, 1,799, 2,051, 2,055; *Wharncliffe*, 109, 110, 111; *Elmhirst*, 1,005, 1,006; *Jackson*, 1,321, 1,693; *Oakes*, 770; *Wheat*, 1,961; *Leader*, 70-8; *Beauchief*, 54, 80; *Newman Bond*, inventories; *Staveley iron*, 12, 13, 14, 15, 16, 17; *Parish records*, PR 3, 7/3, 47/2, microfilm of Penistone parish registers; *Church Burgess Trust*, 105, 107, 625, 1,211, 1,215, 1,216; *Vernon-Wentworth*, 308/2; *former South Yorkshire Record office*, 36/2/1/1; Joseph Dickenson's map (1750).

SHEFFIELD CENTRAL LIBRARY, LOCAL STUDIES: Ralph Gosling's map of Sheffield (1736), S. and N. Buck, 'The East Prospect of Sheffield in the County of York', Local pamphlets, 115, no. 2, Acts of Parliament relating to Sheffield (1739-1894), no. 3, *Sheffield Public Advertiser*, 4 Nov. 1760, *Sheffield Register*, 17 June 1791.

PUBLIC RECORD OFFICE: AO 3/370; E134/17 James I/Mich.7; E134/18 James I/East.21/no.78 York; E134/15 and 16 Chas 1/Hil.10; E317 Derbys. 12 and 20; E317 Yorks. 15 and 58; WO/30/48.

BRITISH LIBRARY: *Lansdowne*, 897; *Woolley*, I, 88.

DERBYSHIRE RECORD OFFICE: quarter sessions records; militia records; 1005 Z/E1, D803/ME3; Peak Forest parish records.

WEST YORKSHIRE RECORD OFFICE: quarter sessions records; Book of Bridges (1752).

BORTHWICK INSTITUTE OF HISTORICAL RESEARCH, YORK: wills and inventories for Yorkshire.

LICHFIELD JOINT RECORD OFFICE: wills and inventories for Derbyshire.

BROTHERTON LIBRARY, LEEDS UNIVERSITY: *Wilson*, VII fos. 78-116, XLIV f. 50, LXVII f. 77, CLIX fos. 50-95, CCVI f. 21.

YORKSHIRE ARCHAEOLOGICAL SOCIETY, LEEDS: *Duke of Leeds*, DD5/5/155; typescript of Sheffield parish registers.

JOHN RYLANDS LIBRARY, MANCHESTER UNIVERSITY: *Bagshawe Eyre*, 5/4/1, 2,383, 2,591B.

DERBY LIBRARY: *Gale* bequest, bundle 3, f. 3,343a; *The Derby Mercury*, 1735 onwards.

BRADFORD LIBRARY: John Warburton map.

NOTTINGHAM UNIVERSITY LIBRARY: *Galway*, G12,362.

NOTTINGHAMSHIRE RECORD OFFICE: *Foljambe*, 334, 617; *Portland*, DDP 65/47, DDP 84/5.

DONCASTER ARCHIVES: AB/MR/1/4; Doncaster parish registers.

BARNSLEY ARCHIVES: Thurlstone enclosure award.

CORPORATION OF LONDON RECORD OFFICE: rental 6.16, f. 18.

2 Original sources in print

a. STATUTES OF THE REALM
5/6 Edward VI c.21; 5 Eliz. c.12 and 13; I James I c.7; 3 William and Mary c.12; 5 George I c.12; 3 George II c.4.

b. JOURNALS OF THE HOUSE OF COMMONS
vols XIV (1702-4), XIX (1718-21), XX (1722-7), XXI (1727-31), XXIII (1737-41), XXVII (1754-7), XXVIII (1757-61).

c. CALENDARS AND CATALOGUES
A. E. Bland, P. A. Brown and R. H. Tawney (eds), *English Economic History: Select Documents* (1914)
W. B. Bunting and L. L. Simpson (eds), *Derbyshire Parish Registers*, XII (1914)
Calendar of Patent Rolls, Westminster (1232-48)
Calendar to the Records of the Borough of Doncaster, 4 vols (1899-1902)
O. Coleman (ed.), *The Brokage Book of Southampton, 1443-4*, II, (Southampton record series, VI, 1961)
C. Drury and T.W. Hall, *The Parish Registers of Sheffield*, 5 vols (1917-27)
C. M. Fraser and K. Emsley (eds), *The Court Rolls of the Manor of Wakefield*, I (1977)
G. L. Gomme (ed.), *Topographical History of Worcestershire and Yorkshire: A classified collection of the chief contents of the Gentleman's Magazine from 1731 to 1868* (1902)
T. W. Hall, *Sheffield 1297 to 1554* (1913)
T. W. Hall and A. H. Thomas, *A Descriptive Catalogue of the Jackson Collection* (1914)
T. W. Hall, *A Descriptive Catalogue of the Edmunds Collection and Court Roll and Parliamentary Survey of the Manor of Eckington* (1924)
T. W. Hall, *A Descriptive Catalogue of Sheffield Manorial Records*, I (1926), II (1928), III (1934)
T. W. Hall, *A Descriptive Catalogue of the Bosville and Lindsay Collections* (1930)
T. W. Hall, *A Descriptive Catalogue of Ancient Charters ... in the Counties of York, Derby, Nottingham and Lincoln* (1935)
T. W, Hall, *A Descriptive Catologue of the Wheat Collection* (1920)
T. W. *Hall, Materials for the History of Wincobank* (1922)
T. W. Hall, *Sheffield and Rotherham from the 12th to the 18th century* (1916)
C. S. James (ed.), *Rotherham Marriage Registers*, I (1914)
J. Lister (ed.), 'West Riding Sessions Rolls, 1597/8-1602', *YAS record series*, III (1888)
J. Lister (ed.), 'West Riding Sessions Records, II', *YAS record series*, LIV (1915)

W. S. Owen and M. Walton, *The Parish Registers of Sheffield*, VI (1981) and VII (1989)
Royal Commission on Historical Manuscripts, Portland, II and VI
SA, *Calendar of the Talbot Correspondence* (1965)
R. H. Tawney and E. Power, *Tudor Economic Documents*, II (1924)
J. Thirsk and J. P. Cooper (eds), *Seventeenth-Century Economic Documents* (1972)
YAS parish registers, XIV (1902)

d. BOOKS

S. O. Addy (ed.), *A Directory of Sheffield published by Gales and Martin in 1787* (1889)
J. Aikin, *A Description of the Country from Thirty to Forty Miles around Manchester* (1798)
E. Baines, *History, Directory and Gazetteer of the County of York*, I (1822)
J. M. Bestall and D. V. Fowkes (eds), *Chesterfield Wills and Inventories, 1521-1603* (1977)
R. Blome, *Britannia* (1673)
W. Bray, *Sketch of a Tour into Derbyshire and Yorkshire* (1783)
J. Brown, *General View of the Agriculture of the County of Derby* (1794)
R. Brown, *et.al.*, *General View of the Agriculture of the West Riding* (1799)
A. J. Browning (ed.), *Memoirs of Sir John Reresby* (1936)
Samuel Buck's Yorkshire Sketchbook, Wakefield Historical Publications (1979),
K. Cameron, *The Place-Names of Derbyshire*, 3 vols (1959)
J. Clare, *The Shepherd's Calendar* (1817)
W. Cobbett, *Rural Rides*, II (1930)
J. C. Cox, *Three Centuries of Derbyshire Annals*, II (1890)
W. Davies, *Agriculture of North Wales* (1810)
D. Defoe, *The Complete English Tradesman* (1726)
D. Defoe, *Tour through the Whole Island of Great Britain* (1962 edition)
W. Dickinson, *Essays on the Farming of Cumberland* (1853)
V. S. Doe (ed.), *The Diary of James Clegg of Chapel en le Frith, 1708-55*, I (1979)
D. Durant and P. Riden (eds), *The Building of Hardwick Hall*, 2 vols (1980-4)
'A Dyurnall, or Catalogue of all my Accions and Expences from the 1st of January 1646[7] — Adam Eyre', *Surtees Soc.*, LXV (1875)
J. Farey, *General View of the Agriculture of Derbyshire*, II (1813) and III (1817)
'A Family History Begun by James Fewtrell', *Surtees Soc.*, LXV (1875)
S. Glover, *History of Derbyshire*, I (1829)
D. Hey (ed.), *The Hearth Tax Returns for South Yorkshire, Ladyday 1672* (1991)
D. Hey (ed.), *Richard Gough: The History of Myddle* (1981)
J. Houghton, *A Collection for Improvement of Husbandry and Trade* (1692)
J. Hunter (ed.), *The Diary of Ralph Thoresby*, I (1830)
'The Diary of Arthur Jessop', *YAS record series*, CXVII (1952)
W. T. Lancaster (ed.), *Letters addressed to Ralph Thoresby*, Thoresby Soc., XXI (1912)
R. E. Leader, *A History of the Company of Cutlers in Hallamshire*, 2 vols (1905-6)
J. D. Marshall (ed.), *The Autobiography of William Stout of Lancaster, 1665-1752* (1967)
W. Marshall, *Review and Abstract of County Reports to the Board of Agriculture: I, Northern Department* (1808)
W. Marshall, *The Rural Economy of Yorkshire*, I (1788)
W. Marshall, *The Rural Economy of the Midland Counties*, I (1796)
H. Martineau, *Guide to the Lakes* (1855)
E. Miller, *The History and Antiquities of Doncaster and its Vicinity* (1804)
P, Morgan (ed.), *Domesday Book; Derbyshire* (1978)
C. Morris (ed.), *The Journeys of Celia Fiennes* (1947)
W. Owen, *Book of Fairs* (1770)
W. Peck, *A Topographical History and Description of Bawtry and Thorne* (1813)
J. Pilkington, *A View of the Present State of Derbyshire*, II (1789)

R. Plot, *The Natural History of Staffordshire* (1686)
E. Rhodes, *Yorkshire Scenery* (1826)
P. Riden, *George Sitwell's Letterbook, 1662-66* (1985)
J. Ronksley (ed.), *John Harrison: An exact and perfect survey and view of the manor of Sheffield, 1637* (1908)
Sketchley's Birmingham, Wolverhampton and Walsall Directory (1767)
A. H. Smith, *The Place-Names of the West Riding of Yorkshire*, I (1961)
L. T. Smith (ed.), *Leland's Itinerary in England and Wales*, 5 vols (1964)
J. Tait, *The Domesday Survey of Cheshire* (1916)
J. Taylor, *The Carriers' Cosmographie* (1637)
Early Prose and Poetical Works of John Taylor, the Water Poet, 1580-1653 (1888)
T. Taylor, *The Antiquities of Sheffield* (1797)
C. Vancouver, *General View of the Agriculture of Devon* (1813)
G. Walker, *The Costume of Yorkshire* (1814)
I. Walton, *The Compleat Angler* (1676)
T. D. Whitaker, *Loides and Elmete* (1816)
G. White, *The Natural History of Selborne, in the County of Southampton* (1788-9)
S. Wilkin (ed.), *Sir Thomas Browne's Works* (1836)
G. C. Williamson, *Trade Tokens Issued in the Seventeenth Century*, 3 vols (1967)
J. Wright, *The English Dialect Dictionary*, 5 vols (1898-1905)
T. Wright, *Dictionary of Obsolete and Provincial English* (1857)

e. ARTICLES
W. A. Carrington, 'Selections from the steward's accounts preserved at Haddon Hall, for the years 1549 and 1564', *DAJ*, XVI (1894), 61-85
J. C. Cox, 'The Woolley Manuscripts, no. ii: an analysis of volumes six to ten', *DAJ*, XXXIV (1912), 81-132
E. Curtis, 'Sheffield in the fourteenth century: two Furnival inquisitions', *THAS*, I, 1 (1914), 31-56
W. G. D. Fletcher, 'Philip Kinder's MS "Historie of Darby-Shire"'; *The Reliquary*, old series, XXII (1881-2), 23 and 181, and XXIII (1882-3), 9
W. H. Hart, 'A list of the "Alehouses, Innes and Tavernes" in Derbyshire in the year 1577', *DAJ*, I (1889), 68-80
C. Kerry (ed.), 'Ashover memoranda by Titus Wheatcroft, AD 1722', *DAJ*, XIX (1897), 24-52
R. Meredith, 'Hathersage Affairs, 1720-35', *THAS*, XI (1981), 14-27
R. Meredith, 'Millstone making at Yarncliff in the reign of Edward IV', *DAJ*, CI (1981), 102-6
'The Chartulary of St John of Pontefract', *YAS record series*, XXV (1898)
B. Stallybras, 'Bess of Hardwick's buildings and building accounts', *Archaeologia*, LXIV (1912-13), 347-98
A. H. Thomas, 'Some Hallamshire Rolls of the fifteenth century', *THAS*, II, 2 (1921), 142-58; 3 (1922), 225-45; 4 (1924), 341-60
'The autobiography of Leonard Wheatcroft', *DAJ*, XXI (1891), 26-60
P. Yeatman, 'The Diary of Benjamin Grange of Bolsover, 1688-1708', *DAJ*, IX (1887), 55-69

3 Secondary works

a. BOOKS
J. Addy (ed.), *A Further History of Penistone* (1965)
W. I. Albert, *The Turnpike Road System in England, 1663-1840* (1972)
D. Alexander, *Retailing in England during the Industrial Revolution* (1970)
C. R. Andrews, *The Story of Wortley Ironworks* (1956)

F. Atkinson (ed.), *Some Aspects of the Eighteenth Century Woollen and Worsted Trade in Halifax* (1956)
J. C. Atkinson, *Forty Years in a Moorland Parish* (1891)
K. Barraclough, *Sheffield Steel* (1976)
C. Binfield and D. Hey (eds), *Mesters to Masters: A history of the Company of Cutlers in Hallamshire* (1997)
K. J. Bonser, *The Drovers* (1970)
E. Buckley and R. Ward, *Sheffield Postal History from Earliest Times to 1850* (1969)
K. Cameron, *English Place Names* (1963)
C. W. Chalklin, *Seventeenth Century Kent* (1965)
J. A. Chartres, *Internal Trade in England, 1500-1700* (1977)
I. S. W. Blanchard, 'Economic Change in Derbyshire in the Late Middle Ages, 1272-1540' (unpublished PhD thesis, University of London, 1967)
A. Clayton, *Hoyland Nether* (1974)
J. T. Cliffe, *The Yorkshire Gentry from the Reformation to the Civil War* (1969)
D. C. Coleman and A. H. John (eds), *Trade, Government and Economy in Pre-Industrial England* (1976)
R. Colyer, *The Welsh Cattle Drovers* (2001), Landmark
J. Crofts, *Packhorse, Waggon and Post: Land carriage and communications under the Tudors and Stuarts* (1967)
W. B. Crump, *Huddersfield Highways Down the Ages* (1949)
W. B. Crump and G. Ghorbal, *History of the Huddersfield Woollen Industry* (1967)
R. Davis, *The Trade and Shipping of Hull, 1500-1700* (1964)
M. J. Dickenson, 'The West Riding Woollen and Worsted Industries, 1689-1770: an analysis of probate inventories and insurance policies' (unpublished Ph.D thesis, University of Nottingham, 1974)
A. E. and E. M. Dodd, *Peakland Roads and Trackways* (2000 edition), Landmark
V. S. Doe (ed.), *Essays in the History of Holmesfield, 1550-1714* (1975)
P. Dover, *The Early Medieval History of Boston, 1086-1400* (1972)
A. D. Dyer, *The City of Worcester in the Sixteenth Century* (1973)
P. Edwards, *The Horse Trade of Tudor and Stuart England* (1988)
B. Elliott (ed.), *Aspects of Barnsley*, V (1998)
B. Elliott (ed.), *Aspects of Doncaster*, I (1997)
A. Everitt (ed.), *Perspectives in English Urban History* (1973)
T. D. Ford and J. H. Rieuwerts (eds), *Lead Mining in the Peak District* (2000), Landmark
J. Guest, *Historic Notices of Rotherham* (1879)
A. R. B. Haldane, *The Drove Roads of Scotland* (1952)
H. Harris, *Industrial Archaeology of the Peak District* (1971)
E. Heaf, *Tideswell Tracks* (1999)
H. Heaton, *The Yorkshire Wollen and Worsted Industries* (1965)
D. Hey, *The Fiery Blades of Hallamshire: Sheffield and its Neighbourhood, 1660-1740* (1991)
D. Hey, *The Making of South Yorkshire* (1979)
D. Hey, *The Rural Metalworkers of the Sheffield Region* (1972)
D. Holland, *Bawtry and the Idle River Trade* (1976)
D. Holland (ed), *New Light on Old Bawtry* (1978)
A. Hopkinson, 'Study of a Village: Killamarsh, 1535-1750', dissertation for the Certificate in Local History, University of Sheffield (1984)
J. Hunter, *South Yorkshire: The history and topography of the deanery of Doncaster*, 2 vols (1828-31)
J. Hunter, *Hallamshire* (ed. A. Gatty, 1869)
D. Hussey, *Coastal and River Trade in Pre-Industrial England: Bristol and its region, 1680-1730* (2000)

W. T. Jackman, *The Development of Transportation in Modern Britain* (1916)
G. Jackson, *Hull in the Eighteenth Century; A Study in Economic and Social History* (1972)
J. G. Jenkins, *The English farm Wagon: Origins and Structure* (1972)
M. Jones, *Trees, Wood and People: Habitat, History and Heritage* (2000)
J. Kenworthy, *The Lure of Midhope-cum-Langsett* (1927)
J. Kenworthy, *Midhope Potteries* (1928)
D. Kiernan, *The Derbyshire Lead Industry in the Sixteenth Century* (1989)
N. Kirkham, *Derbyshire Lead Mining through the Centuries* (1968)
J. D. Leader, *Records of the Burgery of Sheffield* (1897)
R. E. Leader, *Sheffield in the Eighteenth Century* (1905)
G. I. H. Lloyd, *The Cutlery Trades* (1913)`
R. Millward and A. Robinson, *The Peak District* (1975)
H. J. Morehouse, *History and Topography of the Parish of Kirkburton and of the Graveship of Holme* (1861)
J. Parkes, *Travel in England in the Seventeenth Century* (1925)
E. Pawson, *Transport and Economy: The turnpike roads of eighteenth century Britain* (1977)
N. Pevsner, *The Buildings of England: Derbyshire* (1953)
J. Prince, *History of Silkstone* (1922)
A. Raistrick, *Industrial Archaeology* (1972)
A. Raistrick, *Yorkshire Maps and Map Makers* (1969)
A. Raistrick and B. Jennings, *A History of Lead Mining in the Pennines* (1965)
A. F. Roberts and J. R. Leach, *The Coal Mines of Buxton* (1985)
J. Roper, *Early North Worcestershire Sythesmiths* (1967)
M. B. Rowlands, *Masters and Men in the West Midlands Metalware Trades before the Industrial Revolution* (1975)
L. F. Salzman, *Building in England Down to 1540; A documentary history* (1952)
A Seventeenth-Century Scarsdale Miscellany, (Derbyshire Record Society, 1973)
Sheffield Clarion Ramblers' Handbooks
S. Smiles, *Lives of the Engineers: Metcalfe-Telford* (1904)
H. Smith, *The Guide Stoops of Derbyshire* (second edition, 2000)
H. Smith, *The Guide Stoops of the Dark Peak* (1999)
M. Spufford, *Small Books and Pleasant Histories: Popular Fiction and its Readership in Seventeenth-Century England* (1981)
L. Stone, *The Crisis of the Aristocracy, 1558-1641* (1965)
D. F. E. Sykes, *History of Huddersfield and the Valleys of the Colne, the Holme and the Dearne* (n.d.).
J. Thirsk (ed.), *Land, Church and people: Essays presented to Professor H. P. R. Finberg* (1970)
J. Thirsk, *Economic Policy and Projects* (1978)
J. Thirsk (ed.), *Agrarian History of England and Wales*, IV, *1500-1640* (1967) and V, *1640-1750* (1984)
F. Thompson, *The History of Chatsworth* (1949)
J. Thompson, *Doncaster from the Roman Occupation to the Present Time* (1887)
G. L. Turnbull, *Traffic and Transport: An economic history of Pickford's* (1979)
Victoria County History of Derbyshire, II (1907)
Victoria County History of Staffordshire, II (1967)
R. B. Westerfield, *Middlemen in English Business: Particularly between 1660 and 1760* (1915)
T. S. Willan, *The Inland Trade* (1976)
T. S. Willan, *River Navigation in England, 1660-1750* (1936)
T. S. Willan, *The History of the Don Navigation* (1965)
L. A. Williams, *Road Transport in Cumbria in the Nineteenth Century* (1975)
R. G. Wilson, *Gentleman Merchents: The Merchant Community in Leeds, 1700-1830* (1971)
A. Wood, *The Politics of Social Conflict: The Peak Country, 1520-1770* (1999)
D. M. Woodward, *The Trade of Elizabethan Chester* (1970)

b. ARTICLES
J. Blackman, 'The Food Supply of an Indutrial Town: a Study of Sheffield's Public Markets, 1780-1900', Bussiness History, V (1962-3), 83-97
J. H. Brooksbank, 'The Forest of the Peak', 1, 4, (1918), 337-55
L. H. Butcher, 'Archaeological remains on the Wharncliffe-Greno upland, South Yorkshire', *THAS*, VII, 1 (1957), 38
J. A. Chartres, 'Road carrying in England in the seventeenth century: myth and reality', *EcHR*, XXX, 1 (1977), 73-94
R. P. Chope, 'Some old farm implements and operations', *Trans. Devon Archaeological Soc.*, I (1918), 284-8
L. A. Clarkson, 'The leather crafts in Tudor and Stuart England', *AHR*, XIV (1966), 25-39
B. E. Coates, 'The origin and distribution of markets and fairs in medieval Derbyshire', *DAJ*, LXXXV (1965), 92-111
V. M. Conway, 'Stratigraphy and pollen analysis of southern Pennine blanket peats', *Journal of Ecology*, XLII (1954), 117-47
D. Crosley and D. Ashurst, 'Excavations at Rockley Smithies, a Water Powered Bloomery of the Sixteenth and Seventeenth Centuries', *Post Medieval Archaeology, II* (1968), 10-54.
D. Crossley and D. Kiernan, 'The Lead-Smelting Mills of Derbyshire', *DAJ*, CXII (1992), 6-48
W. B. Crump, 'Saltways from the Cheshire wiches' (reprinted 1940 from *Trans. Lancashire and Cheshire Antiquarian Soc.*, LIV)
G. C. Dunning, 'The stone mortar in Little Baddow church', *Medieval Archaeology*, XIX (1975), 161-3
B. Elliott, 'John Foster of Woolley: an early eighteenth century coal master', *South Yorkshire Historian*, 3 (1976), 18-21
D. Gerhold, 'The growth of the London carrying trade, 1681-1838', *EcHR*, XLI (1988), 392-410
D. Gerhold, 'Packhorses and Wheeled Vehicles in England, 1550-1800', *Journal of Transport History*, 14, 1 (1993), 1-26
T. W. Hall, 'Ye racker way', *THAS*, I, 1 (1914), 63-70
H. C. Heathcote, 'Winster Market House', *DAJ*, XXVIII (1906), 169-73
D. Hey, 'Fresh Light on the South Yorkshire saltways', *THAS*, IX, 3 (1967), 151-7
D. Hey, 'The ironworks at Chapeltown', *THAS*, X, 4 (1977), 252-9
D. Hey. 'The Pattern of Nonconformity in south Yorkshire, 1660-1851', *Northern History*, VIII (1973), 86-118
B. P. Hindle, 'Seasonal variations in travel in medieval England', *Journal of Transport History*, IV, 3 (1978), 170-8
B. A. Holderness, 'Credit in English rural society before the nineteenth century, with special reference to the period 1650-1720', *AHR*, XXIV, 2 91976), 97-109
G. G. Hopkinson, 'Road development in south Yorkshire and north Derbyshire, 1700-1850', *THAS*, X, 1 (1971), 14-30
G. G. Hopkinson, 'The business transactions of Richard Dalton, raff merchant, 1739-49', *THAS*, VIII, 1 (1958), 16-18
G. G. Hopkinson, 'The development of the south Yorkshire and north Derbyshire coalfield, 1550-1775', *THAS*, VII, 6 (1957), 295-319
G. G. Hopkinson, 'The charcoal iron industry in the Sheffield region, 1500-1725', *THAS*, VIII, 3 (1961), 122-51
J. Langdon, 'The Economics of Horses and Oxen in Medieval England', *AHR*, 30, 1 (1982), 31-40
R. E. Leader, 'Our old roads', *THAS*, II, 1 (1920), 7-29
R. Meredith, 'The Eyres of Hassop', *DAJ* LXXXIV (1964)

S. C. Newton, 'The gentry of Derbyshire in the seventeenth century', *DAJ*, LXXXVI (1966), 1-30
M. Plant, 'A scythe-stone industry on Beeley Moor', *DAJ*, LXXVIII 1968), 98-100
J. P. Polak, 'The Production and Distribution of Peak Millstones from the Sixteenth to the Eighteenth Centuries', *DAJ*, CVII (1987), 55-72
J. Radley, 'Peak District roads prior to the turnpike era', *DAJ*, LXXIII (1963), 39-50
J. Radley, 'Peak millstones and Hallamshire grindstones', *Trans. Newcomen Soc.*, XIX (1963-4), 165-74
J. Radley and S. R. Penny, 'The turnpike roads of the Peak District', *DAJ*, XCII (1972), 93-109
A. Raistrick, 'The south Yorkshire iron industry, 1698-1756', *Trans. Newcomen Soc.*, XIX (1938-9), 51-86
A. Raistrick and E. Allen, 'The south Yorkshire ironmasters, 1690-1750', *EcHR*, old series, IX (1939), 168-85
M. Rowlands, 'Society and industry in the West Midlands at the end of the seventeenth century', *Midland History*, IV, 1 (1977), 48-60
'Salt Making in Domesday Cheshire' and 'The Cheshire Salt Industry in Tudor & Stuart Times (1485-1714)', Northwich Salt Museum leaflets (n.d.)
L. Stone, 'An Elizabethan Coal Mine', *EcHR*, III, 1 (1950), 97-106
R. E. Sydes and J. Dunkley, 'Excavations in Bawtry', *Archaeology in South Yorkshire, 1990-1991*, (1991), 32-39
J. Thirsk, 'Seventeenth-century agriculture and social change' in J. Thirsk (ed.), *Land, Church and People: Essays presented to Professor H. P. R. Finberg* (1970), 148-77
D. G. Tuxker, 'Millstones, Quarries and Millstone Makers', *Post-Medieval Archaeology*, XI (1977), 1-21
G. L. Turnbull, 'Provincial road carrying in England in the eighteenth century', *Journal of Transport History*, new series, IV, 1 (1977), 17-39
H. S. Twells, 'Mr. Drewry and the Derby wagons', *DAJ*, LXIII (1942), 61-78
H. S. Twells, 'Derby's flying machines and earliest coaches', *DAJ*, LXIV (1943), 64-82
H. S. Twells, 'The beginnings of a turnpike trust', *DAJ*, LXVI (1946), 22-39
M. D. G. Wanklyn. 'The impact of water transport facilities on English river ports, c.1660-c.1760', *EcHR*, XLIX (1996), 1-19
G. H. B. Ward, 'Fox Lane and Whibbersley Crosses', THAS, II, 2 (1921), 137-41
J. R. Wigfall, 'Lady's Bridge, Sheffield', *THAS*, I, 1 (1914), 57-63
J. F. Willard, 'The use of carts in the fourteenth century', *History*, XVII (1932), 246-50

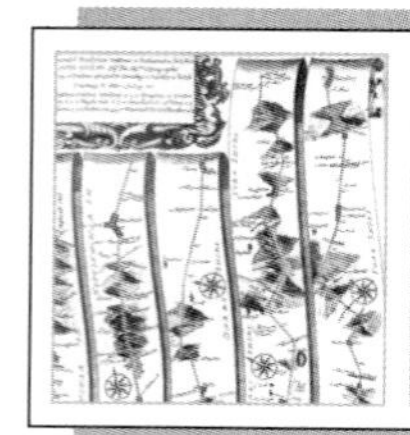

INDEX